Principles of
Test Theories

Hoi K. Suen
Pennsylvania State University

 LAWRENCE ERLBAUM ASSOCIATES, PUBLISHERS
1990   Hillsdale, New Jersey   Hove and London

Lawrence Erlbaum Associates, Inc., Publishers
365 Hillsdale, New Jersey 07642

Library of Congress Catalog Card Number 90-3769

Printed in the United States of America
10 9 8 7 6 5 4 3 2 1

Contents

PART 1

INTRODUCTION

CHAPTER 1

The Psychometric Process

Tests, rating scales, questionnaires, and other measurement procedures are administered routinely in our daily lives. Many people are "tested" at the moment of birth through a rating scale (e.g., APGAR). From that moment on, various characteristics of the person are probed and measured periodically through various educational, psychological, and behavioral measurement tools, including early childhood developmental tests, pre-school readiness tests, various aptitude and achievement tests, intelligence tests, behavioral rating scales, personality inventories, interest inventories, college admission tests, professional licensure tests, not to mention continuous in-class examinations while in school and various attitude and opinion surveys. Additionally, an individual's performances on the job, in athletic competitions, in the arts, and many other areas are rated by judges. Presumably, these rating scores reflect the quality of the individual's performance.

From an institutional perspective, the results of these tests frequently have important influences on the person's placement in schools, admission to universities, and choice of and participation in various professions and activities. At a personal level, the results of these tests frequently influence how the person views him or herself and how others view that person. Because educational and psychological tests and measurement procedures are given such important roles in modern society, it is important to understand how these scores are derived and what information they contain.

The science of developing educational and psychological tests and measurement procedures has become highly sophisticated and has developed into such a large body of knowledge that it is considered a scientific discipline of inquiry in its own right. This discipline is referred to as *psychometrics*. Various aspects of educational and psychological tests and measurement procedures are studied in psychometrics. These include how test questions (called *items*) should be developed, how to select test items, how to transform responses to items into numerical scores, how to assess the quality of these scores, how to interpret these scores, and how to ascertain that the scores are not biased against certain groups of individuals.

At the core of these psychometric questions and issues is the central question: Does the test score indicate what it is supposed to indicate? For example, does the score for an individual from a test called a "reading test" actually indicate the person's reading ability or does it reflect something else? This central question contains the questions of the *reliability* and *validity* of the test score. In the use of a test to measure some characteristic of a person, the questions of reliability and validity can be considered most critical. Unless the answers to these central questions are positive, all other psychometric issues are secondary. A quotation from Stamp (1929) best illustrates the fundamental risk of reliability and validity in measurement:

> The government are very keen on amassing statistics — they collect them, raise them to the nth power, take the cube root and prepare wonderful diagrams. But what you must never forget is that every one of those figures comes in the first instance from the village watchman, who just puts down what he damn well pleases.

At the current stage of development of psychometrics, the answers to the central questions of reliability and validity of scores from tests or other educational/psychological measurement procedures are derived through different mathematical and statistical theories. These theories are referred to as *test theories* or *psychometric theories*. These theories are the primary focus of discussion in this text. Some common extensions of these theories to specific measurement situations, such as *direct behavioral observation* and *criterion-referenced testing,* are also discussed. Finally, some common application issues are reviewed.

It should be noted at this early point that mainstream psychometric theories as they exist today are primarily mathematical and statistical. This does not imply that the answers to psychometric questions are necessarily and exclusively mathematical or statistical ones. Rather, the wealth of knowledge in cognitive psychology has not yet been well integrated into the testing process. A discussion of the role of cognitive psychological theory in testing is provided in chapter 15.

PSYCHOMETRIC INFERENCE

In educational and psychological testing and measurement, the objective is to describe a characteristic of a subject as a numerical score, which represents the quantity of that characteristic of that subject. This characteristic may be overt as with many directly observable behaviors, or covert as with psychological variables such as aptitude, self-esteem, and alienation. A quantitative description of these characteristics allows for comparisons across subjects, comparisons against a criterion, and systematic analyses through statistical or other quantitative techniques.

At first glance, to attain such an objective is deceptively simple. To quantify an overt behavior, we can simply observe the behavior and record its occurrences or assign scores on a rating scale. To measure a covert characteristic, we can construct and administer tests or questionnaires. Through these processes, we can obtain one or more numerical scores for a subject, which we then assume to reflect the quantity of interest for that subject.

A major problem is that one has no basis to assume that the numerical score truthfully and accurately reflects the underlying quantity of interest. The hazard of educational and psychological measurement is that almost anyone can devise his or her own set of rules to assign some numbers to some subjects and believe that these numbers represent the quantities of some characteristics of the subjects. The fact that numbers can be created through various systematic as well as random processes, even through machines, suggests that some so-called test scores may be meaningless numbers. This reality makes it important to distinguish those scores that truthfully reflect the quantity of the characteristic of interest as claimed from those that do not. The ability of test scores to truthfully reflect quantities of a characteristic of interest actually involves a huge inferential leap.

Let us examine what takes place in a typical testing situation. Take for instance the conceptual process involved in measuring something called the "math aptitude" of a subject through a paper-and-pencil multiple-choice examination. In this situation, in order to believe that the score obtained by a particular subject on the exam truthfully represents the math aptitude of the subject, a number of conceptual inferences are made. These conceptual inferences are illustrated in Fig. 1.1.

First, a number of exam questions are constructed. These questions are

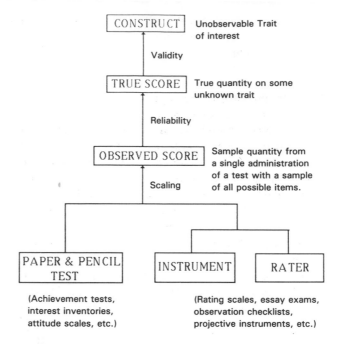

Figure 1.1.   The psychometric process.

referred to as *items*. A subject is asked to provide answers or *responses* to these items. These responses may be in the form of words and sentences as in the case of essay questions, in the form of marks as in the case of multiple-choice items, or in the form of certain task performances such as in the case of performance rating. These items and responses represent the only tangible portion of the entire measurement process. From the responses to the items on a math aptitude test, for instance, we wish to describe the subject's math aptitude as a score or number.

In order to describe the subject's math aptitude as a score, we have to somehow transform these responses into a number. A common approach is to give each correct response a score of 1. In this case, the score for the subject is the number of correct responses. The process of transforming responses into scores is referred to as *scaling*. There are a number of scaling methods or rules for this transformation. Some of these scaling methods are intuitive whereas others are based on statistical theories. We will not discuss various scaling techniques and scoring systems in this book. Interested readers should consult specialized texts such as Maranell (1974) for psychological measurement or Lyman (1978) and Angoff (1984) for educational testing.

The result of this scaling process is a score for each subject. This score is referred to as the *observed* score. When a test such as the math test is given to a subject, because of time and other physical limitations, only a limited number of items or questions can be asked. These items represent a sample of all possible similar math items. In other words, the score obtained by the subject only represents the score on that particular sample of items given at that particular time within that particular physical environment. It may or may not reflect the actual math aptitude of the subject. Hence, that score can best be described as the *observed* score.

If we were able to test the subject on all possible similar items under all conditions at various times, we would be able to obtain a *true score* for that subject. Because we are unable to do so, we infer from our observed score to the true score. That is, we assume that our observed score provides a good indication of the true score. The extent to which the observed score reflects the true score is referred to as *reliability*. The higher the reliability, the better the observed score serves as a stand-in for the true score.

If our math items in fact measure math aptitude, then our true score would be a truthful reflection of the quantity of math aptitude of the subject. However, simply because a test claims and appears to be a math aptitude test does not guarantee that the score actually reflects math aptitude. For instance, for a math test in which subjects are asked to solve math problems based on long verbal descriptions of problem situations, a high score may in fact indicate high reading ability rather than high math aptitude. For this reason, the true score may or may not reflect the quantity of math aptitude. Although it is a true score in the sense that it is the score the subject would obtain on all similar items tested under all different conditions, it is only a truthful reflection of something. This something may or may not be math aptitude.

The ability of the true score to reflect what the test intends to measure is referred to as *validity*. What the test intends to measure is referred to as the *object of measurement*. The object of measurement in most testing situations in education and psychology, such as math aptitude, are psychological *constructs*. A construct is an unobservable trait, attribute, or characteristic of a subject such as math aptitude, achievement, self-concept, or patriotism. These constructs are literally constructed by psychologists to explain some phenomenon. They are useful in that they help explain the differences in behavior among people. For example, in order to explain why Johnny learns how to solve a math problem faster than Jane, we can suggest that Johnny has a higher math aptitude than Jane. As such, a construct may or may not exist in reality. Some (e.g., Nunnally, 1978) have suggested that the question of the objective existence of a construct is moot, as long as the construct is useful in explaining and predicting behaviors.

Essentially, in a testing situation, we first devise a scaling rule to change a set of responses into a numerical observed score. Next we infer that the observed score faithfully reflects a true score. Finally, we infer that the true score truthfully reflects the quantity of a construct, which may or may not exist. This chain of inferential leaps takes considerable stretching of the tangible items and responses. To justify these inferential leaps for a particular test, different types of evidence are needed. Some measurement situations such as some direct observations of overt behaviors require less evidence whereas others such as the measurement of intelligence require considerably more evidence.

PSYCHOMETRIC THEORIES

The study of this chain of inferential connections and subsequent implications, derivations, and applications of these relationships is based on psychometric theories. From these theoretical paradigms, a large array of statistical methods and indices have been suggested as appropriate for deriving evidence of reliability and validity for different types of measurement and testing situations (e.g., Berk, 1979, 1984; 1975; Suen, Ary, & Ary, 1985). Others have suggested methods to arrive at the best estimate of true score based on responses directly (e.g., Lord, 1952a; Rasch, 1980).

Unlike most psychological and behavioral theories, which are formulated through insights and experiences and confirmed through empirical data, psychometric theories as they exist today are primarily applied mathematical and statistical models. Consider the process through which a typical behavioral theory is confirmed (a process frequently referred to as the positivistic paradigm as opposed to naturalistic inquiries): Hypotheses are formulated, data are gathered through the measurement of constructs, data are analyzed, and hypotheses are supported. Such a process cannot be applied to confirm psychometric theories because the process of the measurement of constructs, a critical step in the positivistic theory-testing approach, is by itself the phenomenon of interest. Hence, psychometric theories are confirmed through logical deductions and mathematical proofs.

There are two major psychometric theories today: *random sampling theory* and *item response theory* (Bejar, 1983). In random sampling theory, the connection between observed score and true score is viewed essentially as a problem of generalizing from a sample to a larger population or universe. Item response theory, on the other hand, suggests that, if we can understand how each item in a test operates with a subject, we can estimate the true score of the subject directly.

The random sampling theory consists of two approaches: the *classical* theoretical approach (Gulliksen, 1950) and the *generalizability* approach (Brennan, 1983; Cronbach, Gleser, Nanda, & Rajaratnam, 1972). The generalizability theory has been described as a liberalization of measurement theory (Brennan, 1984a) and a conceptual breakthrough (Bakeman & Gottman, 1986). Although developed through a different set of conceptual and statistical assumptions and derivations, the classical theory proves to be a special subset of the more comprehensive generalizability theory in practice. Relatively limited in scope, the classical theory is of both historical and practical significance. It is the theory that has dominated testing for many decades and remains quite popular today despite its inherent limitations.

It has been suggested that what item response theory is to random sampling theory in psychometrics is analogous to what the Einsteinian theory of relativity is to the Newtonian world view in physics (Warm, 1978). Item response theory provides a completely different and more effective way of looking at the psychometric process. Item response theory encompasses a number of slightly different conceptual models. The most common models are the Rasch model (Rasch, 1980), the 2-parameter logistic model and the 3-parameter logistic model (Birnbaum, 1968). These models differ slightly in their assumptions regarding the characteristics of a test item.

The assumptions, logical deductions, and statistical derivations of classical, generalizability, and item response theories will be discussed in detail in later chapters. Additionally, the applications of these theories to solve specific psychometric issues will also be discussed.

SOME COMMON PSYCHOMETRIC ISSUES

Although the basic psychometric process involves only a chain of inferences from a test to a construct, there are numerous variations in terms of data acquisition, score interpretation, and subsequent data analyses. Some of these specific issues are discussed in detail later but are introduced here.

Norm- and Criterion-referenced Interpretations

A test score by itself is a number without a context. As such, a test score *per se,* whether observed, true, or construct, is rarely directly interpretable. For example, an examinee may have answered 80 of a 100-item math aptitude test correctly and obtain a score of 80. What does this score of 80 tell us about the examinee's math aptitude? The answer depends on the difficulty of the test and/or the performance of other similar examinees. The score of 80 may, for instance, indicate low ability if all items in the test are easy. Similarly, the score of 80 may indicate low ability if all other similar examinees score higher than 80.

In order to attach meaning to a test score, some external point of reference is needed. There are two basic orientations in test score interpretation. These are referred to as the *norm-referenced* and *criterion-referenced* approaches. With a norm-referenced interpretation, a test score is interpreted in terms of how well an examinee performs relative to other similar examinees. For example, in an Olympic gymnastics competition, it does not matter whether a contestant obtains a score of 9.8, 8.2, or 6.0. What matters is how many other contestants score higher than this contestant. A contestant who scores higher than all other contestants will be awarded the gold medal regardless of exactly what score is obtained by that contestant.

With a criterion-referenced interpretation, a test score is interpreted in terms of how much of a specific body of knowledge has the examinee mastered. In other words, instead of interpreting the score as a basis to determine how many people score below this person in a norm-referenced fashion, in criterion-referenced testing, we are interested in what exactly does the examinee know and/or can do. These two different interpretations present different problems in the psychometric process. Specifically, in order to interpret a test score in a criterion-referenced manner, more complex evidence is needed to justify the inferential psychometric connection.

Direct Behavioral Observation

Partly because of the huge inferential leap of the psychometric process, operant behaviorists (e.g., Skinner, 1945) have maintained that we should not attempt to measure covert constructs. Instead, we should only observe overt behaviors directly and confine our measurement procedure to what is observable. Early behaviorists believe that scores obtained through the direct observation of behavior are axiomatically reliable and valid (cf. Cone & Foster, 1982). Hence, the entire psychometric inferential process becomes unnecessary. More recent research in observational methods (cf. Suen & Ary, 1989) suggests that observational data are not totally exempted from psychometric considerations, although the level of inference may be lower in some specific situations. Additionally, behavioral observation presents a different set of psychometric problems.

Other Issues

A number of other issues also lead to different implications in the derivation of evidence to support the psychometric inferences. For instance, a test may be used to measure a *cognitive* or an *affective* construct. A cognitive construct is one of knowledge, skill, aptitude, or ability. An affective construct, on the other hand, is one of feeling, attitude, belief, and perception. The major difference between the measurements of these two types of constructs, from a psychometric perspective, is that an item in the former usually has a correct answer. An item designed to measure an affective construct theoretically does not have a correct answer, with the exception of a case in which there is a clear direction of *social desirability*. That is, an item that is written in such a way that a respondent has a desire to respond based on what is socially desirable rather than what he or she actually feels.

The implication of the presence or absence of a correct answer for psychometric considerations is the possibility of guessing. Specifically, when an item has a correct and an incorrect answer, an examinee may provide a correct response through guessing. Guessing behavior in testing is not well-understood today. It can be expected that attempts to guess the correct answer will complicate the psychometric process. When the construct of interest is affective, guessing is generally not a serious concern. However, guessing needs to be taken into consideration when measuring a cognitive construct.

Another issue that needs to be taken into consideration in the psychometric process is the expected use of the test. Test scores may be used as the basis to select individuals for admission or employment, to place students in different courses of study, to classify individuals into different categories, to compare across subjects, to compare across programs, to diagnose specific areas of deficiency, to determine needs for guidance and counseling, and to evaluate the effectiveness of intervention. Dependent on the exact purpose of a test, different amounts of evidence are needed to support the psychometric connection.

In general, when only the mean score of a group is used, such as in the case of comparing programs and evaluating intervention effectiveness, less evidence is needed. When decisions regarding an individual are made based on test scores, such as diagnosis and selection, strong evidence is required. Additionally, some types of evidence are more important for certain situations than others. For instance, when test scores are used for selection, typically a *cut-score* is used. Individuals who score below this cut-score will be rejected, whereas those who score above this cut-score will be accepted. In this type of situation, it is not enough to demonstrate that observed scores in general provide good indications of true scores. It is critical that the observed scores near the cut-score be particularly faithful reflections of true scores.

Because tests are used for many different purposes, different levels of scores are used in different situations. For instance, a question in an opinion poll is essentially a single-item test. In this situation, the questions of reliability and validity are ones of how well that single item reflects the construct of interest. In most educational and psychological testing situations, the total score across a number of items in a test or a questionnaire is used. In these situations, the concerns are how well the total score reflects the construct. In program evaluation, the mean total score across a number of subjects is of interest. In these situations, the concern is how well the mean observed score of the sample of subjects represents the mean construct score of the population. These problems translate into questions of item reliability and validity, total score reliability and validity, and group mean score sampling adequacy.

A major concern with test scores, particularly those that are used as bases for decision-making, is the potential existence of cultural, gender, and other types of *bias*. There are numerous definitions of test bias (Berk, 1982). A useful definition of bias from a psychometric perspective is that a test score is biased when it reflects, in addition to the intended construct, one or more unintended socio-cultural constructs. For instance, subjects with a particular ethnic experience and background tend to systematically obtain lower scores on a reading test and the systematically lower score is not due to lower reading ability but to unfamiliarity with the context of the test items. In this example, the reading test is biased in that the score reflects not only reading ability, but ethnic experience as well.

In the larger perspective, the problem of test bias is one aspect of validity. If the scores on a math aptitude test reflect not only math aptitude but reading ability as well, the test can be said to be biased against poor readers. This definition of test bias reduces the problem to one of the number of constructs being reflected by a test score. To discern the number and nature of constructs being measured by a test score, however, is a technically complex problem. Some of the existing solutions are discussed in detail in later chapters.

With advances in psychometric theories, some other psychometric issues have emerged over the past two decades as important considerations. For instance, prior to the availability of the item response theory, the determination of the cut-score in selection, placement, and classification had been accepted as primarily a judgmental process without meaningful empirical verifications (cf. Shepard, 1984). With item response theory, however, empirical verifications of cut-scores became possible (e.g., Kane, 1987).

Another issue is that of *equating*. Examinees of many large-scaled tests such as the Scholastic Aptitude Test (SAT) are permitted to review items and correct responses after a test has been administered. This implies a serious compromise in test security in that the same items cannot be used again in the next administration of the test because they have now become public information. In essence, each new administration of the test requires a new set of items. This leads to a different psychometric problem: How can we compare test scores across subjects over time when they take different tests with different items? A number of techniques have been developed to make scores from different tests comparable. Some of these will be discussed in later chapters.

A logistically attractive approach to test construction is *item banking*. For the testing of a particular construct (e.g., social science), instead of creating a different test each time the test is needed, one can establish an item bank or a warehouse of test items on that construct. Each time a test is needed, items can be selected in a mix-and-match fashion from this item bank to make up a new test. What is needed in this process is a large number of field-tested items with known properties so that the ability of each new test to reflect the construct is known and the scores from each new test are comparable to those from other tests constructed from the same item bank. Psychometrically, item banking requires the ability to connect each item, rather than the total test score, to the construct.

Finally, at the frontier of testing, a process known as *adaptive testing* or *tailored testing* is envisioned. In conventional testing, all subjects are required to respond to all items in a test. This is a very inefficient process. For a high-ability subject, only a few items are challenging. The rest of the items are too easy and boring. For a low-ability subject, however, most of the items are too difficult and frustrating. A considerable amount of time is wasted in requiring the high-ability subject to respond to easy items and the low-ability subject to respond to difficult items. These responses provide little useful information regarding the ability of the subject. Testing time can be more efficiently used if tests can be tailored, through a computer for instance, such that a subject is required to respond only to items most appropriate for the subject's level of ability. Such a process requires good estimates of subjects' abilities based on a few initial items. Based on these initial items, subsequent items of the test can focus on the appropriate level of difficulty.

OVERVIEW OF CHAPTERS

Because existing psychometric theories are primarily applied mathematical and statistical models, some basic knowledge of statistical principle is needed to follow the logic of these theories. Readers are assumed to have knowledge in introductory statistics including such techniques as correlation, analysis of variance, and regression. A number of other mathematical and statistical concepts are, however, needed for the discussion of specific aspects of psychometrics. In chapter 2, some basic quantitative concepts are presented. These include brief reviews of quadratic function, derivatives, optimization algorithms, Bayesian statistics, and matrix algebra. Readers without a firm grasp of these concepts are suggested to read this chapter before proceeding to subsequent chapters.

In chapters 3, 4, 5, and 6, the essence of random sampling theory is presented. Specifically, in chapter 3, the core reasoning of the classical theory of measurement as well as some of its practical implications are presented. In chapter 4, the conceptual framework of generalizability theory is discussed. The statistical process involved in generalizability theory is discussed in chapter 5. Conventional item analytic techniques are discussed in chapter 6. Whereas the classical theory and generalizability theory establish the conceptual process to derive evidence of reliability, conventional item analytic techniques are methods to maximize the reliability.

In chapters 7, 8, and 9, the core concepts and mathematical reasoning of item response theory are discussed. The focus of discussion in chapter 7 is the assumptions and various models of, and the psychometric information derived from, item response theory. In chapter 8, various methods of estimating subjects' abilities with known item characteristics are discussed. In chapter 9, methods of estimating item characteristics and subject abilities simultaneously are discussed.

Although generalizability theory can be employed in some situations to derive evidence of validity, all three theories are essentially conceptual processes to establish the connection between observed and true scores. As such, evidence of validity is needed beyond the application of these theories in order to demonstrate that the observed score reflects the construct. In chapters 10 and 11, various types of validity evidence are discussed. Additionally, the conceptual and statistical differences and similarities between reliability and validity are explored.

In chapters 12 through 15, various applied issues are discussed. In chapter 12, issues related to criterion-referenced score interpretation, such as systematic error, reliability, and cut-score determination methods are discussed. The issues of direct observation of behavior and the application of psychometric theories in these situations are the focus of discussion in chapter 13. Chapter 14 provides a discussion of methods to detect item bias. Chapter 15 provides brief discussions of an array of other psychometric issues and an overview of some of the current conceptual concerns and general trends.

CHAPTER 2

Some Mathematical and Statistical Concepts

Readers of psychometric literature often find their progress hindered by a lack of familiarity with the mathematical language of the discipline. Although a mastery of complex mathematics is not necessary to gain a basic understanding of various psychometric theories, knowledge of the conceptual nature of some of the mathematical and statistical tools — beyond introductory statistics — used frequently in psychometrics will facilitate an understanding of the logic of various measurement theories. In this chapter, relevant features of quadratic functions, derivatives, optimization algorithms, Bayesian statistics, and linear algebraic analogs of matrix algebra are reviewed in very general conceptual terms.

QUADRATIC FUNCTIONS

A *quadratic function* is a curvilinear relationship in which the value of the dependent variable is the square of the value of the independent variable or variables. For example, $Y = X^2$ is a simple quadratic function. If $X = 3$, then $Y = 9$. What is special about a quadratic function is that when there is more than one independent variable, the function takes on a gestalt quality in that the square of the dependent variable is more than the sum of the squares of the independent variables. For example, if $Y = (X + Z)^2$, then Y does not equal $X^2 + Z^2$, but is equal to $X^2 + Z^2 + 2XZ$. On the other hand, if $Y = (X - Z)^2$, then $Y = X^2 + Z^2 - 2XZ$. To generalize to K independent variables, if

$$Y = (X_1 + X_2 + \ldots + X_k)^2$$

then

$$Y = X_1^2 + X_2^2 + \ldots + X_k^2 + 2X_1X_2 + 2X_1X_3 \ldots + 2X_{k-1}X_k,$$

$$= \sum_{i=1}^{k} X_{(1)}^2 + 2 \sum_{i \neq j} X_i X_j.$$

Similarly, if

$$Y = (X_1 - X_2 - \ldots - X_k)^2$$

then

$$Y = \sum_{i=1}^{k} X_{(1)}^2 - 2 \sum_{i \neq j} X_i X_j.$$

The quadratic function is used extensively in the derivations of properties of a test in classical and generalizability theories. Its use is common, for example, in describing the relationship between the variance of a composite (total) score and those of its constituent parts. To illustrate, Y is the sum or total of the scores on three items: X_1, X_2, and X_3. For the convenience of illustration, the scores of X_1, X_2, and X_3 can be alternatively expressed through linear transformations as deviation scores x_1, x_2, x_3. Specifically, x_1 is X_1 minus the mean of X_1 across subjects, and so on. A notation E (i.e., expected value of) can be used to denote "the average of." With this notation, Ex_i^2 becomes an alternative expression of the variance of X_i and Ex_ix_j is the covariance between X_i and X_j. If $Y = X_1 + X_2 + X_3$, then

$$\text{Variance of } Y = \sigma_Y^2$$

$$= Ey^2$$

$$= E(x_1 + x_2 + x_3)^2.$$

Hence, this becomes a quadratic equation,

$$\text{Var}(Y) = Ex_1^2 + Ex_2^2 + Ex_3^2 + 2Ex_1x_2 + 2Ex_1x_3 + 2Ex_2x_3$$

$$= \text{Var}(X_1) + \text{Var}(X_2) + \text{Var}(X_3) + 2[\text{Cov}(X_1X_2) + \text{Cov}(X_1X_3) + \text{Cov}(X_2X_3)],$$

where Var represents "the variance of" and Cov represents "the covariance between." This relationship between the variance of a composite score and the variances and covariances of its constituent parts proves to be quite useful. It can be used, for example, to show that the variance of the total score of a test is larger than the sum of item variances.

DERIVATIVES

Derivative is another term for slope, or the amount of change in the dependent variable Y per unit increase in the independent variable X. The most common derivatives encountered in psychometrics are the *first derivative* and the *second derivative*. The first derivative is the slope of the relationship between X and Y. The second derivative is the slope of the slope.

With the familiar linear regression $Y = bX + a$ commonly used in statistical analysis, the slope is b. Another way to describe this slope is that *the first derivative* of Y is b. The first derivative can be expressed as dY/dX, which reads "the first derivative of Y with respect to X." Alternatively, the relationship between X and Y can be expressed as $Y = f(X)$, or Y is a function of X. With these notations, the first derivative can be expressed as $f'(X)$ or $df(X)/dX$. In subsequent discussions, the notation $f'(X)$ is used for first derivatives. Hence, for a linear function $Y = 3X + 2$, $f'(X)$ is 3, which reads "the first derivative of $Y = 3X + 2$ with respect to X is 3".

Whereas the slope of $f'(X)$ of a linear function is a constant at all values of X, the slope of a curvilinear function changes as X changes and can be expressed as another function of X. For example, for the polynomial relationship $Y = 7 + 80X - 2X^2$ (See Fig. 2.1a), the slope changes as X changes. These changing slope values can be expressed as a first derivative function of X, $f'(X) = 80 - 4X$ (See Fig. 2.1b). The relationship between $f'(X)$ and X, in turn, has its own slope. The second derivative, denoted alternatively as $f''(X)$ or d^2Y/dX^2, describes the slope of the first derivative function, $f'(X)$. With our example, $f'(X)$ is a linear function, hence, $f''(X)$ is a constant -4 (See Fig. 2.1c). However, if $f'(X)$ is also a curvilinear function, $f''(X)$ becomes another function, rather than a constant. One can theoretically derive the 3rd derivative (i.e., the slope of the slope of the slope) and so forth.

The most frequent application of the first derivative in psychometrics is in item response theory. For example, let us assume that the X in Fig. 2.1a represents a person's possible true scores and Y represents the probability that that particular person has the corresponding true score. In Fig. 2.1a, the true score with the highest probability is 20. Hence, the most probable true score for this person is 20. Note in Fig. 2.1a that the slope of the curve

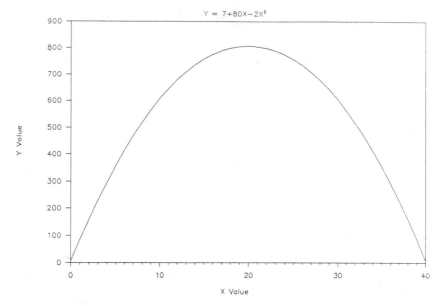

Figure 2.1a.　A quadratic function

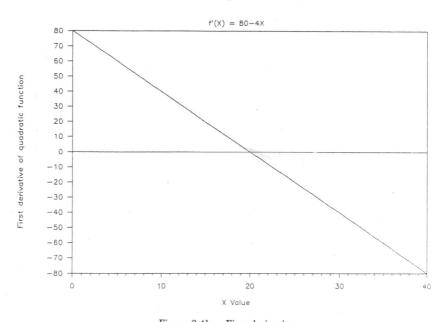

Figure 2.1b.　First derivative

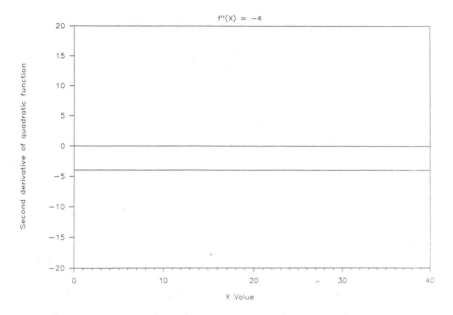

Figure 2.1c.   Second derivative

is positive when X is less than 20 and is negative when X is more than 20. At the point of maximum likelihood (i.e., the highest probability, $X = 20$), the slope is neither positive nor negative, but is zero. Given that the highest probability point also has a zero slope, it is quite convenient to find the maximum likelihood value of X by setting $f'(X)$ to zero and solving the resulting equation. With our example, the slope is $f'(X) = 80 - 4X$. To find the maximum likelihood X, set $80 - 4X = 0$. Through algebraic conversions, $X = 20$, or the maximum likelihood estimate of the person's true score is 20.

The second derivative $f''(X)$ is useful in item response theory for a process known as the Newton-Raphson procedure, a class of functions known as information functions, and other processes. We discuss these in the chapters on item response theory. For now, it suffices to recognize $f''(X)$ as the slope of $f'(X)$.

OPTIMIZATION ALGORITHMS

Related to the use of first and second derivatives to determine some maximum likelihood, minimum likelihood, or optimal values is a class of mathematical procedures known as optimization methods. The use of optimization methods is most commonly found in business operations research. These methods are increasingly being used to resolve complex psychometric problems today. Essentially, in many situations, optimal values (e.g., maximum likelihood) can be found by setting the first derivative to zero and solving the subsequent equation, as in the previous polynomial example. In many complex psychometric situations, however, the subsequent equation may not be solvable through algebra. In these situations, optimization techniques are employed.

Unlike statistics and algebra in which solutions are found through mathematical operations, optimization techniques literally search for the solution systematically. As such, optimization techniques are not so much mathematical operations; rather, they are mathematical strategies. An analogy is when a person cannot find his or her keys. Instead of trying to remember where the keys were placed, the person systematically searches the room until the keys are found.

Optimization techniques are typically not expressed in the familiar format of statistical equations. Rather, they are expressed in the form of algorithms, or procedures. These algorithms are typically so complex that they cannot be followed without the aid of a computer. As can be imagined, the concern in optimization is not only accuracy but efficiency as well.

Many psychometric problems are highly complex and cannot be solved through familiar statistical and mathematical techniques. Increasingly, psychometricians are utilizing optimization techniques to search for solutions. An example of the application of optimization techniques is the use of a procedure known as the *Newton-Raphson* procedure in item response theory. Other recent examples of the application of these techniques in measurement include Suen and Lee (1985) in behavioral observation, Sanders, Theunissen, and Baas (1989) in generalizability theory, and Stocking and Lord (1983), Suen and Lee (1989), and Xiao (1989) in item response theory. Some optimization algorithms or strategies which have been used in psychometric research include *linear programming, Newton-Raphson, golden section search, branch and bound integer programming,* and *generalized reduced gradient* method. The choice of method is determined by the nature of the data, the desired accuracy, and the desired efficiency.

BAYESIAN STATISTICS

Bayesian statistics are a special statistical and decision-making paradigm. Bayesian techniques have been used to solve a variety of psychometric problems. However, the most relevant feature of Bayesian statistics for the topics in this text is the Bayesian estimation of conditional probabilities.

A conditional probability is the probability that some event B is true given that some other event A is true, whereas an unconditional probability is simply the probability that some event B is true without any given condition. A conditional probability is symbolically denoted as $P(B|A)$ or "probability of B given A" and an unconditional probability is simply denoted $P(B)$ or "the probability of B." Logical deduction tells us that $P(B|A) \neq P(A|B)$. To borrow Carver's (1978) example, the probability that a person is dead given that the person was hanged is high. However, given that a person is dead, the probability that the person was hanged is quite low. In other words, $P(\text{dead}|\text{hanged}) \neq P(\text{hanged}|\text{dead})$.

To estimate $P(B|A)$ from knowledge of $P(A|B)$, Bayesian statistical techniques are needed. Based on the Bayes Theorem of conditional probability,

$$P(B|A) = \frac{P(A|B)P(B)}{P(A|B)P(B) + P(A|\text{not } B)P(\text{not } B)} \qquad (2.1)$$

where $P(B)$ is the unconditional probability of B. For example, if the proportion of nurses in the U.S. population is 0.01, the proportion of females among all nurses is 0.90, and the proportion of females among non-nurse individuals is 0.50, then $P(\text{female}|\text{nurse}) = 0.90$, $P(\text{nurse}) = 0.01$, $P(\text{female}|\text{not nurse}) = 0.50$, and $P(\text{not nurse}) = 0.99$. Given these probabilities,

$$P(\text{nurse}|\text{female}) = \frac{(.90)\,(.01)}{(.90)\,(.01) + (.50)\,(.99)} = .02,$$

which is substantially less than the $P(\text{female}|\text{nurse})$ of .90.

In Bayesian language, the unconditional probabilities $P(B)$ and $P(\text{not } B)$ in Equation 2.1 are called *prior* probabilities, $P(A|B)$ and $P(A|\text{not } B)$ are *sample* probabilities, the product $P(A|B)P(B)$ is called *likelihood,* and $P(B|A)$ is called *posterior* probability. Thus, the basic Bayesian process is to combine prior information with sample information to derive likelihood that leads to posterior information.

For polychotomous variables, if the unconditional probability of B having a value of B_i is $f(B_i)$, there are a total of K probable B values, and the conditional probability distribution of $(A|B_i)$ can be represented by a function $g(A|B_i)$, then Equation 2.1 can be generalized as:

$$p(B|A) = \frac{g(A|B)f(B)}{\sum_{i=1}^{K} g(A|B_i)f(B_i)},$$

if B is a discrete variable; and

$$p(B|A) = \frac{g(A|B)f(B)}{\int g(A|B)f(B)},$$

if B is a continuous variable. The integration sign, $\int$, can be viewed conceptually as a continuous-variable version of Σ.

The estimation of posterior probabilities through the Bayesian process has been integrated into various psychometric techniques, particularly in item response theory. To illustrate, true score is unknown. However, we can deduce, based on sampling theory, how observed scores may be distributed among individuals with the same true score. If the probability of obtaining different observed scores for a given true score can be characterized by a function $G(X|T)$, and if we made an *a priori* assumption that people's true score distribution is a function $F(T)$ (e.g., normal distribution) then we can treat $F(T)$ as the prior distribution and $G(X|T)$ as the likelihood distribution. Through the Bayesian process, the posterior distribution $P(T|X)$ can be derived. By examining the values of $P(T|X)$ at different true scores, we can deduce the most probable true score for a person given a particular observed score.

MATRIX ALGEBRA

Matrix algebra is a system of mathematical short-hand. It serves as a stand-in for the more time-consuming long-hand linear algebra in that a large amount of data and equations can be expressed efficiently in a single matrix algebraic equation. As with short-hand systems in the English language, the purpose of matrix algebra is to facilitate efficient communication. As the English short-hand does not change the fundamental grammar of the English language, matrix algebra does not change the fundamental nature of linear algebra. Given the complexity of psychometric theories, relationships among variables are often succinctly summarized in matrix algebra notations. It is therefore useful to recognize some of the more common matrix algebra symbols and to relate them to their simpler linear algebraic analogs.

In matrix algebraic language, a single number (e.g., 23) or a single equation that leads to only one value (e.g., $2X + 10$ where $X = 5$) is called a *scalar*. Many scalar values organized systematically into rows and columns form a *matrix*. Each scalar in a matrix is referred to as an *element*. For example,

	Item				
	1	2	3	4	5
Subject 1	3	4	1	2	2
Subject 2	2	2	1	3	1
Subject 3	4	5	5	3	4

is a 3 row by 5 column matrix representing the item-by-item scores of 3 subjects on a 5-item test. The elements (or cells) inside the matrix are the item scores for the corresponding subject on the corresponding item. In linear algebra, a letter is used to represent a variable. In matrix algebra, a bold-face upper-case letter is used to represent the entire matrix. For instance, we may refer to the above subject-by-item matrix as $\mathbf{A}$ or $\mathbf{X}$.

Mathematical operations are performed on the entire matrix as a unit of analysis. Hence, for additions and subtractions, we have $\mathbf{A} + \mathbf{B}$ and $\mathbf{A} - \mathbf{B}$, which are totally analogous to similar operations in linear algebra. For multiplications and divisions, however, the processes are considerably more complex. Because of rules of multiplication and considerations for the differences between rows and columns, $\mathbf{AB} \neq \mathbf{BA}$. We do not dwell on the operations of matrix algebra here. Interested readers are advised to consult textbooks on matrix algebra. For our purpose, it suffices to recognize $\mathbf{AB}$ and $\mathbf{BA}$ are multiplications of matrices $\mathbf{A}$ and $\mathbf{B}$.

A special notation frequently encountered in psychometrics is the *transpose of a matrix*. For example, $\mathbf{A}'$ is the transpose of the matrix $\mathbf{A}$. The transpose of a matrix is obtained by literally flipping the rows and columns of a matrix. With our previous subject-by-item matrix, for instance, the transposed matrix is one in which the items become rows and the subjects become columns. The transposed matrix is important because due to rules of matrix multiplication the square of a matrix (e.g., $\mathbf{A}^2$) does not equal the matrix multiplied by itself (i.e., $\mathbf{A}^2 \neq \mathbf{AA}$). Rather, the square equals the matrix premultiplied by its transpose (i.e., $\mathbf{A}^2 = \mathbf{A}'\mathbf{A}$).

Another important notation is the *inverse of a matrix*. For example, the inverse of $\mathbf{A}$ is denoted $\mathbf{A}^{-1}$. The inverse of a matrix is analogous to the reciprocal of a number. Whereas in conventional mathematics 10^{-1} is equivalent to $1/10$, $\mathbf{A}^{-1}$ is conceptually equivalent to $1/\mathbf{A}$. In matrix algebra, one cannot divide a matrix directly by another matrix. Instead, one can multiply a matrix by the inverse of another matrix, much in the same way that $3/10$ produces the same result as $3(10^{-1})$. The derivation of the inverse of a matrix is very complex. For our purpose, $\mathbf{AB}^{-1}$ can be conceptually viewed as matrix $\mathbf{A}$ divided by matrix $\mathbf{B}$.

A matrix that has only one row or one column is called a *vector*. It is symbolized by a lower-case, bold-face letter (e.g., $\mathbf{a}$). When a vector is added to or subtracted from a vector, the result is another vector. However, when a vector is multiplied by a vector, the result is not a vector but a scalar. For example, if $\mathbf{a} = [2\ 8\ 3]$, the square of $\mathbf{a}$, which is $\mathbf{a}$ multiplied by its transposed vector $\mathbf{a}'$, equals 29. Finally, when a matrix is premultiplied by a row vector, the result is another vector.

PART 2

RANDOM SAMPLING THEORY

CHAPTER 3

Classical Theory

The classical theory (Gulliksen, 1950) is the earliest theory of measurement. Despite the development of the more comprehensive and sophisticated generalizability and item response theories in the past two to three decades, the classical theory of measurement maintains a strong influence among testing and measurement practitioners today. With the exception of some large-scale testing projects, many tests in existence today continue to provide evidence of data quality based on the classical approach.

The classical theory is also referred to as the classical *reliability* theory because its major task is to estimate the reliability of the observed scores of a test. That is, it attempts to estimate the *strength* of the relationship between the observed score and the true score. It is also sometimes referred to as the *true score theory* because its theoretical derivations are based on a mathematical model known as the *true score model*.

THE TRUE SCORE MODEL

When a test is administered to an individual, the observed score for the individual represents the ability of that individual on that particular sample of items administered at that particular occasion under a particular set of conditions. Many factors may affect the performance of the subject. The subject may perform differently had a different set of items on the same content area been used, had the test been given at a different time or under a different set of personal and environmental conditions.

If we were able to administer the test to the same subject under all possible conditions at different times using different possible items, we would have many different observed scores for that subject. The mean of all these observed scores would be the most unbiased estimate of the subject's ability. This mean is defined as the *true score*.

The observed score from any single administration of a test with a particular sample of items is most likely different from this true score. This difference is called *random error score* or simply *error*. Mathematically, this relationship can be expressed as:

$$x = t + e, \tag{3.1}$$

where x is the observed score, t is the true score, and e is the error score. An interesting and somewhat tautological derivation of the true score model in Equation 3.1 is that, in the long run, the expected error is zero. Specifically, if we use the symbol E to represent "the average of" or "the expected value of," then, in repeated administrations of the test:

$$E(x) = E(t) + E(e). \tag{3.2}$$

Because $E(x)$ is by definition true score t and $E(t)$ is t, the expected e is zero. Therefore, although the observed score from a single administration of a test contains error, the average over many administrations of the test contains little error.

RELIABILITY ESTIMATION

Reliability is the strength of the relationship between the observed score and the true score. This can be expressed as the Pearson's correlation between the observed score x and the true score t; that is ρ_{xt}. This correlation is referred to as the *reliability index* (Crocker & Algina, 1986). The stronger the relationship, the better x reflects t. If this relationship is very strong as indicated by a high Pearson's r, one can view x as a linear transformation of t. That is, x is essentially t expressed on a different scale. Unfortunately, we cannot estimate ρ_{xt} directly from observed data because t values are unknown. However, it is possible to estimate the squared value of ρ_{xt}.

ASSUMPTION OF INDEPENDENCE

If we were to use the italicized t to represent $(t-\bar{t})$, x to represent $(x-\bar{x})$, and e to represent $(e-\bar{e})$, then, Et^2 is the variance of t or *true score variance* or simply *true variance*, Ex^2 is the variance of x or *observed score variance* or simply *observed variance*, Ee^2 is the variance of e or *error score variance* or simply *error variance*, *Ext* is the covariance between x and t, and *Ete* is the covariance between t and e. Because the Pearson's r between X and Y is:

$$XY = \frac{\text{Covariance between } X \text{ and } Y}{(\text{Std. Dev. of } X)\,(\text{Std. dev. of } Y)}$$

ρ_{xt} can be expressed as:

$$\rho_{xt} = \frac{Ext}{\sqrt{Ex^2 Et^2}}. \tag{3.3}$$

Given the true score model $x = t + e$, Equation 3.3 can be rewritten as:

$$\rho_{xt} = \frac{E(t + e)t}{\sqrt{Ex^2 Et^2}}$$

$$= \frac{Et^2 + Ete}{\sqrt{Ex^2 Et^2}}. \tag{3.4}$$

An assumption can be made that true score is unrelated to error score; that is, the amount of error made at any particular single administration of a test to a subject is independent of the true score for that subject. This is referred to as the *assumption of independence*. This assumption suggests that $Ete = 0$ or the covariance between t and e is zero. Given this assumption, the square of the reliability index ρ_{xt} as expressed in Equation 3.4 becomes:

$$\rho_{xt}^2 = \frac{(Et^2 + Ete)^2}{Ex^2 Et^2}$$

$$= \frac{(Et^2)^2}{Ex^2 Et^2}$$

$$= \frac{Et^2}{Ex^2}$$

$$= \frac{\text{true variance}}{\text{observed variance}}. \tag{3.5}$$

In other words, the square of the reliability index becomes the proportion of observed variance which is true variance. This squared reliability index is referred to as the *reliability coefficient*. Although it is not possible to estimate ρ_{xt} directly from observed data, it is possible to estimate ρ^2_{xt} when a particular set of assumptions known as *parallel tests assumptions* are met.

PARALLEL TESTS ASSUMPTIONS

If two tests, A and B, designed to measure the same ability, are both given to the same group of subjects, the true score t for each subject remains the same on both tests. The Pearson's r between the two sets of observed scores becomes:

$$r_{AB} = \frac{Ex_A x_B}{\sqrt{Ex_A^2 Ex_B^2}}$$

$$= \frac{E(t + e_A)(t + e_B)}{\sqrt{Ex_A^2 Ex_B^2}}$$

$$= \frac{Et^2 + Ete_A + Ete_B + Ee_A e_B}{\sqrt{Ex_A^2 Ex_B^2}} \tag{3.6}$$

Given the assumption of independence, the second and third terms of the numerator in Equation 3.6 become zero and drop out of the equation. Hence:

$$r_{AB} = \frac{Et^2 + Ee_A e_B}{\sqrt{Ex_A^2 Ex_B^2}} \tag{3.7}$$

This correlation can be used to estimate reliability coefficient $\hat{r}_{xt}^2$ if we assume that the two tests, A and B, meet the parallel tests assumptions. The parallel tests assumptions refer to a set of assumed mathematical relationships between tests A and B. A complete set of these assumptions can be found in Nunnally (1978) and detailed derivations and proofs of these assumptions can be found in Lord and Novick (1968).

Of particular relevance to our discussion here are two specific assumptions: (a) Scores on Tests A and B have the same variance or $Ex_A^2 = Ex_B^2$, and (b) the errors in Tests A and B are mutually independent or $Ee_A e_B = 0$. Given these two assumptions, the second term in the numerator of Equation 3.7 becomes zero and drops out of the equation. Further, the denominator can be written as a general observed variance Ex^2. Equation 3.7 becomes:

$$r_{AB} = \frac{Et^2}{Ex^2} = \rho_{xt}^2 = \text{reliability coefficient.} \tag{3.8}$$

In other words, if we can identify two tests that can be assumed to meet the parallel tests assumptions, the Pearson's r between the observed scores on the two tests becomes the squared correlation between the observed and the true score.

It is important to point out that when a Pearson's r between two parallel tests is used to estimate the reliability coefficient of either of the two essentially interchangeable tests, the resulting statistic is no longer a Pearson's r, but the r-squared between true and observed scores. Whereas Pearson's r ranges from -1.00 to $+1.00$ in values, the reliability coefficient that is an r^2 or *proportion* of variance can only range from 0 to 1. Unlike Pearson's r, a negative reliability coefficient is nonsensical and uninterpretable. Such a negative reliability coefficient implies that the parallel tests assumptions have been violated and the two tests cannot be used to estimate reliability.

ERROR VARIANCE AND STANDARD ERROR OF MEASUREMENT

Given the true score model $x = t + e$, the observed score variance, based on the quadratic function discussed in chapter 2, is:

$$Ex^2 = E(t + e)^2$$
$$= Et^2 + 2Ete + Ee^2. \qquad (3.9)$$

Given the assumption of independence, the second term in Equation 3.9 becomes zero and drops out of the equation. Hence:

$$\text{Observed variance} = \text{True variance} + \text{Error variance.} \qquad (3.10)$$

If observed variance (Ex^2 or σ_x^2) contains only true and error variances and reliability coefficient ρ_{xt}^2 is the proportion of observed variance that is true variance (Et^2 or σ_t^2), it follows then that $(1 - \rho_{xt}^2)$ is the proportion of observed variance which is error variance (Ee^2 or $\hat{\sigma}_e^2$). (Note: It is customary to denote reliability coefficient as ρ_{xx}. The notation $\hat{\rho}_{xt}^2$ is used throughout our discussion of classical theory to avoid confusion with Pearson's r.) Because observed variance is simply the variance of the observed test scores, when reliability coefficient is known, it is possible to estimate error variance as:

$$\hat{\sigma}_e^2 = \hat{\sigma}_x^2(1 - \hat{\rho}_{xt}^2)$$
$$= \text{observed variance } (1 - \text{reliability coeff.}). \qquad (3.11)$$

As the square root of a variance is a standard deviation, the square root of an error variance is a *standard error of measurement*. As we can use any standard error to build confidence intervals, we can use the standard error of measurement $(\hat{\sigma}_e)$ to build confidence intervals around an observed score. For example, we can be 95% certain that the true score of a subject who has an observed score of x is between $(x + 1.96\hat{\sigma}_e)$ and $(x - 1.96\hat{\sigma}_e)$.

ESTIMATION OF TRUE SCORE

If through two parallel tests, a high ρ_{xt}^2 is obtained, the observed score x is highly related to the true score t. The observed score can be viewed as a linear transformation of the true score or the true score expressed on a different scale. As such, for a norm-referenced interpretation in which a person's performance is interpreted relative to the performance of other similar individuals, the rank order of people based on the observed scores is very similar to that based on the true scores. Hence, the observed score is an effective substitute for the true score.

If, for whatever reason, the actual true score is desired, reliability information can be used to estimate a subject's true score. Because the reliability coefficient obtained from two parallel tests is the square of the correlation between observed and true scores, the square root of $\hat{\rho}_{xt}^2$ can be used directly to estimate true score t through linear regression. Specifically, the square root of reliability coefficient is the Pearson's r between observed and true scores. In a standard score regression equation in which the z-score of the independent variable is used to predict the z-score of the dependent variable, the regression coefficient, or beta weight, is equal to Pearson's r. Taking advantage of this relationship, we can estimate the true z-score (z_t) based on the observed z-score (z_x) through:

$$\hat{z}_t = \hat{\rho}_{xt} z_x$$

$$= z_x \sqrt{\hat{\rho}^2 xt} \qquad (3.12)$$

Because in practice, when $\hat{\rho}_{xt}^2$ is high, the observed score x is an effective linear transformation of true score t, the regression in Equation 3.12 is redundant and is of theoretical interest only.

STRATEGIES TO ATTAIN PARALLEL TESTS

Within the classical theory, once $\hat{\rho}_{xt}^2$ is estimated, reliability, error variance, and standard error of measurement can be estimated. Yet, the ability to estimate $\hat{\rho}_{xt}^2$ depends on our ability to identify two tests that meet the parallel tests assumptions. The Pearson's r between two tests that do not meet the parallel tests assumptions only indicates the strength of the relationship between those two particular sets of test scores and does not indicate the relationship between observed and true scores. That is, it does not indicate the degree of reliability of either test. Hence, it is important that tests that meet the assumptions be identified.

A simple method of attaining two parallel tests is to use the same test twice in a test-retest design. That is, administer the same test to the same group of subjects at two different points in time. Because the same test is being used in both administrations, the two sets of scores can be assumed to have met the parallel tests assumptions. Hence, the Pearson's r between the scores in the first and second administrations provide an estimate of ρ_{xt}^2. Unfortunately, the meeting of the parallel tests assumptions in test-retest is only approximated but not guaranteed. Because of such factors as practice effect and growth from the time of the first to that of the second administration, the true scores of subjects may have changed. If the two sets of scores do not contain identical true scores, the parallel tests assumptions are violated. To signify that the Pearson's r in a test–retest design only attempts to approximate ρ_{xt}^2, this r is referred to as the *coefficient of stability*. It represents one strategy to attain parallel tests.

An alternative strategy is to deliberately construct two equivalent versions of a test (e.g., forms A and B). The parallel tests assumptions are assumed met because both versions are deliberately constructed to be as similar as possible. Both versions can be administered to the same group of subjects and the Pearson's r between the two sets of scores can be considered an estimate of ρ_{xt}^2. Although the two versions are supposed to be equivalent, there is no guarantee that they do in fact meet the parallel tests assumptions. Hence, the Pearson's r in this situation is referred to as the *coefficient of equivalence* and is an approximate attempt to estimate ρ_{xt}^2. One major drawback of this strategy is the expense in the construction of two versions of the same test.

A more efficient alternative to the equivalent tests strategy is to construct only one test but split the items in the test into two halves and treat the scores from the two half-tests as if they were scores from two equivalent versions of a test. The resulting Pearson's r between the scores on the two half-tests is referred to as the *split-half reliability* and is one form of the *coefficient of internal consistency*. Assuming the two equivalent halves have met the parallel tests assumptions, the split-half reliability is then an approximate estimate of ρ_{xt}^2.

A major drawback of the split-half strategy is that the Pearson's r between the two halves reflects only the reliability of scores from half of the test. It can be demonstrated that the longer (more items) a test, the higher the ρ_{xt}^2 of the total score of the a test (Lord, 1957). Hence, the Pearson's r in a split-half strategy will provide an underestimation of ρ_{xt}^2 of the total score of the test because, for the purpose of reliability estimation, the test has essentially been reduced to half of its actual length. The underestimation of ρ_{xt}^2 can be corrected through the application of the Spearman-Brown prophecy formula.

The Spearman-Brown prophecy formula is a general purpose process to estimate the effects of shortening or lengthening a test on ρ_{xt}^2. Specifically, if the length of a test is to be changed by a factor of K, the reliability of the total score of the changed test, $\rho_{xt}^2{}^*$, is:

$$\rho_{xt}^2{}^* = \frac{K\rho_{xt}^2}{1 + (K-1)\rho_{xt}^2} \qquad (3.13)$$

where ρ_{xt}^2 is the reliability of the original test. A mathematical proof of the Spearman-Brown formula can be found in Lord and Novick (1968) and in Crocker and Algina (1985).

The Spearman-Brown formula can be applied to correct for the underestimation of the split-half reliability. Specifically, because the split-half reliability is the reliability of the score from half of the test, to estimate the reliability of the total score on the overall test, we can set $K = 2$ in Equation 3.13. Subsequently, the corrected reliability of the total test score reduces to:

$$\rho_{xt}^2{}^* = \frac{2\rho_{xt}^2}{1 + \rho_{xt}^2} \qquad (3.14)$$

where ρ_{xt}^2 is the Pearson's r between the two halves of the test.

Another drawback of the split-half reliability strategy to attain parallel tests is that there are numerous ways of splitting the test; each will likely lead to a different split-half reliability estimate. Which then is the best estimate of ρ_{xt}^2? To resolve this dilemma, the most comprehensive way to attain parallel tests internally within a single test is to split down to the item level. That is, we may treat each individual item as a parallel single-item test. For a test with K items, we would have K parallel single-item tests. From observed data, we can find the Pearson's correlations between all possible pairs of items. The average of all these Pearson's rs would be the best estimate of the reliability of a single item. This average r can then be corrected through Spearman-Brown to estimate the $\rho_{xt}^2{}^*$ of the total score across all these items. That is, for a test with K items,:

$$\rho_{xt}^2{}^* = \frac{K\bar{\rho}_{xt}^2}{1 + (K-1)\bar{\rho}_{xt}^2} \qquad (3.15)$$

where $\bar{\rho}_{xt}^2$ is the average Pearson's r between all possible pairs of items. The result of this process is known as the *standardized item Alpha* and is the most comprehensive approach within the internal consistency strategy to attain parallel tests.

For a test with K items, Equation 3.15 implies the need to compute $K(K-1)/2$ Pearson's correlation coefficients — a formidable task. For example, for a relatively short 20-item test, Equation 3.15 implies the computation of 190 Pearson's coefficients. As an alternative, the lower bound (or conservative estimate) of the standardized item Alpha can be estimated more efficiently through:

$$\alpha = \frac{K}{K-1} \left(1 - \frac{\Sigma \sigma_i^2}{\sigma_x^2}\right) \tag{3.16}$$

where σ_i^2 is the variance of the ith item and σ_x^2 is the total score variance. This is a conservative estimate of Equation 3.15 and is the most common form of *Cronbach Alpha*.

In cognitive testing, item scores are frequently dichotomous in nature (i.e., correct|incorrect, right|wrong). When all items are dichotomous, σ_i^2 in Equation 3.16 is mathematically equivalent to pq, where p is the proportion of subjects with positive scores and q is the proportion of subjects with negative scores on that item. The resulting reliability estimate,

$$KR - 20 = \frac{K}{K-1} \left(1 - \frac{\Sigma pq}{\sigma_x^2}\right), \tag{3.17}$$

is referred to as *Kuder-Richardson Formula-20* or *KR-20*. It is a special case of Cronbach Alpha as expressed in Equation 3.16 when all items are dichotomous.

Another approach known as *Kuder-Richardson Formula-21* or *KR-21* is a quick estimate of the lowest possible *KR-20* for a given set of data. Although computationally, *KR-21* is more efficient than any of the above strategies, conceptually, it is quite far removed from the original idea of attempting to estimate ρ_{xt}^2 through the Pearson's r between tests that meet the parallel test assumptions. KR-21 is defined as:

$$KR - 21 = \frac{K}{K-1} \left[1 - \frac{\hat{\mu}(K - \hat{\mu})}{K\sigma_x^2}\right], \tag{3.18}$$

where $\hat{\mu}$ is the mean total score across the subjects. Figure 3.1 provides a graphic summary of the classical process to estimate reliability and the various strategies used to attain parallel tests.

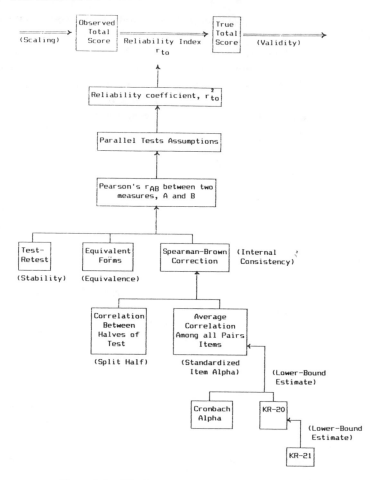

Figure 3.1. The Process of Classical Reliability Theory

CONCEPTUAL AND PRACTICAL IMPLICATIONS

As can be seen in this chapter, the logical and mathematical derivations of classical theory are rather convoluted. When applied to practical testing situations, the extent to which observed Pearson's r actually reflects ρ_{xt}^2 depends on whether the data meet the critical assumptions of independence and parallel tests. Whether two or more tests in practice actually meet the parallel tests assumptions, despite the various strategies employed, is a matter of conjecture and cannot be substantiated empirically. There is no known method to test the extent to which these parallel tests assumptions are met from a given set of test data.

Despite the large arrays of strategies to attain parallel tests that have led to a variety of coefficients (i.e., stability, equivalence, internal consistency), having more than one reliability coefficient with the classical theory is inherently self-contradictory. The objective is to estimate ρ_{xt} (i.e., the reliability index) through ρ_{xt}^2 (i.e., the reliability coefficient), and there can be only one ρ_{xt}^2. Various coefficients are different attempts to estimate ρ_{xt}^2. As such, for a given set of observed test data, only one of the many possible coefficients is the best estimate of ρ_{xt}^2. That is, only one of the many strategies has most successfully attained parallel tests. It is conceptually unacceptable within classical theory to suggest, for instance, that a test has high stability but low internal consistency or that the test is high in both stability and internal consistency. Stability and internal consistency can only be viewed as two different ways of estimating the same ρ_{xt}^2.

This inability to accommodate more than one reliability estimate becomes most apparent when the standard error of measurement is considered. When there is more than one reliability estimate, there is also more than one standard error of measurement. For the same subject, there would be more than one confidence interval around the same observed scores. The overall result becomes uninterpretable.

An important consideration in the classical approach to estimate reliability is that, despite the fact that Pearson's r is employed as the tool, the result is not a Pearson's r but an r^2 between observed and true scores. As such, a reliability coefficient does not contain the usual characteristics of a Pearson's r. For instance, when computing the mean of a number of Pearson's rs, the Fisher's zeta-transformation (Fisher, 1921) is employed to correct for the skewed distribution of rs. However, when computing the mean of a number of reliability coefficients, as in the case of Equation 3.15, despite the fact that these reliability coefficients have been estimated through the Pearson's r procedure, Fisher's zeta-transformation is inappropriate.

Because there is only one reliability coefficient, there is only one error variance and one standard error of measurement. It is thus necessary to assume that the same error variance applies to all observed scores on the same test; that is, all observed scores share the same error variance. When building confidence intervals, the same standard error of measurement is applied regardless of the exact observed score. Yet, it can be argued that the probability of a subject obtaining an extremely high score or an extremely low score because of random score fluctuation is much lower than that of obtaining a medium score. Hence, the error variance around extreme scores cannot be as high as those around the mid-range of scores. Although there is only one standard error of measurement, one would apply this standard error with caution when the observed score is an extreme score. Lord (1959a) has derived a method for the estimation of error variances at extreme scores which should be applied in those situations. According to Lord's derivation, extreme scores have smaller standard errors of measurement than mid-range scores.

EXTENSIONS OF CLASSICAL THEORY

An important limitation of the classical theory is that it is applicable to the establishment of reliability of the total score from a norm-referenced paper-and-pencil test only. That is, it is useful for the estimation of reliability only. Further, the result indicates only the reliability of the total score across the items, or a linear transformation of this total score. Finally, it indicates the reliability of the total score only if this total score is to be interpreted in a norm-referenced manner. In some measurement situations, however, one may wish to estimate the reliability of a score other than that of the total score. For two of these situations, classical theory can be extended to derive the appropriate reliability estimate.

First, in many measurement situations, a researcher is interested in the difference between the total scores on two tests. For instance, a researcher may be interested in the gain score in a pretest-posttest situation and analyses or interpretations are made on the gain score. Simply because both the pretest and the posttest total scores are reliable does not automatically imply that the observed gain score accurately reflects the true gain score. The reliability of the gain score can be assessed through a direct extension of the Classical Theory. Using x to represent the deviation total score on one test (e.g., pretest) and y to represent that on the other test (e.g., posttest) and d to represent the difference between x and y, let us examine the nature of the observed difference score:

$$d = y - x.$$

Based on the quadratic function, the variance of the observed difference score, σ_d^2, becomes:

$$
\begin{aligned}
\sigma_d^2 &= Ed^2 \\
&= E(y - x)^2 \\
&= Ey^2 + Ex^2 - 2Exy \\
&= \sigma_y^2 + \sigma_x^2 - 2Cov(x,y).
\end{aligned}
\tag{3.19}
$$

Because a Pearson's r between x and y is, by definition,

$$r_{xy} = \frac{Cov(x,y)}{\sigma_x \sigma_y}$$

through algebraic conversion,

$$Cov(x,y) = r_{xy}\sigma_x\sigma_y \, .$$

Hence, Equation 3.19 becomes:

$$\sigma_d^2 = \sigma_y^2 + \sigma_x^2 - 2r_{xy}\sigma_x\sigma_y. \tag{3.20}$$

Using the same reasoning process, the variance of the true difference score, $\sigma(t_d)^2$, is

$$\sigma(t_d)^2 = \sigma(t_x)^2 + \sigma(t_y)^2 - 2Cov(x,y), \tag{3.21}$$

where $\sigma(t_x)^2$ is the true score variance on the pretest and $\sigma(t_y)^2$ is the true score variance on the posttest. Based on earlier discussions of the Classical Theory,

true score variance = observed variance × reliability coefficient.

Hence, Equation 3.21 becomes:

$$\sigma(t_d)^2 = r_{tx}^2\sigma_x^2 + r_{ty}^2\sigma_y^2 - 2Cov(x,y)$$
$$= r_{tx}^2\sigma_x^2 + r_{ty}^2\sigma_y^2 - 2r_{xy}\sigma_x\sigma_y, \tag{3.22}$$

where r_{tx}^2 and r_{ty}^2 are the reliabilities of the pretest and posttest score respectively. Because the reliability coefficient of the difference score is, by earlier definition, true difference score variance divided by observed difference score variance, by combining Equations 3.20 and 3.22, this reliability can be estimated by:

$$\text{Reliability of difference score} = \frac{r_{tx}^2\sigma_x^2 + r_{ty}^2\sigma_y^2 - 2r_{xy}\sigma_x\sigma_y}{\sigma_y^2 + \sigma_x^2 - 2r_{xy}\sigma_x\sigma_y}. \tag{3.23}$$

Thus, a reliable pretest score and a reliable posttest score do not guarantee a reliable difference score. In general, the higher the pretest and posttest scores *and* the lower the correlation between these two scores, the higher the reliability of the difference score.

In other situations, a researcher may wish to assess the reliability of a single item or the reliability of the new total score when new items are added to the test. For example, in research, subjects' responses to some specific items in the test are sometimes compared across different groups. For this purpose, the reliability of the total score on the test is inappropriate. Rather, the researcher needs to assess the reliability of the single item. In these situations, the Spearman-Brown Prophecy formula defined in Equation 3.13 can be applied directly. For instance, if the reliability of the total score on a 10-item test is 0.85 and one wishes to assess the reliability of a single item, K in Equation 3.13 becomes 1/10 or 0.1 and ρ_{xt}^2 is 0.85. Using Equation 3.13, the reliability of a single item on this test is 0.36. On the other hand, if one wishes to estimate the reliability of this test if 10 more similar items are added, K becomes 2 and, through Equation 3.13, the reliability of the total score on the new 20-item test is 0.92.

CHAPTER 4

Generalizability Theory: Conceptual Framework

Although many psychometricians (e.g., Bartke, 1966; Burt, 1936; Ebel, 1951; Haggard, 1958; Hoyt, 1941; Jackson & Ferguson, 1941; Lindquist, 1953) had paved the way to the Generalizability Theory of Measurement, it was formally introduced by Cronbach, Gleser, Nanda, and Rajaratnam (1972). The generalizability theory is different from the classical theory in a number of important respects. Perhaps the most important difference is that of perspective. Specifically, within generalizability theory, reliability is considered within the context of a testing situation. Recall that in classical theory, measurement error is described through a rather vague concept called random error without any specific context. Within generalizability theory, however, measurements are viewed within a specific context of measurement situation.

From a technical perspective, the generalizability theory has at least two advantages over the classical theory. First, the restrictive parallel tests assumptions are avoided in generalizability theory. Instead, a weaker assumption called *randomly parallel tests assumption* is made. This weaker assumption is sometimes referred to as the *domain-sampling approach* (Nunnally, 1978). With this assumption, two tests are said to be randomly parallel if it can be assumed that the items in the two tests are random samples drawn from the same pool of possible items. It is important to note that this is not a complete change of assumptions from the classical theory. Rather, it is a relaxation of assumptions in that the randomly parallel test assumption is a prerequisite to the classically parallel tests assumptions.

A second important technical advantage of the generalizability theory is its ability to assess multiple sources of measurement error. To assess measurement errors in generalizability, an analysis of variance (ANOVA) technique is used. Unlike classical theory that yields a single reliability coefficient through a Pearson's *r*, the ANOVA in generalizability can yield as many reliability coefficients as there are questions of reliability. Whereas for the same set of measurement data, the classical theory cannot accommodate the idea of having more than one reliability coefficient, the generalizability approach can yield as many reliability coefficients as the number of reliability questions posed. Additionally, specific information regarding the amounts and sources of measurement errors is also derived.

THE NATURE OF SCORE VARIANCES

To follow the logic of generalizability theory, it is important to understand the nature of the statistical concept of variance. We know from introductory statistics that a distribution of scores can be summarized by a number of univariate statistics. Central to these statistics are the mean and the variance. The mean is the arithmetic average of all scores. As a measure of central tendency, the mean is usually interpreted as the typical score among the subjects. That is, the mean is used to represent all the scores. An important deficiency of the mean is that, in most applied situations, it is inaccurate, although unbiased, in representing the scores of most of the individuals. In many situations, there may in fact be no one with a score equal to the mean score.

The variance can be viewed as a qualifier for the deficiency of the mean. Specifically, the variance provides an index of the total amount of score deviations from the mean. In other words, the variance indicates the amount of error in using the mean to represent the scores of all subjects. The fact that variance is a measure of the amount of error is important. A small variance indicates that the mean is relatively accurate in describing the score of the typical subject, whereas a large variance indicates a lack of accuracy.

This characteristic of the variance makes it a very useful statistic for psychometrics. Knowing the magnitude of variances would provide useful information about the amount of measurement error, or the *lack of reliability*. Analyzing variances in a set of pilot test scores from a particular measurement situation would hence provide useful information regarding measurement error and reliability.

TYPES OF VARIANCES

For a given set of test data, there are different sources of score variation. These different sources have different implications about the characteristics of the testing situations. To facilitate discussion, we consider several hypothetical situations involving an essay exam. First, consider a situation in which a single subject was asked to respond to a single essay question. After reading the essay response, a judge assigned a score of 6 out of 10 points for this subject on the essay. In this situation, we have no way of knowing whether the score of 6 represents the true score of the subject. There is insufficient information to make such a reliability assessment.

If the same judge were asked to score the same essay on different days and the judge consistently assigned a score of 6, we could conclude that the judge was perfectly reliable. That is, there is a high level of *intrajudge reliability*. If the judge assigned different scores to the same essay on different days, however, we may conclude that there is a lack of intrajudge reliability. A good measure of the degree of intrajudge reliability is the variance of the scores on different days from the same judge. The *larger* this variance, the *lower* the intrajudge reliability, and the *larger* the intrajudge error.

If, instead of asking the same judge to score the same essay several times, we asked several judges, each with a perfect intrajudge reliability, to score the same essay one time, we would have several scores from several judges. The variance across these scores are not intrajudge error, because these judge have perfect intrajudge reliabilities, but are *interjudge error*. The smaller this variance, the higher the *interjudge reliability*.

In a third situation, a single judge with perfect intrajudge reliability, was asked to score the responses to several essay questions in an exam from a single subject. Although, for each question, the judge provided an identical score on different days, the scores for different questions were different. That is, there is a variance of scores across the questions (i.e., items). This variance is neither intrajudge nor interjudge error because the judge has perfect intrajudge reliability and there is only one judge, but inter-item error. It is an indication of the lack of *internal consistency* across the items within the same exam.

In a fourth situation, a test of several essay questions with perfect internal consistency was given to a number of subjects. Several judges with perfect intrajudge and interjudge reliabilities were used to score these tests. The scores of different subjects turned out to be different. The variance across these scores is neither interjudge, intrajudge, nor interitem error, but is *variance across subjects*.

The above hypothetical scenarios demonstrate several types of variances. Knowledge of the magnitudes of these variances helps to determine the reliability of test scores.

True and Error Variances

The existence of intrajudge, interjudge, and interitem variances is undesirable. They indicate the *lack* of reliability. The larger these variances, the larger the measurement error. Therefore, these variances can be referred to as *error variances*. Variance across subjects, however, is precisely the target of the exam. Specifically, the purpose of giving an exam to a number of subjects is to differentiate the levels of abilities among these subjects. Score variance across the subjects is not measurement error but an indication of the dispersion of scores, or the amount of differences across these subjects. Hence, variance across subjects can best be described as *true variance*.

Intrajudge, interjudge, and interitem variances used in the four scenarios are only three examples of error variances. In testing and measurement, errors can be introduced from an unlimited number of sources. Hence, there are many other sources of error variances. Variances across scores between a test and a retest, between two parallel forms, across different physical settings, and across different testing locations are examples of some other sources of error variances. Although true variance is generally variance across subjects, there are exceptions. For example, in single-subject research, there is only one subject and hence no variance across subjects. In these situations, the true variance may be variance across points in time or observational sessions depending on the purpose of the measurement.

DESIGN CONSIDERATIONS

The application of Classical Theory is limited to paper-and-pencil norm-referenced situations. The Generalizability Theory, however, is applicable to virtually all types of measurement situations ranging from paper-and-pencil tests to the rating of artistic performances. In other words, the Generalizability approach can be used to assess the quality of scores from numerous measurement situations. Because different measurement situations imply different ways of obtaining scores to reflect different constructs, a thorough understanding of the data collection design for each individual measurement situation is of central importance. It is critical that the various characteristics of a measurement design be considered so that data can be analyzed appropriately through the Generalizability approach. The following are some important design considerations.

Object of Measurement

The most important task is the proper identification of the object of measurement. The object of measurement is the entity that we wish to describe through a numeric score. In most educational and psychological measurement, the object of measurement can generally be described by whom to measure and what to measure.

In the classical approach, the object of measurement is relatively apparent. In conventional paper-and-pencil testing, attempts are made to standardize all other testing conditions. That is, what the test administrator says, the amount of time available, and so forth are fixed. Additionally, only the total score across a number of items is used as the indicator of ability. Under such attempts to standardize measurement conditions, there are only two sources of score variation: variance across people and variance of unspecified sources or random variance. In this case, it is clear that the purpose of the measurement is to differentiate abilities across people. The object of measurement is people.

With the generalizability approach, it is possible to assess multiple sources of variation. This is particularly useful when some aspects of the measurement condition is permitted to vary or when new dimensions are deliberately added to the measurement condition. For example, in addition to items, raters may be involved. As dimensions of measurement are added, the object of measurement is not as clearly defined as in classical theory. It is clear in classical theory that "abilities of people" are the objects of measurement. In a generalizability analysis in which raters are involved, both raters and examinees are people. Yet, dependent on the object of measurement, the appropriate generalizability analysis will change.

A well-studied case that accentuates the importance of the proper identification of the object of measurement is the common faculty evaluation process used in most universities. In the faculty evaluation situation, four different variables are involved: faculty, student, item, and course. *People* as the object of measurement is not as clear-cut anymore since both faculty and students are people. Yet, different objects of measurement imply different psychometric analyses. For example, most offices of institutional research analyze the reliability of faculty evaluation questionnaires through a classical Cronbach Alpha. With this analysis, the implied object of measurement is "individual *student's perception* of his/her own teacher's teaching ability." Although this is good information, it can hardly be equated to "individual faculty member's teaching ability." To properly assess the reliability of faculty evaluation in measuring "individual faculty member's teaching ability" requires a generalizability analysis as suggested by Gillmore, Kane, and Naccarato (1978). Further, because faculty members will only teach courses of their own specialization and it is extremely unlikely that a professor of literature will teach mathematics courses, the analysis can be further modified to a different generalizability analysis in which the courses taught by a specific instructor is considered fixed. With this analysis, the object of measurement would become "individual faculty member's ability to teach courses of his or her own specialization." Hence, different objects of measurement may imply different psychometric analyses.

The proper identification of the object of measurement is important in generalizability because, within a measurement situation, there can be many different sources of score variance. With the exception of variance across the object of measurement, all other variances are indications of measurement error. However, the variance across the object of measurement is not error but true variance. Conceptually, we hope to be able to attain a measurement situation in which the true variance, or variance across the object of measurement is large while the variances associated with all other sources are small.

Take, for instance, a situation in which several judges rated a number of compositions from a number of examinees. Let us say that in this situation we have a large score variance across judges. If the object of measurement is "examinees' composition abilities," we have a large amount of measurement error because the same composition can obtain different scores depending on which judge is employed. However, if the object of measurement is "individual judge's perception of the compositions," the large variance across judges becomes desirable. With this latter object of measurement, we are interested in distinguishing Judge A's from Judge B's perception. Differences across judges are no longer measurement error but genuine differences across the object of measurement. Therefore, dependent on the desired object of measurement, different variances may take on different meanings.

Facets of Measurement

As illustrated earlier in the different types of variances, in a measurement situation, there are many possible sources of score variation. One of these sources is the object of measurement. That is, the variation across one of the dimensions of the measurement situation is true variance due to the differences across the objects of measurement. All other sources are then sources of measurement error. These sources of measurement error are referred to as *facets* of measurement. For example, a geography examination is given to a number of examinees. Each examinee is asked to provide answers in the form of essays to several questions. The essays by all examinees are rated by a number of judges. There are three sources of score variations: variations across examinees, across judges, and across questions or items. If the object of measurement is examinees' knowledge in geography, then judges and items become sources of error or facets. Hence, the measurement design is referred to as a two-facet design.

The individual cases within a facet are known as *levels* of a facet. For example, in the geography exam, if there are five essay items and the responses are to be judged by four raters, the item facet then has five levels and the judge facet has four levels.

Random versus Fixed Facets

Measurement facets may be random or fixed. With a random facet, the levels within the facet in the psychometric analysis are considered a random sample of all possible levels of that facet. Future administrations of the measurement procedure may employ different levels of that facet. In our geography example, if the four raters are considered a random sample of all similar raters and if future administrations of the geography exam may use a different set of similar raters, the rater facet is considered random. On the other hand, a facet is considered fixed if all future administrations of the measurement procedure employ the exact levels being employed in the analysis. In our example, if the same four raters would always be used in all future administrations of the exam, the rater facet would be fixed. A common term used in everyday language for a fixed facet is *standardization*. That is, when the rater facet is fixed, we may described raters as standardized.

An interesting characteristic of a fixed facet is that when a facet is fixed, it becomes part of the object of measurement. For example, in an Olympic diving competition, contestants perform their routines at a particular pool with a particular diving board. If the object of measurement is "individual contestant's diving skills," questions may be raised as to whether the contestant would obtain the same score had the contestant performed at a different pool, at a different diving board, in a different temperature, and so forth? These become facets of measurement or sources of measurement error. However, if we were to standardize the pool, the diving board, and temperature so that contestants would always be evaluated under the same set of conditions, these sources of measurement error would be eliminated.

Objects of measurement can be more reliably measured, and with better validity, when facets are fixed than when they are not. The trade-off, however, is that the object of measurement is restricted. If we were to fix the pool, diving board, and temperature in the diving competition, the object of measurement is no longer "individual contestant's diving skills" but "individual contestant's diving skills at the assigned pool, at the assigned diving board, and in the particular temperature."

The more facets that are fixed, the better the reliability and validity of the scores. However, as more facets are fixed, the object of measurement becomes more restricted and may be less meaningful. If all facets are fixed, there is no measurement error, but the object of measurement would not be meaningful at all. Recall the hypothetical scenario in which a single judge assigned a score of 6 out of 10 points to an essay of a subject. In that situation, we questioned whether the same score would be obtained by that subject if the same judge were to score the same essay at a different time, if the same essay were scored by a different judge, and if a different essay by the same subject were judged. Hence, we have three facets: error across time, error across judges, and error across items. These measurement errors would be eliminated if we fixed all three facets. That is, we would use only this judge at this time to score this particular item. Assuming that all other conditions are equally fixed, the score of 6 out of 10 is then perfectly reliable. However, it is only a reliable indication of the subject's ability as viewed by this judge at this time on this item. When the object of measurement is severely restricted as in this case, the meaningfulness of the score becomes questionable. In other words, there is a trade-off between reliability–validity and the importance of the object of measurement.

To apply the generalizability theory, at least one facet must be random. Conceptually, this is reasonable because if all facets are fixed, the score is perfectly reliable and there is no need to assess reliability. However, the object of measurement is extremely limited.

The Nature of True Score

In classical theory, true score is defined in a very general manner. Specifically, the true score for an individual in classical theory is operationally defined as the mean observed score over repeated measurements of the same individual. In this view, true score is a constant characteristic of the person and for each person, there can only be one true score. This operational definition suffers from a lack of measurement context. That is, it does not specify the conditions of these repeated measurements (Feldt & Brennan, 1989).

From the above discussions of objects and facets of measurement, within the generalizability conceptual framework, there can be many different measurement procedures. A different procedure may imply a different (e.g., more restrictive) object of measurement and different sources of measurement error. Therefore, true score is not a static characteristic of an individual object of measurement (e.g., ability of a person). Rather, for a given individual, there can be different true scores, depending on the measurement design, the facets that are permitted to change (i.e., random facets), and the sources of measurement error (e.g., Nitko, 1983). A corollary of the ideas of multiple sources of measurement error and multiple true scores is that there are multiple reliability coefficients for the measurement of the same construct.

Data Collection Designs

The process through which measurement scores are gathered may be crossed or nested. In a crossed design, all objects of measurement are measured under all identified levels of all facets. In a nested design, however, objects of measurement are measured under some but not all identified levels of one or more facets. In our geography example, if all five essays from all examinees are rated by all four raters, we have a fully crossed design. But, if the essays by some examinees are rated by judges A and B while those of other examinees are rated by judges C and D and no judge rated all examinees, we have a nested design in which judges are nested within examinees. In general, a crossed design is more informative than a nested design in that more specific information regarding sources of measurement error can be obtained. However, the logistic requirements for data collection in a fully-crossed design are, in many situations, impractical.

G-study and D-study

With the proper object of measurement, the potential sources of measurement, and a tentative measurement design identified, the remaining questions are what are the magnitudes of error associated with each facet of measurement and how much would these measurement errors be reduced if the measurement procedure were further restricted. The process through which the magnitudes of error associated with each random facet in the tentative measurement design are estimated is referred to as the *generalizability study* or *G*-study. In a *G*-study, the purpose is to estimate the variances associated with various facets of measurement.

After these variances are estimated through a *G*-study, consequences of various changes in the measurement design can be investigated to seek the optimal design. For instance, one may investigate the reduction of error as a result of treating some of the facets as fixed; that is, how much improvement in reliability can be obtained if certain facets were standardized. One may also investigate the reduction of error as a result of using more than one level in a facet. For instance, we may investigate the reduction in measurement error if, instead of one rater, we always use the mean score across two raters as the score for the object of measurement. These investigations of various scenarios are referred to as *decision studies* or *D*-studies.

The stages of *G*-study and *D*-study are in fact not a new feature applicable only within a generalizability framework. Within classical theory, we also have available a *G*-study and a *D*-study in a much more restricted sense. Specifically, in classical theory, all facets are generally assumed standardized and the only random facet is items. When we compute a reliability coefficient in classical measurement, we are not exactly estimating variances. However, we are estimating the proportions of variances. Given that there is only one facet, estimating the classical reliability is analogous to estimating variances associated with the total test score across items. From a certain perspective, this is analogous to a *G*-study in which the concern is with the variances of the total score. After the reliability is estimated, we may wish to investigate the consequences of increasing or decreasing the number of items through the Spearman-Brown prophecy formula. These investigations are then analogous to *D*-studies. With classical theory, because there is only one facet, we cannot investigate the consequences of treating the only facet (items, test–retest, etc.) as fixed because when the only facet is treated as fixed, there would not be any measurement error.

CHAPTER 5

Generalizability Theory: Statistical Methods

After a conceptual measurement design is determined, data can be gathered through the chosen design. These data can then be analyzed statistically to estimate the magnitudes of various sources of measurement error. The statistical procedure used in generalizability theory is the Analysis of Variance (ANOVA) procedure. Specifically, after data have been gathered, they are analyzed through ANOVA in the G-study stage of the analysis. The purpose of this ANOVA is to estimate variances due to the object of measurement, different facets of measurement, and the interactions among the object of measurement and facets. In the common application of ANOVA in inferential statistical significance testing, the purpose of the ANOVA process is to estimate F-ratios. Based on these F-ratios, decisions are made as to whether to retain or reject null hypotheses. In the generalizability application of ANOVA, however, F-ratios are of no interest at all. Instead, the mean square (MS) estimates are used as the bases to estimate the underlying variance components.

Through ANOVA, MS due to various main effect sources and interactions can be estimated. What is of interest is the underlying population variances (known as *variance components*) and MSs are biased estimates of these variance components. Based on sampling theory, the most probable values of these variance components are estimated from these MSs. The estimation of these variance components from MSs completes the G-study stage of a generalizability analysis. The resulting variance components indicate the most probable expected degree of score variation for a single level of each facet; for example, the expected error associated with a single item, a single rater, and so forth.

In the D-study stage, various application scenarios are posed. For example, what if we have 10, 20, 30 items? What if we use 2, 3, 4 raters? What if the items are fixed? The reliability associated with each application scenario is estimated through various manipulations of the variance components obtained in the G-study. For the purpose of illustration, the statistical procedures for the G- and D-studies of three common measurement designs are discussed below. The use of *Venn Diagrams* to assist the statistical analyses for other more complex designs are also provided.

Figure 5.1 provides a graphic summary of the process of a generalizability analysis. Note that under Scenario 3 in this figure, both evidence of reliability *and* validity are derived. The use of generalizability for validity

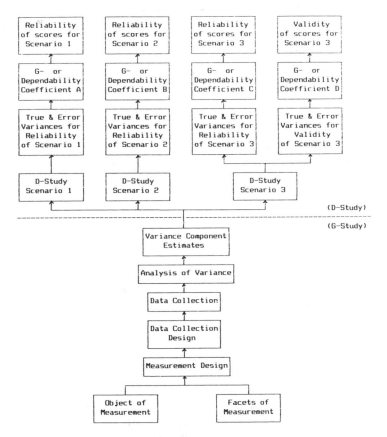

Figure 5.1.   The Process of Generalizability Theory

analysis is discussed in detail in chapter 11. It should be recognized here that, whereas classical theory is primarily an approach to estimate reliability, the generalizability approach can be used to derive evidence of validity as well.

SINGLE-FACET CROSSED-DESIGN

The simplest and most common of all measurement designs is a single-facet crossed design. A common example of this design is a paper-and-pencil multiple-choice test in which all subjects are to respond to all items and all other testing conditions are standardized (or all other facets are fixed). In this example, subjects are the object of measurement and items are the facet of measurement and the only source of measurement error. For discussion, let us say that the test has K items and has been administered to N subjects. The resulting data structure is an N-subject-by-K-item data matrix, with each cell representing the score of a particular subject on a particular item.

G-study

The NxK data matrix can be submitted to a G-study through ANOVA. First, in the usual ANOVA fashion, the mean item score for each subject, the mean subject score for each item, and the grand mean across all items and all subjects can be calculated. Specifically, the mean item score for the ith subject is:

$$\overline{X}_i = (\sum_{j=1}^{K} X_{ij})/K, \tag{5.1}$$

the mean subject score for the jth item is:

$$\overline{X}_j = (\sum_{i=1}^{N} X_{ij})/N, \tag{5.2}$$

and the grand mean is:

$$\overline{X}_i = (\sum_{i=1}^{N} \sum_{j=1}^{K} X_{ij})/NK, \tag{5.3}$$

With this single-subject crossed-design, there are three sources of score variation: subject (s), item (i), and the interaction between subjects and items (si). The sums of squares (SS) for each of these three sources of score variation can be calculated as follows:

$$SS_{\text{subject}} = SS_s = K\sum_{i=1}^{N}\overline{X}_i^2 - NK\overline{X}^2, \tag{5.4}$$

$$SS_{\text{item}} = SS_i = N\sum_{j=1}^{K}\overline{X}_j^2 - NK\overline{X}^2, \tag{5.5}$$

$$SS_{\text{interaction}} = SS_{si}$$
$$= \sum_{i=1}^{N}\sum_{j=1}^{K} X_{ij}^2 - K\sum_{i=1}^{N}\overline{X}_i^2 - N\sum_{j=1}^{K}\overline{X}_j^2 + NK\overline{X}^2. \tag{5.6}$$

The degrees of freedom associated with each of these three SSs are:

$$df_s = N - 1, \tag{5.7}$$

$$df_i = K - 1, \tag{5.8}$$

and

$$df_{si} = (N - 1)(K - 1). \tag{5.9}$$

Hence, the mean squares for each of these three sources are:

$$MS_s = SS_s/(N-1), \tag{5.10}$$

$$MS_i = SS_i/(K-1), \tag{5.11}$$

and

$$MS_{si} = SS_{si}/(N-1)(K-1). \tag{5.12}$$

In the common application of ANOVA, these MS estimates are used to obtain F-ratios for significance testing. In a G-study, however, these are used to estimate the variance components associated with these three sources of score variations: σ_s^2, σ_i^2, and σ_{si}^2. Based on sampling theory, if we were to draw a random sample of N subjects and K items from a population with variance components σ_s^2, σ_i^2, and σ_{si}^2 and calculate the mean squares for the sample data in the manner described in Equations 5.1 through 5.12, it is expected that we would obtain mean square values as follows:

$$EMS_s = \sigma_{si}^2 + K\sigma_s^2, \tag{5.13}$$

$$EMS_i = \sigma_{si}^2 + N\sigma_i^2, \tag{5.14}$$

and

$$EMS_{si} = \sigma_{si}^2 . \tag{5.15}$$

where EMS_s, EMS_i, and EMS_{si} are the expected subject, item, and interaction mean squares. In actual data analysis, if we were to assume that the MS values obtained from a set of empirical data equal the expected mean squares described in Equations 5.13 through 5.15, through algebraic conversions, we can estimate the three variance components as follows:

$$\sigma_s^2 = (MS_s - MS_{si})/K, \tag{5.16}$$

$$\sigma_i^2 = (MS_i - MS_{si})/N, \tag{5.17}$$

and

$$\sigma_{si}^2 = MS_{si} . \tag{5.18}$$

With the values of σ_s^2, σ_i^2, and σ_{si}^2 estimated, the single-facet crossed-design G-study is complete.

D-Study

With these variance components, various measurement scenarios can be posed and the reliabilities of the scores under these scenarios can be estimated. In this chapter we concentrate on only situations in which test scores are to be interpreted in a norm-referenced fashion. Numerous D-study scenarios can also be posed for criterion-referenced score interpretation. These D-studies are discussed in the chapter on criterion-referenced testing. To illustrate D-study scenarios with norm-referenced interpretations, the following are four common single-facet D-study scenarios:

Single Item Norm-referenced Score: One possible scenario is the use of the score on a single randomly-chosen similar item to be interpreted in a norm-referenced fashion to indicate the ability of a subject. When scores are to be interpreted in a norm-referenced fashion, only interaction variances are of concern and the error variance is referred to as *relative error variance*. Relative error variances are frequently denoted by $\sigma^2(\delta)$. It is analogous, but not identical, to random error variance in classical theory.

For the single-item norm-referenced scenario, the amount of measurement error [or relative error variance or $\sigma^2(\delta)$] is represented by the interaction variance σ_{si}^2 from the G-study. The square root of this variance is the standard error of measurement around the score of a single item. Confidence intervals can be established around the score for a single item obtained by a subject in a fashion similar to that of classical theory.

Because in generalizability analysis, there can be many different D-study scenarios, each with its own unique amounts of measurement error, there can be many different reliability coefficients for the same set of G-study data. Additionally, whereas classical reliability implies only a single unspecified source of measurement error (i.e., random error), generalizability can potentially assess multiple sources of error. To distinguish conceptually the potentially multidimensional nature of a generalizability analysis from the unidimensional classical reliability, the term *generalizability coefficient* or simply *G-coefficient* is used to describe the reliability coefficient obtained in the D-study of a norm-referenced scenario.

Recall that reliability is defined as the proportion of true variance. In our single-item norm-referenced D-study scenario, the true variance is σ_s^2 and the error variance is $\sigma^2(\delta)$ or σ_{si}^2. Hence, the generalizability coefficient, which is analogous to classical reliability coefficient, of our single-item norm-referenced score is:

$$E\rho^2 = \sigma_s^2/(\sigma_s^2 + \sigma_{si}^2). \tag{5.19}$$

A generalized version of this G-coefficient which can be applied to other D-study scenarios is:

$$E\rho^2 = \sigma_s^2/[\sigma_s^2 + \sigma^2(\delta)]. \tag{5.20}$$

Like its counterpart in classical theory — the reliability coefficient, the generalizability coefficient is the proportion of observed variance that is true variance and ranges in value from 0 to 1.

Total Score, Norm-referenced: This D-study scenario is similar to the previous scenario except that the score of interest is not from a single item but the total sum (or some linear transformation such as mean) across the K items in the test. For this scenario, the relative error variance $\sigma^2(\delta)$ is σ_{si}^2/K, where K is the number of items in the test. Note that by dividing σ_{si}^2 by K, the $\sigma^2(\delta)$ for this total score scenario can be expected to be smaller than that for the single-item scenario. This is consistent with common sense in that the total score across a number of items can be expected to be more stable than that of a single item.

As before, the square root of this relative error variance is the standard error of measurement for this D-study scenario. This standard error of measurement would be identical numerically to the standard error of measurement one would obtain had one used the Cronbach Alpha approach in classical theory.

Based on the generalized Equation 5.20, the generalizability coefficient for the total score in this D-study scenario is:

$$E\rho^2 \;=\; \sigma_s^2/[\sigma_s^2 + (\sigma_{si}^2/K)].\tag{5.21}$$

Numerically, this G-coefficient will be identical to a classical Cronbach Alpha. If the data were dichotomous, this G-coefficient would also be identical in numerical value to a KR-20 of the same data. Another way to look at the similarities between the classical Cronbach Alpha, KR-20, and standard error of measurement and their counterparts within this D-study scenario is that the classical approach is a special case of the generalizability approach. Specifically, the classical approach is analogous to a single-facet D-study in which one is interested in the error and reliability associated with the total score to be interpreted in a norm-referenced fashion.

Total Score, Norm-referenced, Different Test Length: In this D-study scenario, we wish to assess the error and reliability of the total score if items were added or deleted from the test. More precisely, we wish to assess the consequences if the number of items were changed from K to X. For this scenario, $\sigma^2(\delta)$ is σ_{si}^2/X and the G-coefficient is:

$$E\rho^2 \;=\; \sigma_s^2/[\sigma_s^2 + (\sigma_{si}^2/X)].\tag{5.22}$$

This D-study scenario is analogous to the classical Spearman-Brown process and Equation 5.22 has the same effect as the application of the Spearman-Brown prophecy formula to a classical Cronbach Alpha by setting K in the Spearman-Brown formula in Equation 3.15 to X/(number of items in original test).

Error of the Mean: In statistical analyses, it is often desirable to assess the sampling error associated with using a sample mean $\overline{X}$ to represent the population mean μ. The amount of sampling error is represented by the standard error of the mean, or the square of which—the mean error variance. The limitation of the standard error of the mean and mean error variance is that they assume that the sample scores are perfectly reliable and that the only error in using $\overline{X}$ to represent μ is the error of random sampling fluctuation. However, the scores for the sample obtained through whatever measurement procedure is never perfectly reliable. In other words, the error in using $\overline{X}$ to represent μ contains both sampling and measurement error. Conventional mean error variance, which assumes perfect score reliability, would hence underestimate the amount of error. A more precise indicator of the amount of error in using $\overline{X}$ to represent μ is the mean score variance, denoted by $\sigma^2(\overline{X})$, which takes into consideration both the sampling and the measurement error in using the mean from a sample of N subjects responding to a K item test as an estimate of μ. Statistically,

$$\sigma^2(\overline{X}) = (\sigma_s^2/N) + (\sigma_i^2/K) + (\sigma_{si}^2/NK), \tag{5.23}$$

which indicates the amount of sampling *and* measurement error in using the sample mean total score of the test to represent the population mean. The square root of this mean score variance is thus a more precise estimate of the standard error of the mean.

SINGLE-FACET NESTED-DESIGN

Another common measurement design is a single-facet nested-design. In this design, some levels of the single facet are applied to some subjects while other levels are applied to other subjects. A common example is the scoring of compositions by judges. For example, in the writing portion of a basic skills mastery testing program, all students are assigned the same topic and each student is to write a brief essay on that topic. One hundred trained raters are employed to read and assign a single score to each essay. However, each essay is scored by only 2 of the 100 raters. In other words, the essays for 2 different students are scored by 2 different pairs of raters. In this situation, raters are nested with students and the object of measurement is individual students writing ability. The difference in data structure between a crossed design and a nested design can be represented by the difference in the schema in Figs. 5.2 and 5.3. In these two figures, the shaded areas are ones in which scores are available.

G-Study

The major statistical difference between a crossed design and a nested design is that the main effect variance component due to the nested facet is not separable statistically from the interaction variance component through ANOVA. Consequently, we can only compute an overall error sum of squares, an overall error mean square, and estimate an overall omnibus error variance without knowledge of the contributions of main

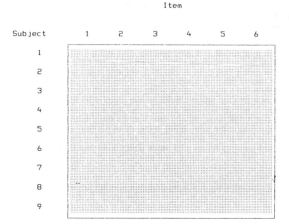

Figure 5.2.   Data Structure of a Crossed Design

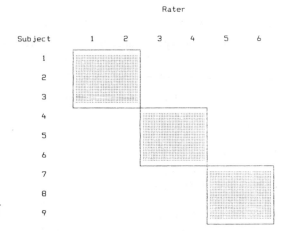

Figure 5.3.   Data Structure of
a Nested Design

effect and interaction error variances. This inability to distinguish main effect from interaction error variances tends to lead to more conservative (lower) generalizability coefficients in the *D*-studies than their crossed design counterparts.

In our writing test example, rater main effect variance is not distinguishable from the interaction variance for our single-facet nested design. Thus, only two variance components are estimated through ANOVA: subject variance (i.e., universe score variance) and an omnibus error variance. If K (e.g., $K = 2$) raters are used to score the essay of each of N subjects, there are then a total of NK raters. The SS for the two variance components are:

$$SS_s = K \sum_{i=1}^{N} \overline{X}_i^2 - NK\overline{X}^2, \tag{5.23}$$

$$SS_{r:s} = \sum_{i=1}^{N} \sum_{j=1}^{K} X_{ij}^2 - K \sum_{i=1}^{N} \overline{X}_i^2, \tag{5.24}$$

where $SS_{r:s}$ is the sum of squares for the omnibus rater-nested-within-subject error term. The degrees of freedom associated with these two SSs are:

$$df_s = N - 1, \tag{5.25}$$

and

$$df_{r:s} = NK - N. \tag{5.26}$$

Thus, the mean squares for these two sources are:

$$MS_s = SS_s/(N-1), \tag{5.27}$$

and

$$MS_{r:s} = SS_{r:s}/(NK - N). \tag{5.28}$$

The expected mean squares for subject and for the nested term are:

$$EMS_s = \sigma_{r:s}^2 + K\sigma_s^2, \tag{5.29}$$

and

$$EMS_{r:s} = \sigma_{r:s}^2. \tag{5.30}$$

Therefore, the two variance components can be estimated by:

$$\sigma_s^2 = (MS_s - MS_{r:s})/K, \tag{5.31}$$

and

$$\sigma_{r:s}^2 = MS_{r:s}. \tag{5.32}$$

D-Study

Statistically, the major difference between a single-facet crossed design and a single-facet nested design is the inability of the latter to separate σ^2_i from σ^2_{si}. Hence, the relative error variances for nested-design D-studies tend to be larger, whereas G-coefficients tend to be smaller, than their crossed design counterparts. This is not because nested designs are inherently less reliable. Rather, nested designs lead to less precise estimates of relative error variance, more conservative estimates of G-coefficients, and thus less informative results. However, when applied, nested designs are often more practicable than crossed designs. We discuss the same four D-study scenarios as in the earlier crossed design:

Single Item Norm-referenced Score: Because of its inability to estimate σ^2_{sr} separately, the relative error variance $\sigma^2(\delta)$ for a single item in a nested design is $\sigma^2_{r:s}$. Similarly, based on Equation 5.20, the G-coefficient for a single item is:

$$E\rho^2 = \sigma^2_s/(\sigma^2_s + \sigma^2_{r:s}). \tag{5.33}$$

Total Score, Norm-referenced: In a similar fashion, the relative error variance for the total score is $\sigma^2(\delta) = \sigma^2_{r:s}/K$. In our writing test example, however, there is only one item (i.e., one essay). The facet of measurement is not items, but raters. Although it is sensible to estimate the reliability of a total score across items, the sensibility of using the total score across raters as an indication of an examinee's ability is not always apparent. A more common practice is to take the average score across raters rather than the total score. Because average scores for the examinees are essentially linear transformations of total scores (i.e., total score divided by K raters), the D-study estimates for the total score apply equally to the average score or any other linear transformation of the total score.

The G-coefficient for this nested design D-study scenario is a direct extension of Equation 5.20 as follows:

$$E\rho^2 = \sigma^2_s/[\sigma^2_s + (\sigma^2_{r:s}/K)]. \tag{5.34}$$

Note that although the cross-design counterpart of this G-coefficient (i.e., Equation 5.21) is numerically equivalent to Cronbach Alpha or KR-20, because of the nested design, this coefficient is not expected to be equivalent to Cronbach Alpha or KR-20, unless the unknown main effect variance component due to raters proves to be zero in value.

Mean Score, Norm-referenced, Different Number of Raters: Again, the relative error variance of the mean score across raters if X instead of K raters were used is $\sigma_{r:s}^2/X$ and the G-coefficient for this mean score is:

$$E\rho^2 = \sigma_s^2/[\sigma_s^2 + (\sigma_{r:s}^2/X)]. \qquad (5.35)$$

Error of the Mean: The mean score variance, $\sigma^2(\overline{X})$, which takes into consideration both the sampling and the measurement error in using the mean from a sample of N subjects rated by K raters each in a nested design as an estimate of μ is:

$$\sigma^2(\overline{X}) = (\sigma_s^2/N) + (\sigma_{r:s}^2/NK). \qquad (5.36)$$

TWO-FACET CROSSED-DESIGN

As discussed earlier, classical psychometric analyses are at least numerically, if not conceptually, equivalent to single-facet crossed design generalizability analyses. Because many standardized paper-and-pencil tests as well as classroom tests used today essentially constitute single-facet crossed design measurement situations, the use of the generalizability approach would lead to results similar to those of classical analyses in many cases. In these situations, the advantage of the generalizability approach is not apparent.

The conceptual as well as statistical advantages of the generalizability approach becomes apparent when one departs from the single-facet crossed design and when one considers situations in which more than one source of error is introduced into the measurement procedure. To provide a focus for discussion, we use a measurement situation in which N_s examinees took an essay exam on history. This history exam has N_i questions and all examinees are required to provide a written answer to all N_i questions. All the written answers on all N_i questions by all N_s examinees are scored by the same N_r raters. In this situation, we have a 2-facet crossed design.

G-Study

With a single-facet crossed design, there are only three variance components. With a two-facet crossed design, however, there are seven variance components. Specifically, there are three main effect components (i.e., *s*, *i*, and *r* in the history exam), three 2-way interactions (i.e., *si*, *sr*, and *ir*), and one 3-way interaction (i.e., *sir*). The mean squares for these seven components can be estimated by:

$$MS_s = (N_i N_r \sum_{i=1}^{N_s} \overline{X}_i^2 - N_s N_i N_r \overline{X}^2)/(N_s - 1), \tag{5.37}$$

$$MS_i = (N_s N_r \sum_{j=1}^{N_i} \overline{X}_j^2 - N_s N_i N_r \overline{X}^2)/(N_i - 1), \tag{5.38}$$

$$MS_r = (N_s N_i \sum_{h=1}^{N_r} \overline{X}_h^2 - N_s N_i N_r \overline{X}^2)/(N_r - 1), \tag{5.39}$$

$$MS_{si} = (N_r \sum_{i=1}^{N_s} \sum_{j=1}^{N_s} \overline{X}_{ij}^2 - N_i N_r \sum_{i=1}^{N_s} \overline{X}_1^2 - N_s N_r \sum_{j=1}^{N_i} \overline{X}_j^2$$
$$- N_s N_i N_r \overline{X}^2)/(N_s - 1)(N_i - 1), \tag{5.40}$$

$$MS_{sr} = (N_i \sum_{i=1}^{N_s} \sum_{h=1}^{N_r} \overline{X}_{ih}^2 - N_i N_r \sum_{i=1}^{N_s} \overline{X}_1^2 - N_s N_i \sum_{h=1}^{N_r} \overline{X}_h^2$$
$$- N_s N_i N_r \overline{X}^2)/(N_s - 1)(N_r - 1), \tag{5.41}$$

$$MS_{ir} = (N_s \sum_{j=1}^{N_i} \sum_{h=1}^{N_r} \overline{X}_{jh}^2 - N_s N_i \sum_{j=1}^{N_i} \overline{X}_j^2 - N_s N_r \sum_{h=1}^{N_r} \overline{X}_h^2$$
$$- N_s N_i N_r \overline{X}^2)/(N_i - 1)(N_r - 1), \tag{5.42}$$

and

$$MS_{sir} = (\sum_{i=1}^{N_s} \sum_{j=1}^{N_i} \sum_{h=1}^{N_r} X_{ijh} + N_i N_r \sum_{i=1}^{N_s} \overline{X}_i^2 + N_s N_r \sum_{j=1}^{N_i} \overline{X}_j^2 + N_s N_r \sum_{h=1}^{N_r} \overline{X}_h^2$$
$$- N_r \sum_{i=1}^{N_s} \sum_{j=1}^{N_i} \overline{X}_{ij}^2 - N_i \sum_{i=1}^{N_s} \sum_{h=1}^{N_r} \overline{X}_{ih}^2 - N_s \sum_{i=1}^{N_i} \sum_{j=1}^{N_i} \overline{X}_{jh}^2$$
$$- N_s N_i N_r \overline{X}^2)/(N_s - 1)(N_i - 1)(N_r - 1). \tag{5.43}$$

Based on these *MS* values, the seven variance components can be estimated through:

$$\sigma_s^2 = (MS_s - MS_{si} - MS_{sr} + MS_{sir})/N_i N_r, \tag{5.44}$$

$$\sigma_i^2 = (MS_i - MS_{si} - MS_{ir} + MS_{sir})/N_s N_r, \tag{5.45}$$

$$\sigma_r^2 = (MS_r - MS_{sr} - MS_{ir} + MS_{sir})/N_sN_i \,, \tag{5.46}$$

$$\sigma_{si}^2 = (MS_{si} - MS_{sir})/N_r \,, \tag{5.47}$$

$$\sigma_{sr}^2 = (MS_{sr} - MS_{sir})/N_i \,, \tag{5.48}$$

$$\sigma_{ir}^2 = (MS_{ir} - MS_{sir})/N_s \,, \tag{5.49}$$

$$\sigma_{sir}^2 = MS_{sir} \,. \tag{5.50}$$

As can be seen, when new facets are added, the statistical estimation procedure becomes increasingly complex. In general, computer programs are used to perform these complex estimation procedures. Bell (1985) reviewed various ANOVA programs to assess their appropriateness for generalizability analysis. Through his analysis, it was found that the specialized GENOVA program (Crick & Brennan, 1983) and the VAR-COMP procedure in SAS (1985) are the two most appropriate programs to assist in the estimation of variance components in a G-study. Feldt and Brennan (1989) also recommended BMDP8V (Dixon & Brown, 1979) as a useful program for generalizability analyses.

D-Study

With a 2-facet design, the number of D-study scenarios that can be investigated is greatly expanded beyond those of a single-facet study. This is not only because there are more variance components. In addition, with more than one facet to consider, one can investigate the consequence of standardizing (or treating as fixed) one of the two facets. With the numerous possible D-study scenarios, it is difficult to explore all of them. Instead, three general "rules of thumb" are presented below:

1. The relative error variance $\sigma^2(\delta)$ for a given D-study scenario in which X raters are used to score Y questions on the exam (Note: X and/or Y can be 1) is $(\sigma_{si}^2/Y + \sigma_{sr}^2/X + \sigma_{sir}^2/XY)$. In other words, the relative error variance for a multifacet D-study is the sum of all interaction variance components that interact *with the object of measurement* and is divided by the desired number of levels. X and Y can be any desired number. For example, Y may be 1.

2. The G-coefficient of the total score across Y questions across X raters with a norm-referenced interpretation is $\sigma_s^2/[\sigma_s^2 + \sigma^2(\delta)]$ which is then:

$$E\rho^2 = \sigma_s^2/(\sigma_s^2 + \sigma_{si}^2/Y + \sigma_{sr}^2/X + \sigma_{sir}^2/XY) \tag{5.51}$$

Again, this coefficient would apply to total score, mean score, and any other linear transformation of the total score.

3. For a facet that is treated as fixed, the interaction between that facet and the object of measurement is no longer error but is a part of the restricted object of measurement. Therefore, the interaction variance between that facet and the object of measurement is part of true variance. Thus, if we treat items as fixed in this 2-facet design, $\sigma^2(\delta) = (\sigma_{sr}^2/X + \sigma_{sir}^2/XY)$ and the G-coefficient for this fixed facet D-study scenario is:

$$E\rho^2 = (\sigma_s^2 + \sigma_{si}^2/Y)/(\sigma_s^2 + \sigma_{si}^2/Y + \sigma_{sr}^2/X + \sigma_{sir}^2/XY) \qquad (5.52)$$

On the other hand, if we treat raters as fixed, then $\sigma^2(\delta) = (\sigma_{si}^2/Y + \sigma_{sir}^2/XY)$ and the G-coefficient is:

$$E\rho^2 = (\sigma_s^2 + \sigma_{sr}^2/Y)/(\sigma_s^2 + \sigma_{si}^2/Y + \sigma_{sr}^2/X + \sigma_{sir}^2/XY) \qquad (5.53)$$

SAMPLE SIZE CONSIDERATIONS

The key to generalizability analyses is the variance components estimated in the G-study stage, which are the building blocks for all subsequent D-studies. The accuracy of these variance estimates are therefore important. In general, the larger the sample of people and the number of levels of each facet, the more stable the variance estimates (Smith, 1978). The stability of a variance estimate is indicated by the variance of the variance estimate.

When the number of levels for a facet is small, it is possible that negative variance estimates are obtained. A negative variance is nonsensical and uninterpretable because variances are squared numbers and are, by definition, positive. To avoid possible negative variance estimates, the sample sizes of subjects and facets should ideally be large. In practice, this may not be attainable. For example, it may be logistically difficult to have more than two or three raters rating the performance of a subject. In these cases, negative variance estimates may result.

Cronbach et al. (1972) suggested that negative variance estimates should default to zero. A problem with this tactic is that variance estimates for different main effects and interactions are mutually related. When one estimate is artificially changed from negative to zero, many other variance estimates are affected and biased. Brennan (1983) suggested that negative variance estimates should default to zero. However, when estimating other variance components, the original negative value for this variance component be retained to avoid the biased effect. Shavelson and Webb (1981) proposed a tentative Bayesian approach that restricts all possible variance estimates to positive values. Marcoulides (1987) proposed a maximum likelihood estimation of variance components that will also lead to positive variance components only. Shavelson, Webb, and Rowley (1989) reviewed these methods and concluded that, with most real datasets, these methods provided very similar estimates of variance components and G-coefficients.

VENN DIAGRAMS

As new facets are added, not only is the statistical analysis more complex, the task of conceptually sorting out the different variance components and the number and nature of possible D-study scenarios increases in complexity geometrically. Whereas a single-facet crossed design has only 3 variance components to consider, a 2-facet crossed design has 7 components, a 3-facet crossed design has 15 components and a 4-facet crossed design has 31 variance components. Fortunately, computer programs are available to assist in the estimation of these variance components. However, the conceptual problem of sorting out these variance components in various combinations to answer different D-study questions remains formidable. Examples of multifacet generalizability analyses can be found in Brennan (1983), Webb and Shavelson (1981), and Webb, Shavelson, and Maddahian (1983).

A useful conceptual aid to grapple with the complexity of multifacet D-studies is the Venn Diagram. When no more than 3 facets are crossed, Venn Diagrams can provide a clear perspective on D-study scenarios. The limit of 3 crossed facets is caused by the physical difficulty of drawing more than 3 crossed facets. (Note that Venn Diagrams can be used for D-studies with more than 3 facets, as long as only 3 facets are crossed and the remaining facets are nested.)

In the use of Venn Diagrams in generalizability analysis, a circle is used to represent each facet and the object of measurement. Overlapping areas between circles are used to represent interaction. Nonoverlapping areas are used to represent main effects. For the purpose of D-studies, all variance components are assumed to have been divided by the appropriate number of levels.

Figure 5.4 is a Venn Diagram representing a single-facet crossed design in which subjects (s) is crossed with items (i). In this study, subjects are the object of measurement. Note that one circle is used to represent subjects and another circle is used to represent items. This diagram can be separated into three segments. The nonoverlapping area of the subject circle represents the σ_s^2 or true variance component. The nonoverlapping area of the item circle represents the σ_i^2/N_i or item main effect component

Subject   Item

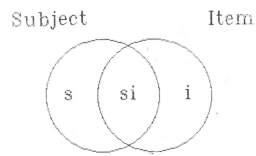

Figure 5.4. Venn Diagram for a
Single-Facet Item Crossed Subject
Design

divided by the desired number of items in the D-study scenario. The overlapping area between the two circles represents σ_{si}^2/N_i or the interaction between subject and items divided by the number of items in the D-study scenario.

In general, for norm-referenced score interpretation, only the circle representing the object of measurement and all the main effects and interactions within that circle are of interest. (The generalizability of criterion-referenced testing is discussed in a later chapter.) The relative error variance or $\sigma^2(\delta)$ is the sum of all interactions within this circle. In this simple single-facet crossed design, $\sigma^2(\delta) = \sigma_{si}^2/N_i$, where N_i is the number of items in the D-study scenario, because there is only one interaction term in this circle. The G-coefficient is the proportion of the circle that is main effect. In this case, the G-coefficient is the proportion of the circle that is σ_s^2. Therefore, the G-coefficient is $\sigma_s^2/[\sigma_s^2 + (\sigma_{si}^2/N_i)]$.

Figure 5.5 is a Venn Diagram for a single-facet nested design in which raters (r) are used to rate subjects (s) but raters are nested within subjects. Note that there are only two variance components and the rater circle is nested within the subject circle. Because for norm-referenced purposes, the components within the subject circle are of interest, $\sigma^2(\delta)$ equals $\sigma_{r:s}^2/N_r$, where N_r is the number of raters in the D-study scenario. The G-coefficient is the proportion of the subject circle that is σ_s^2. In other words, the G-coefficient is $\sigma_s^2/[\sigma_s^2 + (\sigma_{r:s}^2/N_r)]$.

Figure 5.6 is the Venn Diagram for a 2-facet crossed design. In this design, subjects are to respond to N_i items and their responses are rated by

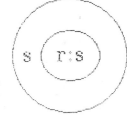

Figure 5.5. Venn Diagram for a
Single-Facet Rater Nested in a Subject Design

N_r raters. There are seven segments in this diagram. Again, for norm-referenced testing, only the segments within the subject circle are of interest. However, when there is more than one facet involved, it is possible to investigate D-study scenarios in which some of the facets are treated as fixed. When a facet is fixed, the two-way interaction between that facet and the object of measurement becomes part of the restricted object of measurement.

In Fig. 5.6, if we wish to treat items as fixed, the object of measurement is conceptually "subject's ability to respond to these particular items" not "subject's ability." In this case, σ_{si}^2/N_i is no longer error. Hence, $\sigma^2(\delta) = \sigma_{sr}^2/N_r + \sigma_{sir}^2/N_iN_r$ and G-coefficient $= [\sigma_s^2 + (\sigma_{si}^2/N_i)]/[\sigma_s^2 + (\sigma_{si}^2/N_i) + (\sigma_{sr}^2/N_r) + (\sigma_{sir}^2/N_iN_r)]$. On the other hand, if we wish to treat raters as fixed, the object of measurement becomes "subject's ability as seen by these particular raters." In this D-study scenario, $\sigma^2(\delta) = \sigma_{si}^2/N_i + \sigma_{sir}^2/N_iN_r$ and G-coefficient $= [\sigma_s^2 + (\sigma_{sr}^2/N_r)]/[\sigma_s^2 + (\sigma_{sr}^2/N_r) + (\sigma_{si}^2/N_i) + (\sigma_{sir}^2/N_iN_r)]$. Finally, if we wish to keep both item and rater facets as random, the object of measurement is "subject's ability," $\sigma^2(\delta) = \sigma_{si}^2/N_i + \sigma_{sr}^2/N_r + \sigma_{sir}^2/N_iN_r$ and G-coefficient $= \sigma_s^2/[\sigma_s^2 + (\sigma_{si}^2/N_i) + (\sigma_{sr}^2/N_r) + (\sigma_{sir}^2/N_iN_r)]$.

A relatively complex design is the design of a typical faculty evaluation (Gillmore, Kane, & Naccarato, 1978). In this design, students-as-raters (s) are nested within courses (c), courses are nested within faculty members (f) and they all cross items (i). With "individual faculty member's teaching ability" as the object of measurement, we have a 3-facet (i.e., students, courses, and items) nested design. Figure 5.7 is a Venn Diagram representing this design. For norm-referenced interpretation, only the segments within the faculty circle are of interest. For a D-study in which all facets are considered random and each faculty member teaches N_c courses, each course has N_s students, and the evaluation questionnaire has N_i items, the G-coefficient is the proportion of the non-overlapping σ_f^2 within the faculty circle. That is,

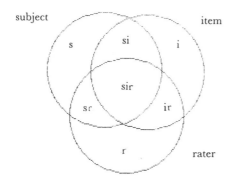

Figure 5.6. Venn Diagram for a 2-Facet Subject Crossed Item Crossed Rater Design

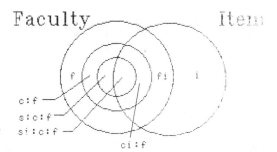

Figure 5.7. Venn Diagram for
Faculty Evaluation Design

$$G\text{-coefficient} = \sigma_f^2 / [\sigma_f^2 + (\sigma_{c:f}^2/N_c) + (\sigma_{s:c:f}^2/N_cN_s)$$
$$+ (\sigma_{si:c:f}^2/N_iN_cN_s) + (\sigma_{ci:f}^2/N_cN_i) + (\sigma_{fi}^2/N_i)]$$

This coefficient assesses the reliability of using the mean (or total) score across N_i items, across N_s students in each course, and across N_c courses taught by the faculty member to indicate the "teaching ability" of the faculty member. Because all facets are treated as random, we are essentially measuring the faculty member's general ability to teach any randomly chosen courses. This D-study scenario is unrealistic in that faculty members generally only teach courses of their own specialization, not any randomly chosen courses. Hence, a more appropriate D-study is to treat courses as a fixed facet. The object of measurement becomes the faculty member ability to teach a particular set of N_c courses and $\sigma_{c:f}^2$ becomes part of the true variance. Thus, for the D-study in which courses are treated as fixed, the G-coefficient is:

$$G\text{-coefficient} = [\sigma_f^2 + (\sigma_{c:f}^2/N_c)]/[\sigma_f^2 + (\sigma_{c:f}^2/N_c) + (\sigma_{s:c:f}^2/N_cN_s)$$
$$+ (\sigma_{si:c:f}^2/N_iN_cN_s) + (\sigma_{ci:f}^2/N_cN_i) + (\sigma_{fi}^2/N_i)]$$

CHAPTER 6

Conventional
Item Analysis

Whether a paper-and-pencil test, a rating scale, or a self-report questionnaire is used, a test is most frequently made up of a number of items (although there *can* be single-item rating scales). Conceptually, if we know the quality of each item in a test, we should be able to deduce the quality of the total test score. Minimally, knowledge of the quality of each item should provide indications of the reliability of the total score. Unfortunately, within classical and generalizability theory, there are no established procedures through which one can deduce the reliability of the total score from known characteristics of individual items. However, knowledge of the characteristics of individual items can guide us in the improvement of the test, and thus maximize the ultimate reliability of the total score.

Various indices of item characteristics can be estimated through item analysis. It should be pointed out that the item analytic techniques discussed in this chapter may best be described as conventional item analyses. This is because a different set of item characteristics can also be derived through item response theory discussed in the next chapter. The item characteristics within item response theory can, in fact, provide information to estimate the quality of the total score and to estimate the true score of examinees. In any event, conventional item analysis can provide information to guide the selection from a pool of items the best items that can enhance the reliability of the total score.

The general strategy is to first determine the number of items needed for the actual administration of the test. This can be determined by such factors as the amount of test time available and the approximate amount of time it takes to respond to each item. A pool of items larger than the number needed is then generated. This pool of items is administered to a pilot sample of subjects similar in characteristic to the examinees for whom the test is intended. Data from this pilot study can then be analyzed to derive item characteristic indices. These indices are used to guide the revision of the test to produce a final test with maximum reliability.

PROBABILITY OF GUESSING

For a multiple-choice or true/false item, an inherent phenomenon is the probability that an examinee without the necessary knowledge can guess correctly. It is reasonable to assume that item score is affected by guessing. Because the total score is the sum of individual item scores, the probability of guessing would thus influence the reliability of the total score.

Unlike other item statistics, the probability of guessing correctly for a given item is not derived empirically through an item analysis. Rather, it is based on assumption and how we think test takers without the necessary knowledge behave. Unfortunately, guessing behavior is not well understood today. Although there have been a number of studies on guessing behavior (e.g., Bliss, 1980; Diamond & Evans, 1973; Lord, 1975), they have not produced results that can be translated into techniques to remove the effect of guessing on item scores. We generally assume that people without the necessary knowledge to select the correct answer would guess at random. Based on the *random guessing model,* for a multiple-choice item with m options, the probability that a subject can answer an item correctly through guessing is thus $1/m$.

There are reasons to believe that the random guessing model does not match reality. The answer to a multiple-choice item is made up of several options. One of these options is the correct answer. All other options are incorrect and are referred to as *distractors.* Dependent on the quality of the distractors, the probability of a correct guess by an individual who cannot identify the correct answer may be higher or lower than chance. That is, the probability of a correct guess may not be $1/m$.

There are two views regarding the probability of a correct guess. One view suggests that people who do not know the correct answer generally have some partial knowledge (Crocker & Algina, 1986; Lord, 1952b). Based on this partial knowledge, they are able to eliminate some distractors. Thus the probability of choosing the correct response is enhanced. For instance, on a 4-option multiple-choice item, an examinee who does not know the correct response has a 25% chance of guessing correctly if the examinee indeed guesses at random. However, if the examinee has some partial knowledge and is able to eliminate two of the three distractors as implausible, the examinee would have to choose from only two remaining options. If the examinee guesses at random at this point, the probability of a correct guess becomes 50%, not 25%. With this view, the probability of guessing right is higher than $1/m$.

An alternative view goes in an opposite direction. According to this view, when constructing a test, item writers deliberately generate distractors that are not only plausible, but attractive (Lord, 1974). It is suggested that examinees without the necessary knowledge to choose the correct option would be attracted to these incorrect options. Hence, the probability of a correct guess is lower than $1/m$. Clearly, more research is needed to investigate the effects of guessing on item as well as total score.

Currently, for a lack of better knowledge, it is frequently assumed that random guessing is an adequate representation of guessing behavior. Conceptually, guessing would render the observed score not representative of true scores, thus affecting the reliability of the observed score. In order to maximize the ability of the observed score in representing the true score (i.e., reliability), the effects of guessing should be removed from the observed score (Also see Lord, 1975). Based on the random guessing model, the *correction for guessing* is attained through:

$$X_c = R - [W/(m - 1)], \tag{6.1}$$

where X_c is the corrected score, R is the number of right answers, W is the number of wrong answers, and m is the number of options in each of the multiple-choice items in the test. Using this correction for guessing to assign scores to examinees is also referred to as *formula scoring*.

Diamond and Evans (1973) found that corrected scores based on the random guessing model did not show higher reliability than their uncorrected counterparts. Conceptually, it is reasonable to assume that guessing should lower score reliability. However, there is no evidence to support the correction for guessing based on the random guessing model. A better model is needed to remove the effects of guessing.

ITEM DIFFICULTY

Another characteristic of an item is its degree of difficulty. The difficulty of an item can be described statistically as the proportion of subjects who can answer the item correctly. This is referred to as the *item difficulty index*. This label is an unfortunate misnomer in that the higher the difficulty index, the *easier* the item. Statistically, the item difficulty index for an item is also known as the *p-value* of that item. The higher the *p*-value, the easier the item. The *p*-value of an item can be estimated based on the proportion of subjects in the pilot study who responded to the item correctly. For an item that is scored dichotomously (i.e., 1 and 0), the difficulty estimate is also equal to the mean item score across the subjects in the study.

For a dichotomous item with a true difficulty index of *p,* the true item variance is *pq.* True total score is the sum of true item scores. Following our earlier quadratic function, true total score variance for an *N*-item test, using deviation score notations, is then:

$$Et^2 = E(x_1 + x_2 + x_3 + \ldots + x_N)^2$$

$$= \sum_{i=1}^{N} x_i^2 + 2 \sum_{i \neq j} x_i x_j \tag{6.2}$$

In other words, total true score variance is a function of item true variance and covariances across items. More precisely:

$$\sigma_t^2 = \sum_{i=1}^{N} \sigma_i^2 + 2 \sum_{i \neq j} r_{ij} \sigma_i \sigma_j \tag{6.3}$$

The larger the individual true item variances as well as the correlations among the items, the large the true total score variance. For a given observed score variance, the larger the true score variance component, the higher the reliability of the observed score. The true score variance is maximized when all true item variances and the correlations among the true item scores in the test are maximized.

For a dichotomous item, true item variance is at its maximum value of 0.25 when $p = q = 0.5$. Therefore, the true item score variance is maximized when the mean true item score is 0.5. To maximize total score reliability, it is desirable to maximize true item score variance; and true item score variance is maximized when the true item difficult is 0.5. In other words, an item that would help to maximize total score reliability is one for which half of the examinees have the true ability to answer correctly.

As discussed earlier, with an objective test consisting of multiple-choice or true/false items, it is possible for the examinee to guess the correct answer. Because of the possibility of guessing, an item with a true difficulty of 0.5 would not have an observed difficulty index of 0.5. Rather, the observed difficulty index from the pilot study would reflect a combination of the 50% of the examinees with the true ability and some other proportion of the remaining examinees who guessed correctly.

Without guessing, it would be desirable to select items that have p-values around 0.50 in the pilot study. However, with guessing, the desired p-value would be higher than 0.50. Based on the random guessing model, the most desirable p-value for an m-option multiple-choice item would be:

$$p' = .5 + .5/m. \qquad (6.4)$$

where p' is the observed p-value that would maximize true item variance. Thus, for a true/false item, the desired p-value is $0.5 + 0.5/2 = 0.75$. Similarly, the desired p-value is 0.67 for a 3-option item, 0.62 for a 4-option item, and 0.60 for a 5-option item. Choosing items with p-values around its appropriate desired p-value would enhance the reliability of the total score.

Also discussed earlier, there is evidence that the random guessing model is unrealistic. Depending on how examinees actually guess, the desired p-values may be higher or lower than the above desired values suggested by the random guessing model. Based on a simulated study, Lord (1952b) found that the reliability of the total score is improved if a p-value of 0.85 for a true/false item, 0.77 for a 3-option item, and 0.74 for a 4-options item is used to select items.

In the use of p-values as a basis for item selection and test revision, two points are important to note. First, the purpose of selecting items with p-values close to the ideal p-values is to maximize total score reliability. If the reliability of the total score is already acceptably high, consideration of other item characteristics, such as discrimination (to be discussed next), are more important. Second, it is sometimes desirable to retain some items with extreme p-values even though they depart significantly from the ideal p-value. Including items with extremely high p-values intermittently throughout the test may serve as motivators for examinees with low abilities, who may otherwise be discouraged and frustrated by the test. Including items with extremely low p-values may present challenges to examinees with high abilities, who may otherwise be bored by the simplicity of the test.

ITEM DISCRIMINATION

The purpose of testing is to differentiate among people with different ability levels. A good item should be able to discriminate those with high from those with low ability. That is, an item is an effective one if those with high ability tend to answer it correctly and those with low ability tend to answer it incorrectly. The reliability of the total score is maximized when all items in the test have high discrimination power. Therefore, in item analysis, it is desirable to estimate the discrimination power of the items so that items with high discrimination can be selected. There are a number of *item discrimination indices* that can be estimated from the data in a pilot study. Two popular ones—the *D-index* and the *point-biserial correlation*—are discussed in this chapter.

The D-Index

The *D*-index, or the *discrimination index,* is a direct expression of the idea that subjects with high ability should tend to respond correctly while subjects with low ability should tend to respond incorrectly. To determine if this has indeed occurred with a given item, the subjects in the pilot study can be divided into a high-ability group and a low-ability group. The proportion of people in each of the two ability groups who have answered the item correctly can be calculated. If the item has good discrimination power, the proportion of the high-ability group answering the item correctly should be substantially higher than the proportion of the low-ability group. The D-index is the difference between these two proportions. That is,

$$D = p_h - p_l, \tag{6.5}$$

where p_h is the proportion in the high-ability group and p_l is the proportion in the low-ability group. The *D*-index would range in value from -1.00 to $+1.00$. A negative D value would indicate that the item is doing the opposite of what it is supposed to do; that is, low-ability examinees have a higher tendency of answering it correctly. The higher positive value the D index, the better the discrimination of the item.

A consideration in computing the *D*-index is how to divide the people in the pilot study into a high-ability and a low-ability group. In practice, these two groups are identified based on their total scores on the test. Based on total scores, we may divide the subjects into an upper-half and a lower-half and consider them to be high-ability and low-ability groups. Alternatively, we may use only the upper third and lower third, or some other cut-off points, to identify the two groups of subjects.

Conceptually, when an upper half/lower half division is used, the difference between the two groups is minimized. Examinees who are just above and just below the cut-off are not very different. Treating them as high-ability and low-ability subjects would reduce the sensitivity of the *D*-index. The sensitivity of the *D*-index can be enhanced if more extremely different groups are used. For example, one may use the upper and lower third, or the upper and lower 10%, and so on. The trade-off, however, is that as more extreme groups are used, the sample size is reduced, and the D-index becomes unstable. Kelley (1939) demonstrated that the optimal levels of sensitivity and stability can be attained if the upper 27% of the subjects are used as the high-ability group and the lower 27% used as the low-ability group. It has been found (e.g., Beuchert & Mendoza, 1979), however, that when the pilot sample is large, the 27% rule is not necessary.

Despite its conceptual and computational parsimony, the D-index has a major limitation. As a sample statistic, it does not have a known sampling distribution. Thus, there is no basis to judge how well the D-index computed from a pilot sample represents the true discrimination power of the item, either through significance testing or through parameter estimation. Nor do we know whether the sample D value is a biased or an unbiased estimate of the true D value.

Point-biserial Correlation

A popular alternative to the D-index is the point-biserial correlation. The point-biserial correlation is a computationally simplified Pearson's r between the dichotomously scored item and the total score. With the total score used as an estimate of ability, the point-biserial correlation would indicate the extent to which ability is related to responses to an item. Computationally, the point-biserial correlation is:

$$r_{pb} = \frac{(\mu_1 - \mu_x)}{\sigma_x} \sqrt{p/q}, \tag{6.6}$$

where μ_1 is the mean total score among examinees who have responded correctly to the item, μ_x is the mean total score for all examinees, p is the item difficulty index for the item, q is $(1-p)$, and σ_x is the standard deviation of the total score for all examinees.

The point-biserial correlation computed through Equation 6.6 tends to somewhat overestimate the discrimination of the item. This is because the item score is part of the total score. The correlation between scores on the item and the total score is thus somewhat inflated because the item score is embedded in the total score. This inflation is negligible for a long test. However, for a short test, the inflation may be important. The inflation can be removed by

$$r_c = \frac{r_{pb}\sigma_x - \sigma_i}{\sqrt{\sigma_i^2 + \sigma_x^2 - 2r_{pb}\sigma_x\sigma_i}}, \tag{6.7}$$

where r_c is the corrected point-biserial, r_{pb} is the original point-biserial, σ_x is the total score standard deviation, and σ_i is the item standard deviation and is equal to $\sqrt{pq}$.

ANALYSIS OF DISTRACTORS

The item difficulty index and the item discrimination index are useful only to the extent that they help to identify problematic items in the pilot pool. By themselves, these statistics provide no hint as to how to improve the item, and subsequently the test. The apparent choice is to delete the problematic items. However, the deletion of items from the pilot pool is not always the best course of action.

There are at least two situations in which item deletion is undesirable. First, although the deletion of problematic items would improve the reliability of the total score, it would also shorten the test. As reliability is a direct function of test length (Lord, 1957), deletion of items would reduce the reliability of the total test score. There is a trade-off in that the enhancement of reliability is somewhat moderated by the shortening of the test. Second, and more importantly, the items in a test are assumed to be a random sample of the universe of possible items in the domain. The extent to which the items in the test is a representative sample of the universe of items in the domain is referred to as *content validity,* which is discussed in further detail in a later chapter. Some items may be considered critical elements of the domain and cannot be deleted without compromising the content validity of the test. When such an item has poor item characteristics, it would be undesirable to delete this item. When this situation occurs, it may be better to analyze the content of the item and revise the item accordingly.

Information that could help the revision of an item may be obtained through an inspection of the response pattern to the item. Poor item statistics may be due to ineffective distractors. Specifically, responses to the distractors can be analyzed to identify "defective" distractors. To detect poor distractors, the option-by-option responses of the high-ability group and and low-ability group can be examined. A good distractor is one that appears plausible such that a low-ability person is attracted to it. However, it should not be ambiguous as to attract high-ability people. Table 6.1 presents the response patterns of the high- and low-ability groups to a particular item.

The example is a multiple-choice item with 4-options. Option B is the correct answer. In this item, Option A is a relatively good distractor in that more low-ability than high-ability people were attracted to this option. In other words, as a distractor, it did what it was supposed to do. Option C

TABLE 6.1
Response Pattern of an Item

	Options			
	A	B*	C	D
High-ability group	7	15	0	28
Low-ability group	37	5	0	8

*Correct answer

is an ineffective distractor. It is probably so obviously implausible as an answer that no one, with high- or low-ability, chose this option. The use of this distractor did not seriously affect the quality of the item. However, this distractor has probably inflated the observed item p-value. Additionally, the item can be improved if a more effective distractor can be generated to replace this one.

Option D is a very poor distractor. It is an option that appeared plausible only to individuals with high ability. One possible explanation is that the content of this option may have appeared plausible only to individuals who have the knowledge to see its plausibility. As a distractor, this option is doing exactly opposite to what it is supposed to do. This distractor is a definite candidate for revision. We should inspect the content of this distractor to identify possible ways to improve it or to replace it entirely.

ITEM RELIABILITY

An item statistic that is not frequently used in practice is the *item reliability index*. It is defined as $\sigma_i r_{pb}$, where σ_i is the item standard deviation and r_{pb} is the point-biserial correlation between the item and the total score. With dichotomous items, the item reliability index would be equivalent to $r_{pb}\sqrt{p_i q_i}$. Item reliability is maximized when both r_{pb} and $p_i q_i$ are maximized. Because r_{pb} is maximized when we select items with high discrimination and $p_i q_i$ is maximized when we select items with $p_i = 0.5$, the assessment of this item reliability index is redundant.

PART 3

ITEM RESPONSE THEORY

CHAPTER 7

Basic Concepts of Item Response Theory

Although the classical theory contains many limitations, it has served us well for many decades. The development of the generalizability theory has expanded the application of the classical theory to many measurement situations beyond standardized paper-and-pencil testing. With conventional item analysis and classical or generalizability reliability assessment, measurement procedures that can yield scores with good reliabilities have been attained. However, the use of classical theory, generalizability theory, and conventional item analytic techniques will also lead to a number of important limitations.

LIMITATIONS OF RANDOM SAMPLING THEORY

In conventional item analysis, when we assess the difficulty of an item, a p-value is derived. This p-value represents the proportion of people in the sample who have responded correctly to the item. The higher this p-value, the easier the item. However, unless the sample of people used is very large and is representative of the overall population, this p-value is not stable. Specifically, it only indicates the proportion of people *in the sample* who have responded correctly to this item. If the sample happens to contain mostly people of high abilities, the p-value would indicate that the item is relatively easy, when it may be difficult for the overall population. Conversely, a low p-value from a sample of people with low abilities may erroneously imply that the item is difficult for the overall population. Hence, the ability of the conventional p-value to indicate the difficulty level of an item is dependent on having a representative sample of individuals in the pilot study. Such a sample is not always attainable and in any event cannot be guaranteed.

The conventional p-value is essentially a probability statement. For an item with a p-value of, say, 0.75, we can state that the probability that a randomly selected subject from the population will respond correctly to this item is 75%. Even when the pilot sample is representative of the population, this remains a very general statement that does not take into account the differences in ability. For individuals with high ability, the actual probability of a correct response is higher than 0.75, whereas for individuals with low ability, the probability is less than 0.75. The p-value of 0.75 can only be considered an average difficulty across all ability levels. It would be more informative if we could express the p-values as a function of ability.

In classical theory, a single reliability estimate is obtained. Although more than one reliability estimate can be obtained in generalizability theory, there is only one reliability estimate for each D-study scenario. From this reliability estimate, we can derive a standard error of measurement that expresses the expected distribution of error around an observed score. As in the case of the conventional p-value, these reliability and standard error of measurement estimates do not take into account the differences in abilities. For a given test, not all scores are equally reliable. Some scores contain more measurement errors than others. Expressed differently, with a given test, we can measure certain ability levels more reliably than other levels. As with p-values, classical or generalizability estimates of reliability can best be described as an average reliability across all ability levels. It would be more informative if we could estimate reliability as a function of ability so that we might identify which scores are more trustworthy than others within a given measurement procedure.

Perhaps one of the most important limitations of measurement procedures analyzed through classical or generalizability is the difficulty in comparing scores across similar tests. This limitation becomes most apparent when one compares conventional educational and psychological measurement procedures against measurement in the physical sciences. If we were told, for instance, that the temperature in Miami is 85° and the temperature in Chicago is 20° Fahrenheit today, we would generally accept that it is colder in Chicago than it is in Miami, in spite of the fact that the two temperatures are obviously measured by two different thermometers.

We do not generally question the difference in temperature even if we know that the two temperatures were measured by two different *types* of thermometers. This is because the Fahrenheit scale has been standardized. The same cannot be said about educational and psychological measurement. If we were told that Johnny in Chicago scored 80 correct out of 100 questions on a reading comprehension test and Megan in Miami scored 40 out of 100, we cannot immediately conclude that Johnny has a higher level of reading comprehension. Instead, we would ask if they took the same test. It is possible that Megan took a more difficult test and in fact has a higher level of reading comprehension than does Johnny. In other words, the interpretation of educational and psychological test scores are test-dependent. This stems from a lack of a standardized scale that applies across all tests.

It would be ideal if the development of a measurement procedure could be guided by a theory so that the scores on the test would not be test-dependent, if scores could be standardized across similar tests, if separate reliabilities could be estimated for different ability levels, if separate difficulty estimates could be estimated for different ability levels, and that estimates of item statistics and reliabilities were not dependent on the representativeness of the pilot sample. The item response theory holds the promise to be such a theory.

ITEM CHARACTERISTIC CURVE

Item response theory (IRT) is also known as *latent trait theory* or *item characteristic curve theory*. The work of Lawley (1944), Richardson (1936), and Tucker (1946) is generally regarded as having paved the way for the development of IRT. However, the actual development of IRT is due to the independent work of Lord (1952a, 1953) and Rasch (1980). Much of Lord's earlier work was of theoretical interest only in that the solutions were mathematically intractable. The applications of these theoretical works became possible with Birnbaum's (1957) development of mathematical models known as logistic curves. Rasch's independent work proved to be a special case of Birnbaum's mathematical models. Although the mathematical processes became possible with Birnbaum's development, they remain impractical because of the operational complexity of the mathematics. With the development of powerful computers and sophisticated software in the past two decades, however, the application of IRT became practicable. Today, IRT has been and is being used in many large-scale testing programs.

At the core of the IRT is the item characteristic curve (ICC). An item characteristic curve is a description of the relationship between an examinee's ability level on the trait (or construct) being measured by the item and the probability that the examinee will respond to the item correctly. Implicit in any testing procedure is the existence of this relationship. The lack of such a relationship would suggest that the item would not be able to discriminate between those with high ability levels from those with low ability levels. If a test is composed of such items, the test is ineffective in measuring the differences in ability among examinees.

In IRT, the ability level of an examinee on the trait being measured is denoted by θ and is simply referred to as *ability*. The probability that an examinee will respond correctly to the ith item of a test is denoted by $P_i(\theta)$. The basic idea of IRT is that, if the relationship between θ and $P_i(\theta)$ is known for each item in a test, the item characteristics of each item, the ability of each examinee, and the measurement error associated with each score can be derived mathematically. Additionally, the characteristics of any test made up of items with known item characteristics can also be derived. Knowledge of the characteristics of each item will also allow for better solutions in many applied issues such as adaptive testing and equating, which will be discussed in later chapters.

Implicit in conventional item analysis there also exists an item characteristic curve. Recall that the p-value for an item is the probability that an examinee will respond to the item correctly. Because no differentiation in p-value is made among examinees with different ability levels, the implicit ICC in conventional item analysis can best be described as resembling Fig. 7.1. That is, $P_i(\theta)$ is a constant across all values of θ. As discussed earlier in the limitations of random sampling theory, this ICC is counterintuitive and is not an adequate representation of the relationship in that such an item would not be able to discriminate a high-ability from a low-ability examinee. This is not to say that tests constructed with the aid of conventional item analysis cannot discriminate across ability levels. Rather, the p-value provides only a general indication of the average $P_i(\theta)$ without sufficiently specific information. Nevertheless, it is possible that an item may have an ICC resembling Fig. 7.1. In such a case, the item would not be useful for testing purposes.

A relatively more useful item is one with an ICC implicit in a Guttman scale (Guttman, 1944). The ICC for such a scale is a step function. Subjects with a trait level below a certain threshold will have a zero probability of providing a positive response (e.g., a correct response) to the item. However, any subject with a trait level above this threshold will have an absolute certainty of a positive response. Figure 7.2 depicts the step function ICC implicit in the Guttman scale. An item with an ICC resembling Fig. 7.2 would be a very useful item to distinguish examinees

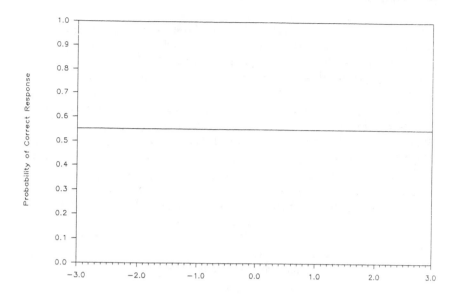

Figure 7.1.   Classical ICC

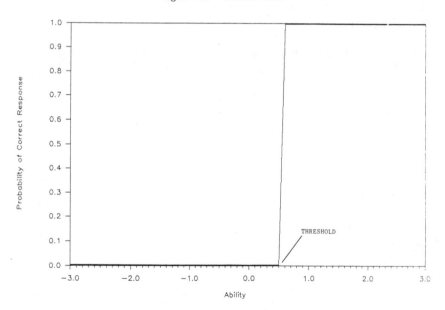

Figure 7.2.   A Guttman Scale ICC

with abilities above the threshold from those with abilities below the threshold. However, it would not be useful in distinguishing two examinees who are both above or both below the threshold.

A more generalized ICC is one in which the relationship between θ and $P_i(\theta)$ resembles an ogive as in Fig. 7.3. The ICC as an ogive function is generally accepted today as a good representation of the relationship between θ and $P_i(\theta)$ and has been confirmed through a number of empirical studies (e.g., Binet & Simon, 1916; Lord, 1980). This ogive function is the theoretical basis for IRT. The ogive function also provides sufficient flexibility such that the classical ICC and the Guttman ICC can be considered special cases of the ogive ICC. Specifically, as the slope of the ogive increases, the ICC approaches a Guttman ICC. As the slope decreases, the ICC approaches a classical constant p-value. Within IRT, when characteristics of the ogive ICC of all items in test are estimated, information regarding the test, ability of subjects, as well as other information can be derived mathematically.

ITEM PARAMETERS AND ABILITY SCALE

Item Parameters

The ogive relationship between θ and $P_i(\theta)$ can be described mathematically through a relationship between θ and three characteristics of the ogive

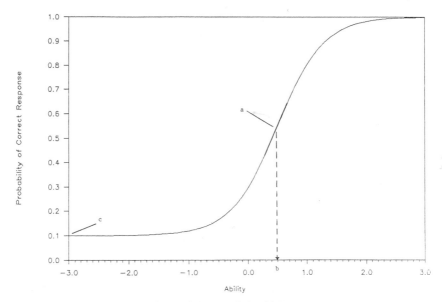

Figure 7.3.   An Ogive ICC

curve. These three characteristics are referred to as item parameters. The first parameter is referred to as the b parameter which is the θ value corresponding to the inflexion point of the ICC. That is, b is the location of the inflexion point on the θ scale (See Fig. 7.3). For a given θ level, if the $P_i(\theta)$ for the ith item is higher than the $P_j(\theta)$ for the jth item, the jth item is more difficult than than ith item. In this situation, the inflexion point of the ICC for the jth item would correspond to a higher θ than does that of the ith item. In other words, the ICC for the jth item would have a higher b value than that of the ith item. Hence, the b parameter is referred to as the *difficulty parameter*.

The second parameter is referred to as the a parameter and is the value of the slope at the inflexion point (See Fig. 7.3). Recall that the ICC implied by a classical p-value is a horizontal line with a slope of zero. With such an ICC, the item cannot discriminate among examinees with different levels of ability. On the other hand, the Guttman ICC has an infinitely high slope at the threshold and has perfect discrimination. In other words, the discrimination ability of an item can be represented by the slope of the ICC. With an ogive curve, however, the slope changes along the θ scale. The slope at the inflexion point would be a convenient point of reference to indicate the discrimination ability of the item. Hence, a is known as the *discrimination parameter*.

The third parameter is referred to as the c parameter and is the lower asymptote of the ICC (See Fig. 7.3). In other words, c is the $P_i(\theta)$ value when θ equals $-\infty$. Conceptually, c is the minimal probability that an examinee can respond correctly to the item since any θ higher than $-\infty$ would have a $P_i(\theta)$ higher than c. An examinee with absolutely no knowledge will still have a probability of c of responding correctly. This probability can be described as the probability of guessing correctly. Hence, c is known as the *guessing parameter*. Because guessing behaviors are not well understood and the value of c is generally lower than pure random guessing, some (e.g., Hambleton & Swaminathan, 1985) have suggested that the c parameter should not be referred to as the guessing parameter, but the *pseudo-chance level parameter*.

Ability Scale Indeterminancy

The θ scale as a measure of ability has no inherently meaningful units of measurement. That is, there are no natural points of reference for the θ scale. For example, for the purpose of distinguishing the abilities of three different examinees, it makes little difference if their scores are 1, 2, and 3, or -5, 0, and $+5$, or 10, 20, and 30. This characteristic of the θ scale is known as the *indeterminancy of the ability scale*. From a mathematical perspective, however, when the θ scale is undefined, the item parameters are unidentifiable (Lord, 1980). Hence, it is necessary to assign some origin for the θ scale so that estimations of item parameters become possible. The most common choice of the θ scale is one in which the mean θ is zero and the standard deviation is 1; that is, the z-score scale. This choice is arbitrary but is as effective as any other. Should a different numerical scale be desired, a new scale can be attained through a linear or curvilinear transformation of the z-score scale.

The use of an unfamiliar θ scale is inconvenient for interpretation (e.g., reporting score to examinees or parents) (Loyd, 1988). It is sometimes desirable to report scores on a true score scale. The true score corresponding to a particular θ_j from an N-item test is:

$$\xi_{\theta_j} = \sum_{i=1}^{N} P_i(\theta_j), \tag{7.1}$$

where ξ is the true score on the raw score scale (i.e., number of item correct).

NORMAL OGIVE FUNCTIONS

The mathematical form of the ogive relationship between $P_i(\theta)$ and θ can be expressed in terms of a, b, c, and θ as follows:

$$P_i(\theta) = c_i + (1 - c_i) \int_{-\infty}^{a_i(\theta - b_i)} \frac{1}{\sqrt{2\pi}} e^{.5(-z^2)} dz. \tag{7.2}$$

This is referred to as the *3-parameter normal ogive item characteristic function*, or the *3-parameter model*. This formidable mathematical model can be simplified if certain assumptions are made. One possible assumption is that no guessing occurs. This assumption is reasonable if the test is, for instance, designed to measure an affective trait. With this assumption, c_i becomes zero for all items and drops out of Equation 7.2. Thus, the normal ogive function becomes:

$$P_i(\theta) = \int_{-\infty}^{a_i(\theta - b_i)} \frac{1}{\sqrt{2\pi}} e^{.5(-z^2)} dz. \tag{7.3}$$

Equation 7.3 is a *2-parameter* (i.e., a_i and b_i) *normal ogive model*. If, in additional to the assumption that $c_i = 0$ for all items, we assume that all items have the same discrimination power (i.e., $a_i = a_j$), the term $a_i(\theta - b_i)$ becomes essentially $\theta - b_i$ multiplied by a constant value. In other words, $a_i(\theta - b_i)$ becomes a linear transformation of $\theta - b_i$. If we were to replace $a_i(\theta - b_i)$ with $(\theta - b_i)$ in Equation 7.3, the result is tantamount to expressing θ and b_i on a new scale. Because the θ scale and, thus, the value of b_i is arbitrary, Equation 7.3 can be further simplified to:

$$P_i(\theta) = \int_{-\infty}^{\theta - b_i} \frac{1}{\sqrt{2\pi}} e^{.5(-z^2)} dz. \qquad (7.4)$$

Equation 7.4 is a *1-parameter normal ogive model* that describes the relationship between $P_i(\theta)$ and θ under the assumption that $c_i = 0$ and that $a_i = a_j$ for all i and j.

Conceptually, the values of b_i, a_i, and c_i are inherent characteristics of the item. As such, their values for a given item are constant and independent of the exact sample of subjects used in the pilot analysis in which the item parameters are estimated. This property of the item parameters is known as the *invariance of item parameters*. Unlike classical *p*-values, which change in values when different samples of examinees are used, IRT item parameters will theoretically retain the same values regardless of exactly what sample of examinees is used.

When item parameters are estimated from sample data—a process known as *item calibration*, the invariance of item parameters will not be apparent. That is, the same items calibrated through two different samples of examinees may in fact show different item parameter values. This is not because of a lack of parameter invariance. Rather, it is due to the indeterminancy of the θ scale. Because the θ scale is arbitrarily set so that the mean of the sample is zero and the standard deviation is 1, different samples in fact would have different θ scales and the values of item parameters are relative to the θ scale. Two different θ scales from two different samples on the same ability trait can be standardized to the same units of measurement through linear transformation. We discuss this in a later chapter when we discuss equating. After linear transformation, the item parameters should have similar values, within the boundaries of random error.

LOGISTIC MODELS

Because of the integration operation in the normal ogive models presented in Equations 7.2 through 7.4, they are mathematically intractable. Birnbaum (1968) demonstrated that these models can be very closely approximated through a mathematically more convenient *logistic function.* Through logistic approximations of the normal ogive functions, the formidable integration operations of the normal ogive functions are avoided. Specifically, the 3-parameter normal ogive function can be closely approximated by the *3-parameter logistic model:*

$$P_i(\theta) = c_i + (1 - c_i) \frac{1}{1 + e^{-Da_i(\theta - b_i)}}, \qquad (7.5)$$

where D is a *scaling factor* and is equal to 1.7. The use of this scaling factor is to ensure that the resulting logistic ogive function will be a close approximation to the normal ogive function. Without this scaling factor, the logistic model would not approximate but would become a linear transformation of the normal ogive function. Given that the θ scale is arbitrary, a linear transformation of the normal ogive function is as informative as the original ogive function. Therefore, the logistic model is sometimes presented without the scaling factor D.

In a similar manner, the 2-parameter and 3-parameter normal ogive function can be closely approximated by the *2-parameter logistic model:*

$$P_i(\theta) = \frac{1}{1 + e^{-Da_i(\theta - b_i)}}, \qquad (7.6)$$

and the *1-parameter logistic model:*

$$P_i(\theta) = \frac{1}{1 + e^{-D(\theta - b_i)}}. \qquad (7.7)$$

The 1-parameter logistic model is mathematically equivalent to what is commonly known as the *Rasch model* (e.g., Wright & Stone, 1979). The Rasch model has been expressed in numerous alternative mathematical forms (e.g., Wright, 1968, 1977). These are essentially mathematical transformations of Equation 7.7. The results of these transformations are such that θ is expressed on a different scale and/or the probability $P_i(\theta)$ is replaced by an *odds ratio.*

Today, the IRT models of interest are primarily the mathematically more "tractable" logistic approximation models. The normal ogive models are only of historical and theoretical interest but are not practical. Although item parameters are invariant across samples of examinees, they are not invariant across IRT models. Dependent on the choice of 1-, 2-, or 3-parameter model, the item parameters are likely to be different. It is therefore important to choose the appropriate model and the choice of model may be determined by a number of considerations. These considerations may be theoretical, practical, and/or statistical.

CHOICE OF MODEL

In cognitive testing through multiple-choice or true/false item formats, the assumptions of zero or minimal guessing and/or equal discrimination across items in the Rasch and 2-parameter models are conceptually against common sense; also there is much contrary empirical evidence (e.g., Birnbaum, 1968; Ross, 1966; Traub, 1983). Therefore, it appears unreasonable to use any but the 3-parameter model. However, with affective measurement, it appears reasonable to assume that guessing does not occur and hence a 2-parameter model is appropriate. Similarly, cognitive tests that do not provide opportunities for guessing (e.g., essay exam, "fill in the blank") can reasonably be assumed to contain items with no or a minimal amount of guessing. Therefore, a 2-parameter model is also appropriate. As for the Rasch model, the variation in item discrimination may be negligible for some tests. In any event, one may deliberately select items from the same domain with minimal guessing and similar discrimination to make up a test. In this case, the Rasch model would be reasonable. From a theoretical perspective, the choice of the model may be determined by what is conceptually reasonable for a given test.

From a practical perspective, the estimation of item parameter and ability is immensely simplified with the Rasch model. Mathematically, the 2- and 3-parameter models suffer from a problem known as *insufficient statistics*, which is discussed in the next chapter. The effect of insufficient statistics is that estimates of item and ability parameters are sometimes unattainable for a given set of observed scores. With the Rasch model only estimates of the b parameter for each item and those of θ for each examinee are needed. These two sets of parameters are essentially nonlinear transformations of their classical p-value and observed score counterparts, the information of which is readily available from classical theory. As such, the likelihood of attaining parameter estimates is immensely enhanced with the Rasch model. In general, the fewer the number of item parameters, the more attainable the estimates of all parameters.

A third consideration in the choice of IRT model is that of *model fitness*. The extent to which the observed data are consistent with the chosen model can be investigated statistically. Many statistical procedures have been developed to test for the fitness of the empirical data to the theoretical model. Some of these include a likelihood ratio test (Andersen, 1973a; Bock & Liebermann, 1970; Waller, 1981), a Q_1 statistic (Yen, 1981), a measure-of-fit (Wright & Stone, 1979), and an analysis of residuals (Hambleton, 1989). Investigations of these statistical techniques have led researchers (e.g., Hambleton, 1989; Traub & Wolf, 1981) to conclude that no single statistical test is adequate. Rather, the assessment of model fitness requires a variety of analyses. Hambleton and Murray (1983), Traub and Wolf (1981), and Hambleton (1989) provided some guidance in the investigation of model fitness.

INFORMATION FUNCTIONS

Recall that the Guttman scale has perfect discrimination between individuals on the two sides of the threshold and the uniform ICC suggested by the classical p-value has no discrimination at all. A generalized description is that the steeper the slope of the ICC, the better the discrimination of the item and the higher the value of the a parameter. There is, however, a tradeoff between discrimination and the range of θ values for which the item is discriminating. Figure 7.4 presents the ICC of two items. With Item A, the a parameter is high and the ability of the item to distinguish examinees between θ_1 and θ_2 is very high. However, the item is relatively ineffective in discriminating among people on the left side of θ_1 or those on the right side of θ_2. Item B has a lower a parameter and the item can discriminate among all examinees within θ_1 and θ_2 to some extent. Note that the range between θ_1 and θ_2 in Item B is wider than that for Item A. In other words, there is a trade-off between the steepness of the slope at the inflexion point (i.e., the a parameter) and the width of the range of θ values for which the item is discriminating. This phenomenon is referred to as the *bandwidth paradox* (Warm, 1978).

The existence of the bandwidth paradox suggested that the a parameter is only a general indication of the discrimination of the item. A high a value would suggest a steep slope at the inflexion point, but at the same time, flatter slopes elsewhere. That is, a high a parameter indicates that the item is more useful than an item with a lower a parameter to distinguish those individuals around the inflexion point, but less useful in distinguishing those with θ values away from the inflexion point. What would be more informative is to describe the ever-changing slope as a function of θ. A steep slope at a certain θ would suggest that the item is discriminating, and thus informative, at that particular θ value.

The informativeness of the item at a particular θ value is also influenced by the amount of error associated with the measurement of that θ value. Recall in our discussion of classical theory that the standard error of measurement is only an average estimate of measurement error. The amount of measurement error is not uniform across all ability levels. The

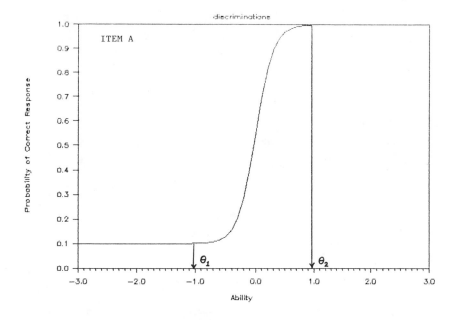

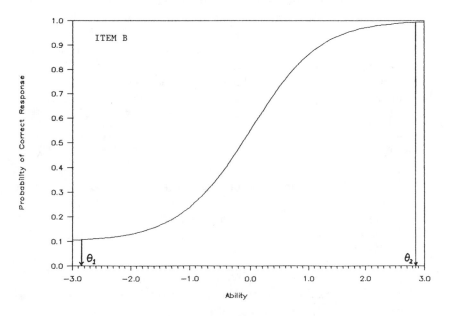

Figure 7.4. Two Items with Different Discriminations

95

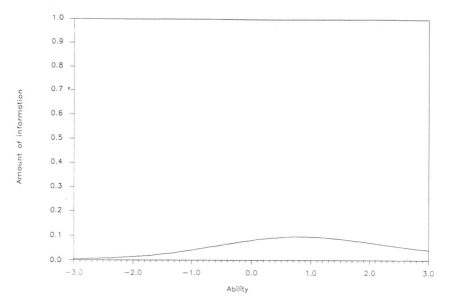

Figure 7.5. Item Information Function

lower the measurement error of an item at a certain θ value, the more informative is that item at that θ value.

The relationship between the informativeness of an item and θ is described by an *item information function*. Although it can be derived mathematically from a different perspective (Hambleton & Swaminathan, 1985; Kendall & Stuart, 1973), the item information function at aparticular θ value is conceptually a ratio of the slope of the ICC and the expected measurement error at that θ. Mathematically, the item information function for the ith item, denoted by $I(\theta, u_i)$ (Hambleton & Swaminathan, 1985), is:

$$I(\theta, u_i) = P'_i(\theta)^2 / P_i(\theta) Q_i(\theta) \tag{7.8}$$

where $P'_i(\theta)$ is the first derivative (or slope) of the ICC at θ and $Q_i(\theta)$ is the probability of an incorrect response, or $1 - P_i(\theta)$. Figure 7.5 presents the graphic form of a possible item information function. When $P'_i(\theta)$ is substituted by the actual derivatives for the three different logistic models, the item information function becomes:

$$I(\theta, u_i) = D^2 a_i^2 Q_i(\theta) \underbrace{[P_i(\theta) - c_i]^2 / (1 - c_i)^2}_{P_i(\theta)} \tag{7.9}$$

for a 3-parameter logistic model,

$$I(\theta, u_i) = D^2 a_i^2 P_i(\theta) \, Q_i(\theta) \tag{7.10}$$

for a 2-parameter logistic model, and

$$I(\theta, u_i) = D^2 P_i(\theta) \, Q_i(\theta) \tag{7.11}$$

for a Rasch model.

A test is made up of a number of items, each with its own item information function. The informativeness of the total score from a test at each θ value is thus the sum of all the item information functions for that θ value (Birnbaum, 1968). The amount of information for the total test score at each θ value expressed as a function of θ, is referred to as the *test information function*, denoted by $I(\theta)$, and defined as the sum of item information at each θ. Hence, for an N-item test,:

$$I(\theta) = \sum_{i=1}^{N} P_i'(\theta)^2 / P_i(\theta) Q_i(\theta). \tag{7.12}$$

Figure 7.6 presents a possible test information function.

The greater the test information function at a given θ, the more discriminating and the less measurement error the test contains at that θ. The error variance in measuring a particular θ value through the test is the

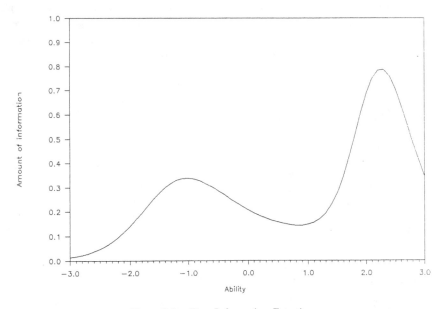

Figure 7.6.   Test Information Function

reciprocal of the test information function. Specifically, measurement error variance, denoted by $V(\theta)$, is:

$$V(\theta) = 1/I(\theta). \qquad (7.13)$$

As the test information function changes with θ, so does the error variance. Each θ value has its own unique error variance. The square root of this error variance is:

$$SE(\theta) = 1/\sqrt{I(\theta)} \qquad (7.14)$$

and is the standard error associated with the θ estimate. $SE(\theta)$ is referred to as the *standard error of estimation* (Hambleton, 1989). Although conceptually this standard error is a direct analog of the classical standard error of measurement, the important distinction is that this standard error is not a statistic, but a function of θ. That is, for a given test, there are many standard errors of estimation.

With the standard error of estimation as an ever-changing function of θ, the concept of a reliability coefficient is more or less irrelevant. Unlike the classical or generalizability reliability coefficients and error variances, the IRT standard error of estimation is theoretically independent of the sample used in the analysis. An important implication of the ever-changing $SE(\theta)$ along the θ scale is that no test is reliable for all examinees. Some tests can produce more reliable scores at a certain score range than others. Every test has a range of θ scores that is best suited for that test.

CHAPTER 8

Conditional Estimation
of Ability

When item parameters a, b, and c for each item in a test are known, not only can the ability of each subject, θ, be estimated, other information such as errors of measurement can be derived as well. Conceptually, if we have the entire population of subjects and we know each subject's true θ, then the proportion of subjects with an identical θ, let us say $\theta = .5$, answering a particular ith item correctly would give us $P_i(\theta)$ at $\theta = .5$. By computing the proportion of subjects at each θ value who have answered that item correctly, we would be able to construct the ICC for that item and the values of a, b, and c can be deduced from the actual ICC. In other words, the problem with IRT parameter estimation is that in order to estimate a, b, and c, we need to know θ; but to know θ we need to know a, b, and c.

In reality, all we have is a set of observed responses to a number of items from a sample of subjects. From these responses, we know the classical difficulty (i.e., p-value) of each item and the raw score of each subject (i.e., x). From these two sets of information, we need to derive four sets of information (i.e., θ, a, b, c). This problem of attempting to estimate more than two sets of parameters from two sets of data is known as the problem of *insufficient statistics*.

The task of estimation becomes immensely simplified if we are willing to make some assumptions. For example, if we are willing to assume that the c parameters for all items are zero (i.e., no guessing) and that the a

parameters for all items are the same (i.e., same discrimination), we would assume that the Rasch model is the appropriate model. With this Rasch model, we would only need to estimate θs and bs. Estimating only θs and bs from the known classical information on item p-values and subject raw scores, we would have sufficient statistics.

However, if we are unwilling to make these assumptions, the tasks of parameter estimation become considerably more complex because of insufficient statistics. All discussions in this chapter assume that the model of interest is a 3-parameter logistic model. From the perspective of parameter estimation, Rasch and 2-parameter models can be viewed as special cases of the 3-parameter model in which the a-parameter is a constant and/or the c-parameter is zero. Therefore, what applies to the 3-parameter model applies to the other two models as well.

ASSUMPTIONS

When a test with N items is administered to K subjects, we are interested in estimating the a, b, and c parameters for each of the N items and the θ for each of the K subjects. In other words, we are interested in estimating $3N$ item parameters and K ability parameters, or a total of $3N + K$ parameters. What is tangible, however, is an N-item-by-K-subject actual response matrix. In order to estimate the $3N + K$ parameters from the $N \times K$ data matrix, an important assumption, known as the assumption of *local independence,* has to be made.

This assumption states that, for a given examinee, the responses to different items are not related. For example, one item does not provide clues to the correct answer for another item. This assumption appears to contradict the conventional idea of internal consistency that suggests that responses to all items are related. There is actually no contradiction. Although local independence is a *conditional* statement, internal consistency is unconditional. That is, under the assumption of local independence, responses to different items are unrelated *for subjects with an identical θ.* Whereas, under the concept of internal consistency, responses to different items are mutually correlated *across all subjects with different θs.*

The idea of local independence is in fact related to the idea of internal consistency. When all items in a test measure only one specific construct, the test is said to be *unidimensional.* With a unidimensional test, internal consistency is expected to be high. At the same time, however, the assumption of local independence is also met. To illustrate, let us say that the $P(\theta)$s for two items with long verbal narratives in a math test are both .7 at a θ of 1. In other words, we would expect that, of all subjects with θs of 1, 7 out of 10 people would answer the first item correctly and 7 out of

10 people would answer the second correctly. Given that all 10 subjects have the same ability, if the same 7 people answered both items correctly, the assumption of local independence is violated in that the response to one item is related to that of another. At the same time, however, the test is not unidimensional. Given that all 10 people have the same ability, the fact that the same 7 people answered both items correctly indicates that those 7 people are high on some other construct (e.g., reading ability) and are being unintentionally measured by those two items. Therefore the test is not unidimensional in that it measures both math and reading abilities. Hence, the assumption of local independence also implies an *assumption of unidimensionality*. The latter is frequently presented as a second assumption of item response theory.

A major drawback of item response theory is that there is a mix of evidence as to whether the estimation procedures and applications of IRT parameters are robust when these two assumptions are violated (Lord & Novick, 1968; Loyd, 1988; Ward, 1986). On the one hand, Dorans and Kingston, (1985), Forsyth, Saisangjan, and Gillmer (1981), and Rentz and Bashaw (1977) found IRT to be relatively robust against the violation of assumptions. On the other hand, Cook, Eignor, and Taft (1984), Loyd and Hoover (1980), and Slinde and Linn (1978) did not find IRT to be robust.

It is therefore important to check for these assumptions. In general, the assumptions of unidimensionality and local independence are equivalent in that when one assumption is met, the other is also met. The most frequently recommended approach to check for these assumptions is factor analysis (cf. Hambleton & Swaminathan, 1985; Lumsden, 1976). Note however that for dichotomous data, ordinary factor analytic techniques will overestimate the number of factors (Hulin, Drasgow, & Parsons, 1983). A more appropriate factor analytic technique is the full-information factor analysis method such as the one developed by Wilson, Wood, and Gibbons (1987). Also note that the equivalence of the assumptions of unidimensionality and local independence is true in general, but is not guaranteed (Crocker & Algina, 1986; p. 343).

THE LIKELIHOOD FUNCTION

Central to all IRT parameter estimation methods is the *likelihood function*. This mathematical function is useful only to the extent that the assumption of local independence is met. When two events are mutually unrelated, the probability of their joint occurrence is the product of the probabilities of the two events occurring individually. For example, for a certain population, half of the people are females. Also half of the people have dark hair.

If gender is not related to hair darkness, the joint probability of randomly selecting a dark-hair female from this population is $0.5 \times 0.5 = 0.25$, or 25% or one-half of one-half. However, if gender is related to hair darkness (e.g., males tend to have dark hair), the joint probability is not .25, but some other value. This characteristic of unrelated events is precisely what is being used in the familiar chi-square test of independence in which the observed probabilities are compared against the joint probabilities of events under the independent scenario, or the products of marginal probabilities.

Based on the logistic function described in the previous chapter, the probability of a particular subject answering a particular item correctly is dependent on the values of θ of the subject and the a, b, and c of the item. If for a 2-item test, the two sets of a, b, and c and the θ of a particular subject are all known, then the probability of the subject answering each of these two items correctly [i.e., $P_1(\theta)$ and $P_2(\theta)$] can be calculated from the logistic function. If these two items meet the assumption of local independence, then, the joint probability of this subject answering both items correctly is the product of the two individual probabilities for the two items, or $P_1(\theta)P_2(\theta)$.

Using a score of 1 to represent a correct answer and a score of 0 to represent an incorrect one, we can use **u** to represent the pattern of response or *response vector* of the subject such that when the subject answers both items correctly, $\mathbf{u} = (1,1)$. Using the same matrix algebraic notations, **a** would represent the vector of the two item discrimination parameters for the two items, or $\mathbf{a} = (a_1, a_2)$. Similarly, $\mathbf{b} = (b_1, b_2)$ and $\mathbf{c} = (c_1, c_2)$. In our example, there is only one subject. Hence, θ is not a vector but a scalar, or a single number. With these notational conventions, the likelihood of **u** $= (1,1)$, given θ, **a**, **b**, and **c** is $P_1(\theta)P_2(\theta)$. Symbolically, this is expressed as $L[\mathbf{u} = (1,1)|\theta,\mathbf{a},\mathbf{b},\mathbf{c}] = P_1(\theta)P_2(\theta)$. To minimize visual complexity, we simply use P to represent $P(\theta)$ for all subsequent discussions. Hence, $L[\mathbf{u}|\theta,\mathbf{a},\mathbf{b},\mathbf{c}] = P_1P_2$.

The probability of answering an item incorrectly is $(1 - P)$, or Q. The above example can be extended to $L[\mathbf{u} = (1,0)|\theta,\mathbf{a},\mathbf{b},\mathbf{c}] = P_1Q_2$, or the joint likelihood of a correct response to the first item *and* an *incorrect* response to the second item, given θ, **a**, **b**, and **c**, is the product of P_1 and Q_2. Hence, $L[\mathbf{u} = (0,1)|\theta,\mathbf{a},\mathbf{b},\mathbf{c}] = Q_1P_2$ and $L[\mathbf{u} = (0,0)|\theta,\mathbf{a},\mathbf{b},\mathbf{c}] = Q_1Q_2$. A convenient way to summarize these likelihoods for the 2-item test is in the form:

$$L[\mathbf{u}|\theta,\mathbf{a},\mathbf{b},\mathbf{c}] = P_1^u Q_1^{1-u} P_2^u Q_2^{1-u}, \tag{8.1}$$

where **u** is the response to the particular item. Given that any number taken to the power of zero equals 1, if $\mathbf{u} = (1,1)$, Equation 8.1 becomes:

$$L[\mathbf{u} = (1,1)|\theta,\mathbf{a},\mathbf{b},\mathbf{c}] = P_1^1 Q_1^{1-1} P_2^1 Q_2^{1-1}$$
$$= P_1^1 Q_1^0 P_2^1 Q_2^0$$
$$= P_1 P_2.$$

Similarly, for $\mathbf{u} = (0,1)$, the likelihood as described in Equation 8.1 will reduce to $Q_1 P_2$. For $\mathbf{u} = (1,0)$, it reduces to $P_1 Q_2$, and for $\mathbf{u} = (0,0)$, it reduces to $Q_1 Q_2$. The principle of Equation 8.1 can be extended directly to a test with N items. In this case, the equation becomes:

$$L(\mathbf{u}|\theta,\mathbf{a},\mathbf{b},\mathbf{c}) = \prod_{i=1}^{N} P_i^{u_i} Q_i^{1-u_i} \tag{8.2}$$

where $\prod$ represents "the product of." Verbally, the likelihood of obtaining a particular response vector $\mathbf{u}$ expressed as 1s and 0s, given $\theta,\mathbf{a},\mathbf{b},\mathbf{c}$ is the product of $P_1^u Q_1^{1-u} P_2^u Q_2^{1-u} \ldots P_N^u Q_N^{1-u}$. This is the *likelihood function* of a single subject with a particular $\mathbf{u}$.

In testing, however, we have K subjects responding to N items leading to, not a single response vector, but a $K \times N$ response matrix, $\mathbf{U}$. If the K subjects are a random sample such that responses across subjects are mutually independent (an assumption required in all testing theories), Equation 8.2 can be generalized to:

$$L(\mathbf{U}|\theta,\mathbf{a},\mathbf{b},\mathbf{c}) = \prod_{j=1}^{K} \prod_{i=1}^{N} P_{ij}^{u_i} Q_{ij}^{1-u_i} \tag{8.3}$$

This is the *joint likelihood function*. Conceptually, it is the mathematical equation that computes the probability that we can obtain a particular response matrix (i.e., the set of N observed item scores each for all K subjects), given that the subjects have abilities of θ and the items have parameters of $\mathbf{a}$, $\mathbf{b}$, and $\mathbf{c}$; and further given that the items are locally independent and the subject scores are mutually independent. This likelihood function serves as the basis for all IRT parameter estimation processes.

CONDITIONAL MAXIMUM LIKELIHOOD ESTIMATE OF DISCRETE ABILITY

The process of estimating the a, b, and c of each item is referred to as *item calibration*. The simplest situation in IRT parameter estimation process is one in which the items on a particular test have been calibrated in previous administrations. The test is given to a subject and we are interested in the ability of this single subject based on this subject's response vector **u** to these items with known parameters. In this situation, the estimation process is referred to as *conditional maximum likelihood estimation* of ability because this estimation process takes place conditional to the knowledge of **a**, **b**, and **c**. For this estimation, the likelihood function reduces to Equation 8.2, which can be used in the following manner: We know **a**, **b**, and **c**. Conceptually, we can use these item parameters to find the likelihood of getting the particular **u** for each of all possible θ values. The θ that produces the largest likelihood is the most probable θ for that subject. This most probable θ is the *maximum likelihood* or best estimate of the subject's ability.

For the purpose of illustration, let us pretend that θ is a discrete scale and there are only seven possible θ values: $-3, -2, \ldots, +3$. We have a 3-item test with item parameters of **a** = (.5, 1, 1.5), **b** = (.5, 0, $-$.5), and **c** = (0, 0, 0). In other words, all three items follow a 2-parameter model (i.e., $c = 0$) and for the first item a = .5 and b = .5, and so on. A subject has a response vector of **u** = (0, 1, 1). That is, the subject responded incorrectly to the first item and correctly to the second and third item. Table 8.1 illustrates how the maximum likelihood estimate of the ability of this subject can be obtained.

In Table 8.1, the first column shows all the possible scenarios. That is, given our finite discrete θ scale, the subject's ability can only be one of these seven values. Column 2 shows the seven probabilities of a correct response to item 1 if the subject in fact has an ability of $-3, -2, \ldots, +3$. These can be obtained by defining a = .5 and b = .5 in all cases, and $\theta = -3$, $-2, \ldots, +3$ successively and applying the 2-parameter logistic function described in the previous chapter each time. For example, for the first scenario that $\theta = -3$, the probability of a correct response to the first item (i.e., P_1) is $1/[1+e^{-.5(-3-.5)}] = .148$. (To simplify computations, the scaling factor $D = 1.7$ is not used in this example.) The values in this column then represent the probability of a correct response if θ is -3, if θ is -2, and so on. Columns 3 and 4 show the results of the same process for items 2 and 3 using a = 1 and 1.5 and b = 0 and $-$.5 respectively. The probability of an incorrect response (i.e., Q) is one minus the corresponding P.

Applying Equation 8.2, the likelihood that the subject would obtain **u** = (0,1,1) is $Q_1 P_2 P_3$. Column 5 shows the likelihoods that the subject would obtain **u** = (0,1,1) should the subject's true θ be $-3, -2, \ldots, +3$. These were obtained by multiplying $(1 - P_1)$ by P_2 by P_3. For example, the likelihood of **u** = (0,1,1) if θ is -3 is $(1 - .148)(.047)(.023) = .001$. As can be seen, the likelihood of obtaining responses 0, 1, 1 is the highest

TABLE 8.1
Conditional Maximum Likelihood Estimate of Discrete Ability

Item parameters				Response vector
Item	a	b		of subject
1	0.5	0.5		0,1,1
2	1.0	0.0		
3	1.5	− 0.5		

(1)	*(2)*	*(3)*	*(4)*	*(5)*
0	P1*	P2**	P3***	Likelihood****
− 3.0	.148	.047	.023	.001
− 2.0	.223	.119	.095	.009
− 1.0	.321	.269	.321	.059
0.0	.438	.500	.679	.191
1.0	.562	.731	.905	.290(maximum)
2.0	.679	.881	.977	.276
3.0	.777	.953	.995	.211

$$*P1 = 1/[1 + e^{- .5(\theta - .5)}]$$
$$**P2 = 1/[1 + e^{- 1.5(\theta - 0)}]$$
$$***P3 = 1/[1 + e^{- 1.5(\theta + .5)}]$$
$$****\text{Likelihood} = (1 - P1)(P2)(P3)$$

when θ is + 1. Hence, the conditional maximum likelihood estimate of this subject's ability is +1, given this finite, discrete scale.

CONDITIONAL MAXIMUM LIKELIHOOD ESTIMATE OF CONTINUOUS ABILITY

In the preceding discussion, the conditional maximum likelihood estimate of ability was obtained by conveniently defining θ as a discrete scale with only seven possible values. In reality, however, the θ scale is continuous with an infinite number of possible values. Therefore, although this discussion presents the principle of conditional maximum likelihood estimation, if the process as described here is used in practice, we would limit people's ability estimates to only a finite number of general categories without a high level of precision.

To obtain the precise conditional maximum likelihood estimate of the subject's ability and to treat the θ scale as continuous and infinite, a more complex process is needed in practice. Conceptually, if we are able to compute the likelihood of each of all possible θ values, we would have many likelihoods, each corresponding to a particular θ value. We can plot these likelihoods against the θ values as shown in Fig. 8.1 The height of the resulting curve at each θ value represents the likelihood of obtaining **u** should the true θ be that value. The highest point on this curve is then the point of maximum likelihood and the θ value corresponding to this point is the maximum likelihood estimate of θ, or θ_{max}.

A useful characteristic of the point of maximum likelihood is that the slope of the curve at that point becomes zero. Note in Fig. 8.1 that the curve is increasing on the left and decreasing on the right of this point and is neither increasing nor decreasing at this point. Hence, to find the maximum likelihood estimate of θ, we can find the θ value at which the slope of the likelihood function becomes zero. Recall from chapter 2 that the slope of a curve can be described by the first derivative of the function. Conceptually, to find θ_{max}, we can find the first derivative of the likelihood function, $f'(L)$, with respect to θ mathematically. We can then set $f'(L)$ to zero and solve the equation to find θ_{max}. The mathematical forms of $f'(L)$ are discussed later in this chapter.

Whereas the principle of finding θ_{max} through the point at which $f'(L)$ becomes zero is relatively straightforward, the actual mathematical process of solving for $f'(L) = 0$ is extremely complex and cannot be accomplished directly. Therefore, in practice, θ_{max} is estimated through optimization algorithms that follow this basic principle without actually solving for $f'(L) = 0$.

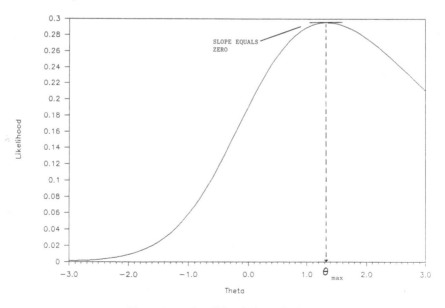

Figure 8.1.   Conditional Max Likelihood

NEWTON-RAPHSON NUMERICAL PROCEDURE

The optimization algorithm most commonly used in IRT parameter estimations today is probably the numerical procedures known as the *Newton-Raphson procedure*. This is a general purpose optimization algorithm that is used to improve an estimate of a maximum or minimum value repeatedly, without actually calculating the exact true value, until the true value is very closely approximated. When applied to IRT, we can start the procedure with any reasonable estimate of θ_{max}, apply Newton-Raphson to improve this estimate, until we are satisfied with the degree of approximation.

The slope of the likelihood function (Fig. 8.1) is the first derivative $f(L)$. Given the curvilinear nature of the likelihood function, the slope at each θ is different, with a slope of 0 at θ_{max}. Conceptually, we can plot the slopes of the likelihood function (i.e., $f'(L)$) against the values of θ. The result would resemble Fig. 8.2. In this plot, the curve intersects the point of zero at θ_{max}.

To start the Newton-Raphson process, a start up estimate of θ is made through any reasonable process (e.g., z score of the subject). We will refer to this start up θ as θ_0 and subsequent improved estimates as θ_1, θ_2, and so on. To demonstrate the principle of Newton-Raphson, let us assume that we have chosen a θ_0 as the start-up value. Figure 8.3 illustrates the

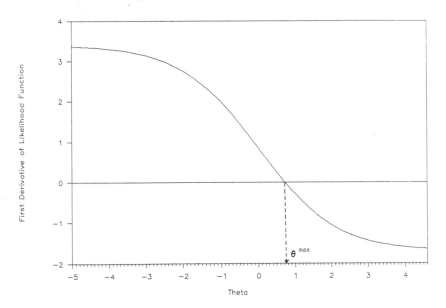

Figure 8.2.   First Derivative of L

Newton-Raphson process. Through Newton-Raphson, we wish to revise our θ successively until θ_{max} is closely approximated.

From Fig. 8.3, we can see that θ_{max} can be approximated if some values h_0, h_1, h_2, and so forth are added successively to the estimate. However, since we do not know where θ_{max} is relative to θ_0, we need some basis to determine the values of h_0, h_1, and so forth so that we are in fact approaching θ_{max}. Additionally, we need to know when we are sufficiently close to θ_{max}.

A convenient basis to determine h is through the slope of the curve. That is, at each revision, h is determined by the slope of the curve at the previous θ estimate. That is, we will improve each θ estimate by the precise amount suggested by the slope of the curve at that particular θ. The slope at a particular point on a curve can be represented by the tangent line (i.e., the line that touches only that one point on the curve). This tangent line can be extended to intersect the line at which $f(L)$ is zero. In Fig. 8.3, the tangent line at the point on the curve corresponding to θ_0 (i.e., Point A) is extended and it intersects the zero line at θ_1. The difference between this intersection point and the original θ_0 can be defined as h_0 that is then added to θ_0 to find the improved θ_1. This process can be repeated. Note that as the improved estimates approach θ_{max}, h decreases. That is, the smaller the h, the closer is the improved estimate to θ_{max}. Hence, the size of h can be used as a criterion to determine if θ_{max} is sufficiently closely approximated. In practice, a criterion of $h < .001$ or $h < .01$ is frequently used.

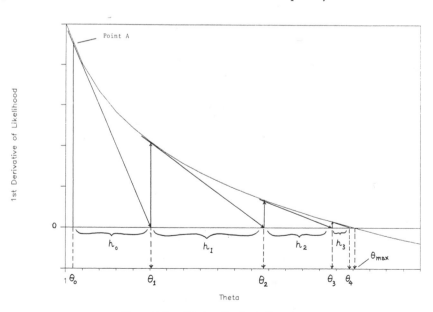

Figure 8.3.   Newton-Raphson Process

The exact value of h at each revision can be obtained as follows: The slope at point A is the same as the tangent at point A and the tangent equals height divided by the base. That is, the slope at point A equals height divided by h_0. The height at θ_0 is the first derivative or the slope of the likelihood function at θ_0 because the curve itself is a curve of the first derivatives. The slope at Point A then is the slope of the slope, or the second derivative, of the likelihood function at θ_0. Or, the slope at Point A is $f''(L)$. Because height divided by base equals the slope of the curve, $f''(L) = f'(L)/h_0$. We do not know h_0, but we can derive $f'(L)$ and $f''(L)$ mathematically. Thus, through algebraic conversion, we can determine h_0 through $f'(L)/f''(L)$ at θ_0. Because $f''(L)$ turns out to be negative mathematically, to improve θ_0, $\theta_1 = \theta_0 - h_0$ is used. This process is repeated until h becomes smaller than .01 or .001 as desired.

When successive h values continue to decrease in size, the Newton-Raphson estimates are said to be *converging*. When h becomes smaller than .001 or .01 as appropriate, the process is said to have converged. If h values continue to increase instead, the process is said to have *diverged*. When the process diverges, θ_{max} cannot be approximated.

LOG LIKELIHOOD FUNCTION

Although the likelihood functions described in Equations 8.2 and 8.3 express the exact likelihood of obtaining a certain response vector or response matrix, they are very inconvenient for the purpose of computation. They involve repeated multiplications of many probabilities leading to extremely small numbers. The computational process can be simplified considerably if likelihood is not expressed as a probability, but a natural log of the probability. For example, a probability of .0000001 can be much more conveniently expressed as $\ln(.0000001)$ or -16.118. In other words, the likelihood can be expressed, not as a decimal number, but the power of 2.718. A probability of .0000001 is $2.718^{-16.118}$.

By expressing likelihood as a natural log (e.g., .0000001 as -16.118), not only can we avoid the extremely small numbers, but the computational process itself becomes simplified. When the log values of a set of numbers are taken, multiplications of these numbers become additions of their log values. Hence, Equations 8.2 and 8.3 can be alternatively expressed as *log likelihood functions* and the multiplications in the likelihood function become additions in the log likelihood function. Specifically, the log likelihood equivalent of Equation 8.2 is:

$$\ln L(\mathbf{u}|\theta \mathbf{a}, \mathbf{b}, \mathbf{c}) = \sum_{i=1}^{N} [u \ln P_i + (1 - u) \ln Q_i] \tag{8.4}$$

and the log likelihood equivalent of Equation 8.3 is:

$$\ln L(\mathbf{U}|\theta\mathbf{a},\mathbf{b},\mathbf{c}) = \sum_{j=1}^{K} \sum_{i=1}^{N} [u \ln P_{ij} + (1 - u) \ln Q_{ij}] \tag{8.5}$$

For the purpose of Newton-Raphson estimation of the conditional maximum *log* likelihood of ability, the first derivatives of the log likelihood function are:

$$1.7 \sum_{i=1}^{N} (u - P_i) \tag{8.6}$$

for the Rasch model,

$$1.7 \sum_{i=1}^{N} a(u - P_i) \tag{8.7}$$

for the 2-parameter model, and

$$1.7 \sum_{i=1}^{N} a(u - P_i)(P_i - c_i)/P_i(1 - c_i). \tag{8.8}$$

The second derivatives of the log likelihood function are:

$$-2.89 \sum_{i=1}^{N} P_i Q_i \tag{8.9}$$

for the Rasch model,

$$-2.89 \sum_{i=1}^{N} a_i^2 P_i Q_i \tag{8.10}$$

for the 2-parameter model, and

$$-2.89 \sum_{i=1}^{N} a_i^2(P_i - c_i)(uc_i - P_i^2)Q_i/P_i^2(1 - c_i)^2 \tag{8.11}$$

for the 3-parameter model.

PROBLEMS WITH MAXIMUM LIKELIHOOD ESTIMATES

When applied, the principle of maximum likelihood estimation encounters a number of technical and conceptual problems. Two major problems are discussed here as the background for the discussion of an alternative approach known as the *Bayesian modal estimation* procedure.

Reversed Conditional Statement

The purpose of the likelihood functions described in Equations 8.2 and 8.3 is to find $L(\mathbf{U}|\theta,\mathbf{a},\mathbf{b},\mathbf{c})$, which essentially addresses the question of what is the probability that the response matrix is $\mathbf{U}$ *given* θ, $\mathbf{a}$, $\mathbf{b}$, *and* $\mathbf{c}$? The maximum likelihood estimate is identified based on this probability. In reality, however, we have no information on either θ, $\mathbf{a}$, $\mathbf{b}$, or $\mathbf{c}$. Instead, we know $\mathbf{U}$. That is, in reality, $\mathbf{U}$ is given while θ, $\mathbf{a}$, $\mathbf{b}$, and $\mathbf{c}$ are unknown. Additionally, we are not interested to know the probability of getting $\mathbf{U}$ because $\mathbf{U}$ is already a certainty. In fact, what we are interested in finding is what is the probability that the abilities and item parameters are θ, $\mathbf{a}$, $\mathbf{b}$, and $\mathbf{c}$, given $\mathbf{U}$. That is, instead of $L(\mathbf{U}|\theta,\mathbf{a},\mathbf{b},\mathbf{c})$, we are in fact interested in $L(\theta,\mathbf{a},\mathbf{b},\mathbf{c}|\mathbf{U})$. Recall that the probability of A given B is not the same as the probability of B given A. Hence, the maximum likelihood approach using the likelihood function may suffer from a problem of reversed conditional statements. The Bayesian approach that can estimate $P(A|B)$ from $P(B|A)$ is needed to resolve this problem. (It is demonstrated later that the maximum likelihood approach proves to be a special case of the Bayesian approach and is thus nonproblematic under certain conditions.)

Infinity Estimates

For a single-item test on which the subject responded correctly, the likelihood function in Equation 8.2 becomes:

$$L[\mathbf{u}|\theta,\mathbf{a},\mathbf{b},\mathbf{c}] = \prod_{i=1}^{N} P_i^u Q_i^{1-u}$$

$$= P$$

$$= c + (1-c)[1/1 + e^{-a(\theta - b)}],$$

which is the ogive function of that item. The P, thus the likelihood, on this ogive function is at its maximum when θ is at the positive infinity. That is, the conditional maximum likelihood estimate of this subject's θ is the positive infinity.

For an N-item test on which the subject responded correctly to all items, the likelihood function is the product of all P values. In other words, the likelihood function is the product of all the individual ogive functions. As the maximum point for each individual ogive function is at the positive infinity, the maximum point of the likelihood function is also at the positive infinity. Hence, the maximum likelihood estimate of the ability of a subject who answers all items on a test correctly is the positive infinity. Conversely, the maximum likelihood estimate of the ability of a subject who answers all items incorrectly is the negative infinity.

Infinity estimates of ability are uninterpretable and conceptually unacceptable. There are at least three approaches to avoid this problem. A common approach is to remove subjects with perfect or zero raw scores from the sample prior to estimation. The effects of this tampering with the sample are unknown. A second approach is to set limits to the θ scale directly. As pointed out in the previous chapter, the θ scale is commonly set on a scale with a mean of zero and a standard deviation of 1. Given such a scale, it can be demonstrated (e.g., Samuelson, 1968) that no examinee in a given sample of N examinees can have a θ value beyond $\pm\sqrt{N-1}$. Minimally, this can be used to set the limits of θ. In practice, θ is frequently limited to within ± 3. With this restriction, the problem of infinite estimates can be avoided. A final alternative is to employ the *Bayesian Modal Estimation* process.

BAYESIAN MODAL ESTIMATE

The Bayesian modal estimation method is based on Bayes' Theorem discussed in chapter 2. To illustrate the principle of this method, we again assume a discrete θ scale as in the example in Table 8.1. Using the same three items in Table 8.1, we can consider a situation in which we wish to estimate the ability of a subject who has answered all three items correctly. Table 8.2 shows the application of Bayesian modal estimation to this situation. Figure 8.4 is a graphic representation of the posterior distribution in Table 8.2.

Note in Column 5 that the maximum likelihood on this finite θ scale is at $+3$ and the likelihood continues to increase from -3 to $+3$. Had the θ scale been continuous and infinite, the likelihood would keep increasing to the positive infinity. That is, using the conditional maximum likelihood approach, the best estimate of the ability of this subject is the positive

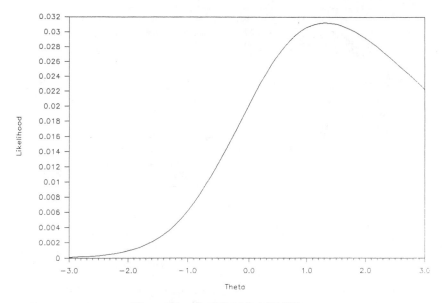

Figure 8.4. Bayesian Modal Estimate

infinity. Additionally, the likelihoods in Column 5 are in fact the probabilities of $\mathbf{u} = (1,1,1)$ given θ, whereas we are actually interested in the probability of θ given $\mathbf{u}$. Recall from the Bayes' Theorem in chapter 2 that the probability that A_j will occur given B has occurred is:

$$P(A_j|B) = P(B|A_j)P(A_j)/[\sum_{i=1}^{K} P(B|A_i)P(A_i)],$$

where K is the number of possible values of A. When applied to our example, A is θ, B is $\mathbf{U}$, and K is 7. Thus:

$$P(\theta_j|\mathbf{u}) = P(\mathbf{u}|\theta_j)P(\theta_j)/[\sum_{i=1}^{7} P(\mathbf{u}|\theta_i)P(\theta_i)]. \qquad (8.11)$$

$P(\theta_j|\mathbf{u})$ is known as the posterior probability, $P(\mathbf{u}|\theta_j)$ is the likelihood (column 5 in Table 8.2), and $P(\theta_j)$ is the prior probability.

If we have some knowledge of the prior probabilities, we would be able to apply Bayes' Theorem. Prior probabilities can be derived either theoretically, based on beliefs, or based on experience. For the purpose of discussion, let us assume that based on previous administrations of the test, we have determined that the distribution of ability score among subjects

TABLE 8.2
Conditional Bayesian Modal Estimate of Discrete Ability

Item parameters							Response vector of subject
Item	a	b					
1	0.5	0.5					1,1,1
2	1.0	0.0					
3	1.5	−0.5					

(1)	(2)	(3)	(4)	(5)	(6)	(7)	(8)
						Likelihood	
θ	P1	P2	P3	Likelihood*	Prior	× Prior	Posterior**
−3.0	.148	.047	.023	.0002	.0500	.00001	.00004
−2.0	.223	.119	.095	.0025	.1000	.00025	.00115
−1.0	.321	.269	.321	.0277	.1750	.00485	.02230
0.0	.438	.500	.679	.1487	.3500	.05205	.23930
1.0	.562	.731	.905	.3718	.1750	.06507	.29916(mode)
2.0	.679	.881	.977	.5844	.1000	.05844	.26868
3.0	.777	.953	.995	.7368	.0500	.03684	.16937
					$\Sigma\ L(u|\theta)P(\theta)$ =	.21751	

*Likelihood = (P1)(P2)(P3)
**Posterior probability = (likelihood × prior)/$\Sigma\ L(u|\theta)P(\theta)$

whose characteristics are similar to the subject in Table 8.2 is that of column 6. This distribution can be used as the prior probabilities. Column 7, which shows the product of columns 5 and 6, thus corresponds to the numerator of Equation 8.11 for all seven possible values of θ. The sum of column 7 thus corresponds to the denominator of Equation 8.11. Column 8, which shows the results of dividing each value of column 7 by the sum of column 7, shows the posterior probability of each of the θ values given $u = (1,1,1)$. Therefore, the problem of reversed conditional statement is resolved. Note also that the posterior probabilities do not continue to increase as we approach infinity and the maximum likelihood estimate based on the mode of the posterior distribution (i.e., mode of column 8) is at +1. Despite the fact that this subject has answered all three items correctly, we do not have a problem of a positive infinity ability score.

Note that the mode of column 7 is also at +1. This is because the values in column 8 are obtained by dividing the corresponding value in column 7 by the same constant number (i.e., the sum of column 7). Hence, all the values in column 8 are directly proportionate to those in column 7. This fact can be used to simplify the process. For the purpose of estimating θ, we are not that interested in knowing the exact probability of θ given u. Rather, we are interested in knowing for which θ this probability is the highest. Because the posterior distribution (column 8) is directly proportionate to (likelihood × prior) (i.e., column 7), the θ with the highest posterior probability is also the θ with the highest (likelihood × prior). So, we can simply use (likelihood × prior) to find the modal estimate of θ without actually computing the posterior probabilities.

For the purpose of illustration, θ was treated as a discrete variable in Equation 8.11. In reality, θ is continuous. Thus, the posterior probability function in Bayesian modal estimation process is more appropriate represented by:

$$f(\theta)|\mathbf{u}) \propto L(\mathbf{u}|\theta)g(\theta), \tag{8.12}$$

where $f(\theta|\mathbf{u})$ is the posterior distribution, $L(\mathbf{u}|\theta)$ is the likelihood function, and $g(\theta)$ is the prior distribution function of the continuous θ scale.

UNINFORMED PRIOR DISTRIBUTIONS

The key to the application of the Bayesian modal estimation procedure is the availability of a prior distribution. As discussed earlier, the prior distribution can be obtained subjectively as a matter of judgment or beliefs, based on past experience, or based on theory. A common prior distribution is the normal distribution. In this case, the exact prior probability for each θ value can be determined by the height of the ordinate at the corresponding z score in a unit normal distribution.

The use of prior distribution or the general Bayesian paradigm is not universally accepted. Some researchers feel that using prior distributions represents a form of prejudice and should be avoided. From the Bayesian perspective, not using a prior distribution is in effect a special case of the Bayesian modal estimation procedure in which the prior probabilities are assumed to be the same for all θ values; that is, a uniform prior distribution of θ.

When one is unwilling to specify a prior distribution, one is essentially saying that there is no basis to determine which θ is more probable and which θ is less probable. In other words, all θ values have the same chance of being the true θ of the subject. In its own way, this has specified a *uniform* prior distribution. A uniform prior distribution is a special type of prior distribution in the Bayesian process and is referred to as an *uninformed* prior distribution.

An interesting characteristic of a Bayesian modal estimation with an uninformed prior distribution is that the result will be identical to that of the non-Bayesian maximum likelihood estimation process discussed earlier in this chapter. That is, the maximum likelihood estimation process is in fact equivalent to a Bayesian modal estimation process with a uniform prior distribution. Let us use the example in Table 8.1 and examine what happens if a uniform prior distribution is specified and the Bayesian modal estimation process is used. Table 8.3 demonstrates this process, and Fig. 8.5 shows the posterior probabilities of Table 8.3.

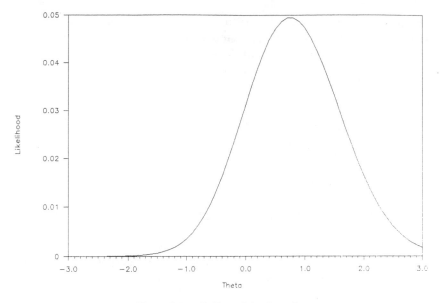

Figure 8.5.   Uniform Prior Bayesian

As with Table 8.1, column 5 in Table 8.3 shows the non-Bayesian likelihood of different θ values. Based on the maximum likelihood process, the most probable value of θ is 1. If we were to specify a uniform prior distribution as in column 6, the probability for each θ is 1/7 or .1429. Using the Bayesian modal estimation process, we find that the modes of both (likelihood × prior) and posterior distribution are also at a θ of 1. In other words, the maximum likelihood process leads to the same estimate of θ as a Bayesian modal estimation process with a uniform or uninformed prior distribution.

Notice that the posterior distribution is directly proportionate to (likelihood × prior) in the Bayesian modal estimation process. Hence, the mode of the posterior can be obtained from the mode of (likelihood × prior). When the prior distribution is uniform, the prior probability is the same for all values of θ. The (likelihood × prior) is essentially likelihood multiplied by a constant. Thus, the non-Bayesian likelihood is directly proportionate to (likelihood × prior), which is in turn directly proportionate to the posterior probability. The maximum likelihood estimation process will yield the same estimate of θ as the Bayesian process with a uniform prior. This also suggests that the problem of reversed conditional statement with the maximum likelihood process is conceptual but nonproblematic in practice.

TABLE 8.3
Conditional Bayesian Modal Estimate of Discrete Ability With a Uniform Prior Distribution

| Item parameters | | | | | | | Response vector |
Item	a	b					of subject
1	0.5	0.5					0,1,1
2	1.0	0.0					
3	1.5	-0.5					

(1)	(2)	(3)	(4)	(5)	(6)	(7)	(8)
						Likelihood	
0	P1	P2	P3	Likelihood*	Prior	× Prior	Posterior**
-3.0	.148	.047	.023	.0009	.1429	.00013	.00088
-2.0	.223	.119	.095	.0088	.1429	.00126	.00851
-1.0	.321	.269	.321	.0586	.1429	.00838	.05657
0.0	.438	.500	.679	.1908	.1429	.02727	.18408
1.0	.562	.731	.905	.2898	.1429	.04140	.27947(mode)
2.0	.679	.881	.977	.2763	.1429	.03948	.26650
3.0	.777	.953	.995	.2115	.1429	.03022	.20400

$$\Sigma \ L(\mathbf{u}|\theta)P(\theta) = .14814$$

*Likelihood $= (1 - P1)(P2)(P3)$
**Posterior probability $=$ (likelihood $\times$ prior)/$\Sigma \ L(\mathbf{u}|\theta)P(\theta)$

CHAPTER 9

Joint Estimation
of Parameters

So far, we have discussed the conditional estimation of θ with knowledge of $a, b,$ and $c,$ which also applies for the conditional estimation of $\mathbf{a},$ given θ, $\mathbf{b},$ and $\mathbf{c},$ and so on. When a test is initially constructed, item parameters are unknown and must be estimated from data. The simultaneous estimation of θ, $\mathbf{a}$, $\mathbf{b},$ and $\mathbf{c}$ is known as *joint estimation*. The joint estimation of these parameters is a much more complex task than its conditional estimation counterpart.

Figure 9.1 provides a general description of the process involved in item response theory. Note that the difference between joint estimation and conditional estimation is whether item parameters have been calibrated previously and are known. Note also that, whereas the classical and the generalizability theories attempts to estimate the magnitude of the relationship between observed scores and true scores, item response theory attempts to estimate the true score itself directly.

PROBLEMS OF JOINT ESTIMATION

Several problems are inherent within the joint estimation of ability and item parameters. First, with the formidably large number of nonlinear equations that need to be solved, computers with large capacities and

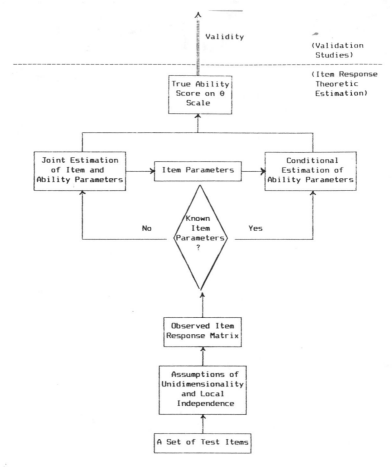

Figure 9.1. The Process of Item Response Theory

complicated algorithms are needed. This suggests some degree of limitation for practitioners. With the rapid advancement in computer technology, we can expect that this problem will disappear quickly. Today, there
are many computer programs available for the joint estimation of item and
ability parameters. Hambleton (1989) reviewed eight such programs.
Many of these programs are available in mainframe as well as microcom-
puter versions.

A second problem is that the likelihood function, and posterior function
in Bayesian modal estimation, is multivariate and nonlinear in nature.
With conditional estimation of the ability of a single subject (or parameters
of a single item), the likelihood function is univariate and is likely to be
unimodal and smooth as depicted in Fig. 8.1. With a joint estimation,
however, this smooth unimodal form is not guaranteed. For a given single

dimension (e.g., θ for a particular subject) in this joint multivariate function, there may be several maxima or modes (Samejima, 1973). This problem is known as the problem of multiple *latent roots*. As such, attempting to estimate the maximum or modal value on that dimension by searching for a slope of zero, such as in the case of the Newton-Raphson process, may lead to a local maximum or local modal estimate, but not the global maximum or mode. Figure 9.2 illustrates a local maximum. In this figure, there are two points at which the slope becomes zero. Using a numerical procedure such as Newton-Raphson or other similar algorithms may lead to the local maximum on the right, instead of the global maximum on the left. Without knowledge of the global maximum, we would conclude that the most probable θ for this subject is 1.7, when it should have been -1.0. Lord (1980) reported that the problem of multiple maxima generally does not occur when the number of items in the test is greater than 20. However, this is based on experience, and is not theoretically guaranteed.

Related to the problem of multiple latent roots is a third problem of minimum estimators. When the likelihood function on a given dimension is not unimodal, not only would the modes have slopes of zero, the troughs would have zero slopes as well. In Fig. 9.3, note that the point of *minimum* likelihood also has a slope of zero. Using a numerical procedure to search for the point at which the slope becomes zero may lead to this minimum likelihood point instead of the maximum likelihood. This problem has been

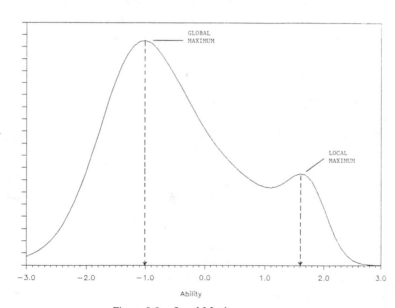

Figure 9.2.   Local Maximum

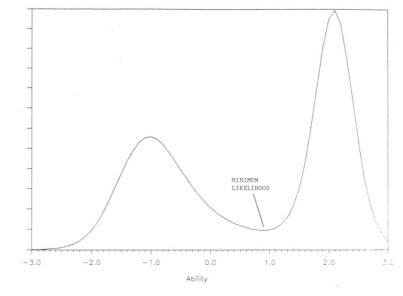

Figure 9.3. Minimum Likelihood

noted by some (e.g., Suen & Lee, 1989) but is not widely reported. The existence of this problem depends on the nature of the joint likelihood function (i.e., the shape of the function, concave or convex) and the numerical algorithm used. The use of Newton-Raphson, for instance, does not safeguard against this problem. When this occurs, the estimated parameter is the *worst* instead of the best estimate. The use of certain algorithms, such as GRG-II (Liebman, Lasdon, Shrage, & Waren, 1986) and MINOS (Murtagh & Saunders, 1987), however, can avoid this problem.

A fourth problem is that of sample size. Conventional statistical wisdom, as well as classical and generalizability theories, generally suggest that the larger the samples of subject and item, the better the estimate. This is only partially true with the joint estimation of item and ability parameters. If we increase the number of examinees without increasing the number of items, the estimates of item parameters will become inconsistent and will not converge to their true values. Conversely, increasing the number of items without increasing the number of examinees will lead to a lack of consistent estimators of ability (Andersen, 1973b). In other words, between items and subjects, increasing one without increasing the other will lead to worse instead of better estimates. Only when both the number of items and the number of examinees are increased simultaneously will the item and ability parameter converge to their true values (Haberman, 1975; Swaminathan & Gifford, 1983).

Finally, when limits are not set for the parameters, the numerical process is unconstrained. With an unconstrained optimization, it is theoretically possible that estimates outside of the acceptable range (e.g., a negative guessing parameter) be obtained. Hambleton and Swaminathan (1985) and Hambleton (1989) suggested that limits should be set for these situations, although they cautioned that such a practice could raise concerns (e.g., Wright, 1977). Suen and Lee (1989) proposed the use of relatively incontrovertible structural constraints in the optimization process. The practicality of their proposal has yet to be demonstrated.

With these limitations in mind, there are several methods available today for the joint estimation of item and ability parameters. The three most popular methods are the joint maximum likelihood estimation, the Bayesian parameter estimation, and the marginal maximum likelihood estimation methods (cf. Hambleton, 1989; Lord, 1986). Additionally, methods are available to approximate item parameter values based on classical statistics (Schmidt, 1977; Urry, 1974, 1977). These approximation methods are sometimes referred to as *heuristic estimation* methods (e.g. Hambleton, 1989).

JOINT MAXIMUM LIKELIHOOD ESTIMATION

We have discussed briefly the joint maximum likelihood estimation method (Lord, 1980) in chapter 8. This method is a direct extension of the conditional maximum likelihood estimation method. For a set of observed dichotomous test data from K subjects responding to N items, the joint likelihood function across all $N \times K$ dimensions is:

$$L(\mathbf{U}|\theta,\mathbf{a},\mathbf{b},\mathbf{c}) \quad \prod_{j=1}^{K} \prod_{i=1}^{N} P_{ij}^{u} Q_{ij}^{1-u} , \tag{9.1}$$

which is a direct extension of the conditional likelihood function across K subjects described in Equation 8.2. As described in chapter 8, the log-likelihood function avoids the numerous multiplications of proportions and is easier to work with than the likelihood function. The joint log-likelihood function is:

$$L(\mathbf{U}|\theta,\mathbf{a},\mathbf{b},\mathbf{c}) \quad \sum_{j=1}^{K} \sum_{i=1}^{N} [u \ln P_{ij} + (1-u) \ln Q_{ij}] . \tag{9.2}$$

The objective is to find a set of θ, **a**, **b**, and **c** values that correspond to the maximum value of the joint log-likelihood function. Operationally, we want to find $K\,\theta$ values, $N\,a$ values, $N\,b$ values, $N\,c$ values such that the first derivative (technically, partial derivative) of Equation 9.2 is zero at these $K\,\theta$ values, $N\,a$ values, $N\,b$ values, and $N\,c$ values *simultaneously*. This is a formidable task.

Currently, this task is commonly performed iteratively. Specifically, some initial values for **a, b,** and **c** are assigned (e.g., based on classical item analysis). These initial values are then treated as if they are the known true values of **a, b,** and **c.** We can then apply the conditional maximum likelihood process as described in chapter 8 to estimate the $K\,\theta$ values through some numerical procedure, such as Newton-Raphson. After all θ values converge within the numerical procedure, the final estimates of θ are then treated as known true values of θ. With these θ values, the values of **a, b,** and **c** are estimated through a similar conditional maximum likelihood process until all **N a, b,** and **c** values converge within the numerical process. These new estimates of **a, b,** and **c** are then treated as known true values and the cycle is repeated to revise the estimates of θ, **a, b,** and **c.** The cycle is repeated until θ, **a, b,** and **c** converge from one cycle to the next, that is, the changes in θ, **a, b,** and **c** from one cycle to the next become negligible.

A common numerical procedure employed in the joint maximum likelihood estimation of parameters is an iterative Newton-Raphson process described in Kale (1962). The most common computer program used for the joint maximum likelihood estimation of parameters is LOGIST (Wingersky, 1983).

BAYESIAN PARAMETER ESTIMATION

The Bayesian parameter estimation procedure (Swaminathan & Gifford, 1986) is also a direct extension of the conditional Bayesian modal estimation procedure described in chapter 8. As with the conditional case, the joint posterior function of the Bayesian parameter estimation process with uniform prior function is directly proportionate to the joint maximum likelihood function.

With a Bayesian parameter estimation based on a K-subject-by-N item response matrix **U,** it is necessary to specify K prior distributions for the K θ values, N prior distributions for the $N\,a$ values, N prior distributions for the $N\,b$ values, and N prior distributions for the $N\,c$ values. It is generally recommended that the prior distributions for θ and **b** be normal distributions. Because the a parameter generally takes on only a positive value, the prior distributions for **a** can best be described as chi-square distributions (Swaminathan & Gifford, 1985). Because the c parameter is restricted within 0 and 1, the prior distributions for **c** can be specified as beta-distributions (Hambleton & Swaminathan, 1985).

Once the prior distributions $f(a_i)$, $f(b_i)$, $f(c_i)$ and $f(\theta_j)$ for the N a, b, and c parameters and for the K θ parameters have been specified, the objective is to find the set of θ, **a, b,** and **c** values that correspond to the maximum value of the joint posterior function. Specifically, the posterior function is:

$$f(\theta,\mathbf{a},\mathbf{b},\mathbf{c}|\mathbf{U}) \propto L(\mathbf{U}|\theta,\mathbf{a},\mathbf{b},\mathbf{c}) \left[\prod_{i=1}^{N} f(a_i)f(b_i)f(c_i)\right] \prod_{j=1}^{K} f(\theta_j), \qquad (9.3)$$

where $f(\theta,\mathbf{a},\mathbf{b},\mathbf{c}|\mathbf{U})$ is the joint posterior function and $L(\mathbf{U}|\theta,\mathbf{a},\mathbf{b},\mathbf{c})$ is the joint likelihood function. The numerical process in the estimation of parameters for Bayesian parameter estimation is similar to that for the joint maximum likelihood estimation. That is, parameters are estimated iteratively. The difference is that, in the Bayesian process, the parameters corresponding to the maximum value of the posterior function $f(\theta,\mathbf{a},\mathbf{b},\mathbf{c}|\mathbf{U})$, not the likelihood function $L(\mathbf{U}|\theta,\mathbf{a},\mathbf{b},\mathbf{c})$, are identified.

When appropriate prior distributions are specified, the Bayesian parameter estimation procedure tends to produce more accurate results (Lord, 1986). However, whereas estimates from a joint maximum likelihood process are unbiased, albeit less accurate, those from a Bayesian parameter estimation process are biased (Hambleton, 1989). The main advantage of the Bayesian parameter estimation procedure over joint maximum likelihood procedure is that estimates of parameters are unlikely to be in an unacceptable range.

MARGINAL MAXIMUM LIKELIHOOD ESTIMATION

Bock and Lieberman (1970), Bock and Aitkin (1981) and Thissen (1982) suggested that the parameter estimation process can be improved if abilities can be removed from the estimation process. With ability parameters removed, we can concentrate on the accurate estimation of the item parameters only. Once this is accomplished, we can then estimate ability parameters through a conditional maximum likelihood or a conditional Bayesian modal estimation procedure.

Based on the conditional likelihood function (i.e., Equation 8.2), the likelihood that a subject will have a response vector of **u** (e.g., 1,0,1,1,. . . ,0), *given* that θ, **a, b,** and **c** are known, is:

$$L(\mathbf{u}|\theta,\mathbf{a},\mathbf{b},\mathbf{c}) = \prod_{i=1}^{N} P_i^u Q_i^{1-u}. \qquad (9.4)$$

The likelihood that a subject will have a response vector of **u,** *regardless* of the actual θ of the subject is then the cumulative likelihood across all possible θ values. If we pretend that the θ scale is discrete, can take on only the seven values $-3, -2, \ldots, 3$, and the subject with the **u** response vector has the same probability of having any one of these 7 θ values, then the likelihood of a **u** response regardless of θ is the sum of the likelihood of **u** given $\theta = -3$ plus the likelihood given $\theta = -2$ plus the likelihood given $\theta = -1$ and so on until $\theta = 3$.

However, the θ scale is not discrete, but continuous. Additionally, θ can take on any value between $-\infty$ and $+\infty$. Finally, the probability of a subject having a particular θ is not the same across all possible θ values. For example, the probability of the subject having a θ of -1000 on a z scale is quite likely to be substantially less than that of having a θ of say 1.5. If we can somehow specify the probabilities of a subject having particular θ values, we can assess the likelihood of u *regardless* of the actual θ value. Specifically, if the distribution of θ across subjects can be described by a function $g(\theta)$, then the likelihood of any one subject having a response vector of u is the integration of all conditional likelihoods for this given u across all possible values of θ, subject to the probabilities of θ as defined by $g(\theta)$. This cumulative probability of a particular **u** regardless of θ is then:

$$L(\mathbf{u}|\mathbf{a},\mathbf{b},\mathbf{c}) = \int_{-\infty}^{\infty} \prod_{i=1}^{N} g(\theta) \, (P_i^u Q_i^{1-u}) d\theta. \tag{9.5}$$

Whereas this is the likelihood of obtaining a particular **u** for any given subject, for a test with N items, there is a total of 2^N possible different response vectors. Hence, the likelihood of obtaining any particular response *matrix* **U** regardless of the subjects actual θ is:

$$L(\mathbf{u}|\mathbf{a},\mathbf{b},\mathbf{c}) = \prod_{i=1}^{2^N} L(\mathbf{u}_i|\mathbf{a},\mathbf{b},\mathbf{c})^{r_i}, \tag{9.6}$$

where r_i is the number of examinees in the sample who have obtained the response vector $\mathbf{u}_i$. The resulting likelihood function $L(\mathbf{U}|\mathbf{a},\mathbf{b},\mathbf{c})$ is called the *marginal likelihood function.* This function can be used to identify the set of **a, b,** and **c** values that correspond to the maximum value of this function through numerical procedures similar to those for the joint maximum likelihood estimation and the Bayesian parameter estimation procedures.

Bock and Aitkin (1981) suggested that the marginal maximum likelihood estimates can be further improved if the distribution of θ, that is, $g(\theta)$ is established empirically through a modification of the EM algorithm formulated by Dempster, Laird, and Rubin (1977). Bayesian prior distributions of **a, b,** and **c** can also be incorporated into the estimation through $L(\mathbf{U}|\mathbf{a},\mathbf{b},\mathbf{c})$ when desired. The BILOG program (Mislevy & Bock, 1984) is designed to produce marginal maximum likelihood estimates. It has been reported (Mislevy & Stocking, 1987) that BILOG is especially suited for small sample sizes.

APPROXIMATION METHODS

Based on Urry (1974, 1977), item parameters can be approximated based on the conventional item difficulty index and the point-biserial correlation discrimination index. Related to the point-biserial correlation is the biserial correlation. The point-biserial correlation is a Pearson's r between a dichotomous variable, such as an item score, and a continuous variable, such as the total score. An item is meant to measure a continuous trait. However, a dichotomously scored item divides the people along this continuous trait into two categories of people—correct and incorrect responses. The biserial correlation coefficient estimates the relationship between the total score and the hypothetical score on the continuous scale underlying the dichotomous item. The biserial correlation between an item and the total score can be estimated from the p-value and the point-biserial correlation of the item:

$$r_b = r_{pb} \sqrt{pq/h(\pi)}, \tag{9.7}$$

where r_b is the biserial correlation for the item, r_{pb} is the point-biserial discrimination index, p is the item difficulty index, q is $(1-p)$, π is the z score that cuts off p proportion of the cases in a unit-normal or z distribution, and $h(\pi)$ is the height or ordinate in the z-distribution corresponding to π.

Lord and Novick (1968) demonstrated that the biserial correlation for an item is related to the a and b parameters of the item. Specifically:

$$r_b = a/(1+a^2), \tag{9.8}$$

and

$$= \pi/b, \tag{9.9}$$

where π, as before, is the z-score that cuts off p proportion of the area in a z distribution. Based on these relationships, Urry suggested that the π can be estimated from the p-value of the item and the biserial correlation for the item can be estimated through Equation 9.7. The a and b parameters can then be approximated through:

$$a = r_b / \sqrt{1 - r_b}, \tag{9.10}$$

and

$$b = \pi/r_b. \tag{9.11}$$

Equation 9.10 and 9.11 are appropriate for a 2-parameter model. For a 3-parameter model, it is necessary to determine an appropriate c value (e.g., based on the random guessing model). The p and q values in Equation 9.7 are then adjusted according to this c value through:

$$r_b = r_{pb} \sqrt{c + (1 - c)p\{1 - [c + (1 - c)]p\}q} / h(\pi). \tag{9.12}$$

This adjusted r_b can then be applied directly to Equations 9.10 and 9.11 to approximate the a and b parameters for the item.

Based on the same principle, Schmidt (1977) derived an approximation procedure to estimate a and b in a 3-parameter model that does not require the estimate of r_b. However, knowledge of the classical KR-20 reliability estimate is needed. Specifically:

$$a = r_{pb} \sqrt{pq} / \sqrt{KR_{20} (1 - c)^2 h(\pi^*)2 - r_{pb}^2 pq}, \tag{9.13}$$

where π^* is the z score that cuts off $(p - c)/(1 - c)$ proportion of the area in a z distribution. The b parameter is approximated through:

$$b = h(\pi^*)\pi^*(1 - c) \sqrt{KR_{20}}/r_{pb} \sqrt{pq}. \tag{9.14}$$

For these approximation methods to produce reliable estimates, there must be at least 80 items and the KR-20 coefficient must be at least .90. The advantage of relative computational parsimony of these approximation methods is somewhat reduced as a result of these requirements. Additionally, an assumption that θ is distributed normally must be met for these methods to produce reliable results. Two computer programs are available for the approximation estimates of item parameters. These are AN-CILLES and OGIVA (Urry, 1977). Swaminathan and Gifford (1983) reported that these programs provide good estimates when the assumption of the normal distribution of θ is met.

SAMPLE SIZE CONSIDERATIONS

Aside from the mathematical problems discussed at the beginning of this chapter, an additional important consideration in the joint estimation of item and ability parameters is the number of items in the test and the number of examinees in the sample. In general, both the number of items and the number of examinees need to be large. As discussed earlier, increasing the number of examinees without a simultaneous increase in the number of items would lead to worse estimates.

The fewer item parameters involved in the model, the less the numbers of items and examinees required for valid estimates. Lord (1980) found that the problem of multiple latent roots identified by Samejima (1973) did not occur with tests with more than 20 items. Hence, a good general rule of thumb is that the number of items must be at least 20. Wright and Stone (1979) recommended a minimum of 20 items and 200 examinees when parameters are estimated within a 1-parameter Rasch model. Hulin, Lissak, and Drasgow (1982) suggested that for a 2-parameter model, there must be at least 30 items and 500 examinees; and for a 3-parameter model, there must be at least 60 items and 1,000 examinees. Hambleton (1989) pointed out that, when there are 80 items in the test, estimates are excellent for all models. When the approximation methods are used, Schmidt (1977) suggested that the test must have at least 80 items. Additionally, Swaminathan and Gifford (1983) found that Urry's (1976) approximation method require very large number of items and subjects to compare favorably against the joint maximum likelihood estimation procedure.

PART 4

VALIDITY

CHAPTER 10

Content and Criterion-Related Validity

In the previous chapters, we have discussed various approaches to connect an observed score to a true score. Within the random sampling theoretic framework, true scores are rarely estimated directly. Rather, the strength of the linear relationship between the observed score and the true score is estimated through a reliability coefficient. When this coefficient is high, the observed score is effectively a linear transformation of the true score. However, a high reliability coefficient only indicates that the observed score is an effective stand-in for the true score. It does not indicate that the score can be interpreted as an indication of the quantity of the construct intended to be measured. In other words, demonstrating reliability alone is not adequate. In addition, we need to demonstrate the validity of the test score so that the score can be meaningfully interpreted.

The alternative label of "latent trait theory" for item response theory can be erroneously interpreted as implying that the scores obtained through this process reflect the quantity of the trait or construct of interest. Through item response theory, an ability score for each subject is obtained. This ability score can best be described as analogous to a classical true score. As such, the ability score is a numeric entity with no intrinsic meaning. To interpret this score as reflecting some construct, evidence of validity is also needed.

THE CONCEPT OF VALIDITY

Conventionally, validity is defined as the extent to which a test measures what it purports to measure. As with the classical reliability coefficient, this view of validity implies the existence of a constant inherent characteristic of a test score. The contemporary view (e.g., Cronbach, 1971; Messick, 1989) of validity has departed from this static perspective. Messick (1989) provided one of the most comprehensive contemporary definitions: Validity is an integrated evaluative judgment of the degree to which empirical evidence and theoretical rationales support the adequacy and appropriateness of inferences and actions based on test scores or other modes of measurement (p.13). This definition suggests that the concept of validity contains a number of important characteristics.

First, as reliability is not the reliability of a test *per se* but the reliability of *using the observed scores* from within a specific set of measurement conditions to represent the true scores, validity is not an inherent characteristic of a test or measurement procedure. Rather, it is the reasonableness of *using the test score* for a particular purpose or for a particular inference. It is incorrect to say that a test or a measurement procedure is valid. A test or measurement procedure itself is neither valid nor invalid. Nor is a test score inherently valid or invalid. Therefore, it is more reasonable to ask "Is this a valid use or interpretation of the test scores?" than "Is this a valid test?".

Second, whereas the reliability of an observed score within a particular measurement procedure can be adequately described numerically through a reliability coefficient, a standard error of measurement, or an information function; validity cannot be adequately summarized by a numerical index. Instead, validity for a particular use of or inference from a test score is *supported* through an accumulation of empirical, statistical, theoretical, and conceptual evidence. As such, there is no single "validity coefficient" for a given measurement procedure. Various statistics called "validity coefficients" commonly reported for measurement procedures are typically numerical descriptors of the *strength* of one of many pieces of empirical evidence.

Third, as there can be many reliability coefficients for a given measurement procedure dependent on the object and facets of measurement, there can be many aspects of validity dependent on the intended use and intended inferences to be made from the test score. Recall that in generalizability theory, a true score is not an absolute entity, but is relative to the measurement conditions. The same examinee may indeed have different true scores dependent upon the defined conditions of measurement. For example, if we restrict the object of measurement, the true score would be different from a less restrictive object of measurement. For a given true score, there are many different ways of interpreting this score. Therefore, a given measurement procedure can lead to both valid and invalid results. Specifically, the scores obtained from this measurement procedure can be valid for certain uses and inferences, but not valid for other uses and inferences.

Finally, because validity is the appropriateness of a particular use of test scores, *test validation* is then the process of accumulating evidence to support this intended use of the scores. As such, validation is a series of on-going and independent processes. These independent processes are essentially independent investigations of the appropriate use or interpretation of scores from a particular measurement procedure. Whereas the estimation of reliabilities involves the definition of measurement conditions and subsequent statistical analyses, test validation involves issues of formal/informal, qualitative/quantitative research designs. Furthermore, reliabilities, once established for a particular object of measurement and a particular set of measurement conditions, remain with that object of measurement and that set of conditions. Validity for a particular interpretation of test scores, however, can be refuted by new evidence.

To accumulate evidence of validity, three types of validation studies are customarily recommended. The results of these three types of studies are commonly referred to as content validity, criterion-related validity, and construct validity. It should be emphasized that these three types of evidence are not distinct categories and that they are not three types of validity. Rather, they are results of three different approaches to the establishment of evidence of validity. Cronbach (1984) referred to them as three different methods of inquiry, rather than three types of validity. Dependent on the intended use of the test scores, not all three types of evidence are needed. Certain types of evidence obtained from certain types of studies may be more appropriate than others for certain score interpretation and usage. For example, when scores are obtained through the direct observation of overt behavior, under certain score interpretations, only evidence of criterion-related validity is needed (Suen & Ary, 1989). In this chapter, we concentrate on issues of content and criterion-related validity. In the next chapter, construct validity and other issues of validity are explored.

CONTENT VALIDITY

From the perspectives of classical theory and item response theory, the items in a test are assumed to be a sample of all possible items that can measure the particular construct of interest. Similarly, from the perspective of generalizability theory, the levels used within each random facet are assumed to be a random sample of all possible levels within the universe of that facet. When these assumptions are met, it would only assure that the items and/or levels are samples of some universe. There is no guarantee that the universe is in fact the one of interest. For example, a test is constructed and the scores are intended to indicate the math aptitude of individuals. The items in this test are assumed to be a random sample of a universe of all possible similar items. Even if this assumption is met, there is no guarantee that this universe of similar items is in fact a universe of math items.

Conventionally, content validity is frequently defined in terms of the sampling adequacy of test items. Considering this definition, content validity is the extent to which the items in a test adequately represent the domain of items or the construct of interest. A definition only in terms of items becomes insufficient for a multi-facet measurement situation. For example, the scores on an essay history test intended to measure "history knowledge as judged by trained high school history teachers" would have poor content validity when these scores are obtained from untrained undergraduate students, even when the items form a good sample of all possible history items. Therefore, a more generalized definition is that content validity is the type of evidence that supports the use of the sample levels of facets as an adequate sample of the intended universe.

Relevance and Representativeness

There are two aspects to the adequacy of the levels of each facet as a sample of its universe: relevance and representativeness (Messick, 1975). To facilitate discussion, we concentrate on a measurement situation involving only an item-facet (e.g., a standardized paper-and-pencil test). To support content validity of scores from this single item-facet measurement procedure, test items must be relevant to the intended use of the score and representative of the relevant domain of items of interest.

A test score is relevant for its intended use when all items in the test are within the domain (or universe) of items of interest. For example, for a test score intended to reflect some generic math aptitude of an individual, all items in the test must be math items. However, for a test score intended to reflect what a student has learned from a series of math instruction, only items related to what had been taught are relevant. Other math items, although important, are not relevant for this intended use of the test score.

When it can be demonstrated that all items are relevant to the intended use of the scores from the test, there is some degree of confidence of content validity. Confidence regarding the content validity of the inference can be further supported if it can be demonstrated that the items form a *representative* sample of the relevant domain. Statistically, the items can be considered a representative sample of the domain of relevant items if the items form a random sample of the domain. This statistical interpretation of representativeness is theoretically sound, but unrealistic. With the exception of some mathematics items, the entire domain of relevant items is rarely identifiable. The process of test development is rarely based on a sampling of relevant item domains. Hence, a more practical interpretation of representativeness is that the items in the test re-presents or reproduces the essential characteristics of the relevant universe of items in the proper proportion and balance (Lennon, 1956). With this interpretation, it is possible to construct, rather than select, items such that the items contain the essential characteristics of the theoretically defined domain of items in the proper proportions.

Content Validity of Paper-and-Pencil Tests

A paper-and-pencil objective testing (e.g., multiple-choice) format has been the predominant measurement procedure. This common measurement procedure is a special case of more general multi-facet measurement designs. In this special case, all measurement conditions are assumed standardized (or fixed) and the only sampling processes involved are the sample of examinees and the sample of items. Content validity, then, is the adequacy of the sample of items.

The content validity of scores from this single-facet measurement procedure can be maximized if the characteristics of the domain of items relevant to the intended use of the scores are defined. The description of these characteristics generally takes the form of behavioral objectives. Each objective describes a particular behavior to be measured (e.g., add two 2-digit numbers with carrying). A list of behavioral objectives thus forms an overall description of the domain to be measured. Items can be constructed based on these objectives. The appropriateness of these items can also be judged by the extent to which each item is relevant to these objectives. As for representativeness, the items can be developed in such a way that the number of items for each objective corresponds to the theoretical proportion or importance of that objective. For example, for a test intended to measure the effects of instruction, the number of items for each objective may correspond to the amount of time spent on that objective during instruction. An alternative to developing a number of items corresponding to the importance of each objective is to weight each item during scoring according to the importance of the item.

Today, there are numerous commercial or so-called standardized tests available. Many of these tests are adopted by local schools for the testing of their students. The advantage of using a standardized test is that national norms are frequently available for the purpose of comparison. The disadvantage is that the scores can have poor content validity for unintended use of the test. Test developers construct tests based on their own set of objectives, for their specified usage, and the test is made up of items from the domain relevant to its intended use. These objectives and the intended use may not match those of a local school. For example, the test publisher of a geography test and a particular local schools may have different ideas of what should be included in a geography test. In this case, the test publisher and the local school have two probably overlapping but different domains of relevant items. When standardized tests are used, the list of behavioral objectives as well as individual items must be examined to ensure that the domain of the standardized test matches that of the local intended use of the test scores. When the domains are not matched, content validity is compromised.

A common use of standardized tests is for the evaluation of instruction. If the purpose is to obtain test scores to reflect the effects of instruction, the behavioral objectives for the test must match the instructional objectives; otherwise, the use of the test scores for instruction evaluation would have poor content validity. The match between test objectives and instructional objects is one form of content validity evidence and is frequently referred to as *curricular relevance* or *curricular validity*.

Content Validity of Multi-facet Measurement

The limited single item-facet sampling orientation of a paper-and-pencil test is frequently not appropriate and often undesirable. For instance, many constructs, such as writing skills, are frequently measured through open-ended essay-type exams. An open-ended essay exam requires judges to assign scores. In terms of sampling, samples in three different dimensions are involved: sample of examinees, sample of items, and sample of judges. In this situation, adequacy of the sample of items as well as the sample of judges needs to be considered. As discussed in the previous section, to assess the relevance and representativeness of items, we need to explicitly define the domain of relevant items through such tools as behavioral objectives. Similarly, to assess the relevance and representativeness of judges, the characteristics of the universe of judges need to be specified.

In our earlier history test example, it would not be sensible to measure history knowledge through an essay exam using any randomly chosen person as a judge. We need to somehow narrow the universe of judges to that of competent judges. Hence, it is necessary to define the characteristics of acceptable judges. For example, "high school history teachers" may be a descriptor of the relevant universe of judges. Hence, for the essay exam, we need to define both the domain of items and the universe of judges. As we assess the representativeness of the items within the domain, we also need to assess the representativeness of the judges used within the universe of judges. When the relevant domains for all facets in a multi-facet measurement procedure have been defined, the resulting multi-faceted domain is known as the *universe of admissible observations* (Cronbach et al., 1972). Content validity can be judged based on the representativeness of a given measurement procedure to the universe of admissible observations.

Another area of measurement that frequently employs a multi-faceted design is performance assessment. This is the measurement of skills or a combination of knowledge and skills used in performing certain tasks. For example, in testing flight skills of airplane pilots, a single item-facet paper-and-pencil test would have poor relevance and representativeness in measuring the ultimate on-the-job performance. The use of a flight simulator would provide better content validity. For another example, a paper-and-pencil rating scale of social competence would have less content validity than, say, an interactive video disc testing procedure in which social situations are depicted to simulate real-life social situations to elicit responses from test takers. In both situations, scores from a paper-and-pencil test would provide poor relevance and representativeness of the object of measurement. Evidence of content validity related to environmental facets is sometimes referred to as *ecological relevance* or *ecological validity*.

Processes of Content Validation

The acquisition of evidence of content validity is primarily a judgmental process. The judgmental process can be formal or informal. The least formal process is a casual overall impression as to whether a paper-and-pencil test *appears* to contain the appropriate items. This loose form of content validity evidence is referred to as *face validity* and is generally considered unacceptable.

A formal judgmental process of content validation is essentially a systematic procedure which arrives at a judgment. For educational testing, an important aid to this process is the identification of the behavioral objectives and the construction of a *table of specifications* or *test blueprint*. A table of specifications is a systematic organization of objectives and relevant levels of cognitive skills to be measured. This table is useful in that it provides the standard on which the test contents can be judged.

Examples of tables of specifications can be found in Gronlund (1981), Nitko (1983) and many other educational testing texts.

In general, the process of content validation involves the definition of the universe of admissible observations, the identification of content-area experts knowledgeable of this universe, and the judgment from these experts on the extent to which actual observations (e.g., scores from items, scores from raters, etc.) are relevant and representative of this universe. With the multi-facet flight simulation test, for instance, it would not be sufficient to identify experts who are knowledgeable of flying. We need to identify experts who can judge the ecological validity of the test procedure.

Although content validation is primarily a judgmental process, various methods have been suggested to summarize expert judgments quantitatively (e.g., Hambleton, 1980; Heuer & Wiersma, 1977; Klein & Kosecoff, 1975; Rovinelli & Hambleton, 1977; Tittle, 1982). Additionally, suggestions have been made to use statistical techniques to derive evidence of content validity. Nunnally (1978) and Tucker (1962) suggested the use of factor analysis to help assess content validity. Nunnally also suggested the use of an internal consistency estimate of reliability to infer content validity. Bohrnstedt (1970) suggested the use of cluster analysis to derive evidence of content validity.

CRITERION-RELATED VALIDITY

Criterion-related validity is the evidence that demonstrates that scores on a test are related to some defined criterion measure of interest. For instance, scores on a particular college entrance exam are intended to be used as predictors of college performance. The criterion measure of interest is then some measure of college performance (e.g., GPA in college). Criterion-related validity is indicated by the strength of the relationship between scores on the college entrance exam and the chosen criterion measure of college performance. For another example, a new and abbreviated version of a career interest inventory is constructed to replace an older version. The criterion measure in this case is the score on the old version and criterion-related validity is indicated by the relationship between the new and the old version. In other words, criterion-related validity is a piece of evidence used to support, not the inference from a test score to some construct, but the appropriate use of scores from the test as an indicator of some criterion. The exact criterion measure to be used is dependent on the intended use of the test scores.

A distinction is frequently made between two types of criterion-related validity: *predictive validity* and *concurrent validity*. There is little substantive difference between these two types of criterion-related validity. The only difference is in the exact time when the criterion measurement is made. Predictive validity is the extent to which the test score can be used to predict the score from a criterion measurement procedure that will take place at some future point in time. Concurrent validity is the relationship between the scores on the test and the criterion measure taken at the same time. In both cases, we are interested in the relationship between scores on the test and the criterion measure taken at some point in time.

The gathering of evidence for criterion-related validity is generally a statistical process and the strength of the relationship between scores on the test and the criterion measure is usually expressed in the form of a Pearson's r. When the term validity coefficient is used in testing, it generally refers to the Pearson's r used as evidence and strength of criterion-related validity.

Relationship Between Reliability and Criterion-Related Validity

Because criterion-related validity is generally expressed statistically through a Pearson's r, the strength of the relationship is influenced by a number of statistical factors. One of these factors is the reliability of the test score.

The strongest possible Pearson's r between the true score for the test and any criterion measure is obtained only when they are either identical or perfect linear transformations of one another. When this occurs, the true score and the criterion measure are totally interchangeable measures on the same or different scales of measurement. Because reliability is the square of the Pearson's r between observed and true score, it is also the square of the relationship between the observed score and the criterion measure. Therefore, the square root of the reliability coefficient (i.e., the reliability index) sets the upper limit of the Pearson's r one can attain from the observed scores and some criterion measure.

This upper limit is attained only if the criterion measure is a perfectly reliable measure of the *same true score*. In reality, even if the criterion measure in fact measures the same true score, there would be measurement errors associated with the criterion measure. Hence, the value of a criterion-related validity coefficient is further limited by the imperfect reliability of the criterion measure. Statistically, the upper limit of a criterion-related validity coefficient is the product of the reliability indices (i.e., square roots of the reliability coefficients) of the test score and the criterion score.

Problem of Restricted Range

Another important and very common factor that influences the magnitude of the observed Pearson's r for criterion-related validity is the restriction of the range of test scores. When the score range is restricted, the observed Pearson's r is reduced. The more severe the restriction, the smaller the observed Pearson's r. This sampling artifact can lead to an erroneous conclusion that there is a lack of criterion-related validity evidence.

Scores on many tests are used as bases for selection. These include, among others, various admission tests, employment tests, and licensure exams. The rationale for the use of these test scores to determine selection is that these tests can predict future performance. To support this inference, evidence of criterion-related validity is needed. Scores for the criterion measure of future performance can only be gathered from subjects who are given a chance to perform. The use of scores on a test for selection would immediately imply that the measure of future performance can only be gathered from subjects whose test scores are above a certain cut-off point. In other words, the range of test scores in the sample for criterion-related validity assessment is restricted as a result of the intended use of the test. A common example is the use of Graduate Record Exam (GRE) scores as predictors of success in graduate programs (cf. Akemann, Bruckner, Robertson, Simons, & Weiss, 1983).

When a particular test score is used directly for selection, it is described as an *explicit selection* on that test score (Lord & Novick, 1968). When scores on a related measure, but not the test score of interest, are used for selection, the influence of the selection decision on the range of scores on the test of interest is indirect. Lord and Novick described this indirect influence as an *incidental selection* on the test score. In either case, the Pearson's r between the test score and the criterion measure will be attenuated. The attenuation due to restricted range of scores is particularly severe with an explicit selection.

If certain statistical assumptions are made, the Pearson's r for the full range of scores can be deduced from the observed Pearson's r for the restricted range in an explicit selection. Specifically, Lord & Novick (1968) demonstrated that, if we can accept the assumption that the true relationship between the test score and the criterion measure is linear and the common assumption of homoscedasticity in linear regression, the criterion-related validity coefficient corrected for the restriction of range is:

$$\rho_{xc} = \sqrt{\frac{1}{1 + \frac{\sigma_{x^*}^2}{\sigma_x^2}\left(\frac{1}{\rho_{x^*c}^2} - 1\right)}} , \qquad (10.1)$$

where ρ_{xc} is the corrected criterion-related validity coefficient, σ_x^{2*} is the variance of the test scores within the group with the restricted scores, σ_x^2 is the variance of the test scores across all subjects in the entire unrestricted score range, and ρ_{x*c} is the correlation between the test score and the criterion measure within the restricted range. It is generally recommended (e.g., Crocker & Algina, 1986) that attempts should be made to attain the full range of scores for criterion-related validity assessment; rather than correcting for restricted range statistically. This is because the assumptions, particularly that of homoscedasticity, needed for the statistical correction are unrealistic; and, in any event, untestable.

CHAPTER 11

Construct Validity
and Other Issues

Evidences of content validity and criterion-related validity discussed in the previous chapter can be considered *ad hoc* in nature (Loevinger, 1957). Specifically, they are relative to the intended use of test scores. With content validity, the main concern is the relevance and representativeness of the content of the measurement procedure relative to a defined domain or universe of admissible observations. When this universe changes, as when a facet changes, content validity is no longer assured. For example, when the same standardized test is used for instructional evaluation in many different schools with different curricular, content validity changes from school to school. With criterion-related validity, the evidence is relative to an intended use of the score only. When scores from one test are used for different purposes, criterion-related validity is no longer assured. Although they provide important evidence to support the appropriateness of the intended use of a test score, neither content validity nor criterion-related validity provides direct evidence to support an inference from a test score to the intended construct. To support such an inference, evidence of construct validity is needed.

CONSTRUCT VALIDITY

Construct validity is the extent to which the scores on a test are an indicator of the theoretical construct of interest. It is important to note that the test score is not equated with the construct (Messick, 1989). Rather, the construct manifests itself through various indicators. Construction validation is the accumulation of evidence to support the test score as one of the many manifestations.

Test scores can be meaningfully interpreted as a manifestation of the construct only when there is sufficient evidence of construct validity. When construct validity is supported, inferences can be made in test interpretation. From the perspective of score interpretation and scientific inference, construct validity is the most important type of validity evidence. For example, when scores from a social science test have content and criterion-related validity evidence, it only indicates that the items are a relevant and representative sample of what appears to be a domain of social science items and that the scores correlate well with some criterion. This does not ascertain that the scores are indicators of social science knowledge.

Because of the importance of construct validity, Loevinger (1957) suggested that construct validity is the whole of validity from a scientific point of view. Messick (1989) further suggested that construct validity embraces and subsumes all forms of validity evidence. Cronbach (1984) contended that all validation is construct validation. The current consensus (cf. Guion, 1977, 1980; Linn, 1980; Messick, 1989; Tenopyr, 1977) seems to be one of moving toward a single unified validity concept. Conceptually, content validity and criterion-related validity can indeed be viewed as limited aspects of construct validity. If one of the many manifestations of the construct is the identified universe of admissible observations, test relevance and representativeness of this universe would be a prerequisite or a preliminary step to construct validity. Similarly, criterion-related validity contributes jointly to the construct validity of both the test score and the criterion measure.

Central to the process of construct validation is a sound construct theory. This theory should specify the internal structure of the construct, how the construct manifests itself in other indicators, and how the construct relates to other variables. Ideally, a sound formal theory about the nature of the construct within the theoretical network of relationships with other variables would be most helpful. In practice, this is rarely attainable. First, all relevant variables within the network may not be identified. Second, not all variables are measurable. Finally, there may simply be no established theory regarding the construct in existence. For the purpose of construct validation, informal propositional statements regarding relationships with other variables as well as the structure of the construct are postulated. These statements are operationalized into researchable hypotheses. Studies are then designed to test these hypotheses. When the result from a construct validation study confirms the hypothesis, both the hypothesis and construct validity are supported. However, if the result does not confirm the hypothesis, we cannot be sure whether it is indicative of a lack of construct validity or that the measure has construct validity but the hypothesis was incorrect.

Methods of Construct Validation

Construct validation is essentially an on-going process of conducting various studies to confirm various hypotheses regarding the internal structure of the construct and its relationships with other variables. Because validation in general is a series of logical and empirical inquiries, construct validation is not different. Various systematic research techniques can be employed for a construction validation study. Methods and research designs that have been used or recommended include logical analysis (Vernon, 1962), experimental studies (Tuinman, Farr, & Bianton, 1972), correlational studies (Darlington, 1970), comparisons across known groups (Sternberg, 1981), generalizability studies (Kane, 1982), multitrait-multimethod matrix (Campbell & Fisk, 1959), multimethod factor analysis (Jackson, 1977), and structural equation modeling (Werts, Jöreskog, & Linn, 1972). We discuss three of these in particular: factor analysis, the multitrait-multimethod matrix, and the generalizability perspective of validity.

FACTOR ANALYSIS

Factor analysis is a group of general purpose statistical techniques designed to reduce a set of variables, measures, or items to a smaller set of common factors. These common factors are the underlying constructs for which the variables, measures, or items are imperfect indicators. Factor analyses may be exploratory or confirmatory in nature. Confirmatory factor analysis techniques have been generally combined with a causal modeling technique known as *path analysis* to form a causal confirmatory technique referred to as *structural equation models* or *latent covariance structure models*. In the following discussion, we only discuss conventional exploratory factor analytic methods. Readers interested in structure equation modeling should consult specialized texts such as Jöreskog and Sörbom (1979, 1983).

Factor analysis is applicable for content validation, criterion-related validation, or construct validation studies (Nunnally, 1978). However, because of its ability to explore underlying constructs common among a group of measures or variables, it is particularly suited for construct validation studies. Internally, factor analysis can empirically demonstrate if the interrelationships among items within a test are consistent with the theoretical internal structure of the construct. Externally, factor analysis can provide evidence to demonstrate whether the relationships between scores on the test and other variables are consistent with the theoretical network of relationships. For the purpose of discussion, we concentrate on the internal structure of the construct. The process applies equally to the external structure when item scores are replaced with test/variable scores.

The general idea behind the use of factor analysis to investigate the internal structure of a test is that the item scores are imperfect manifestations of a small set of underlying common factors (or latent variables). These factors and their interrelationships form the internal structure of the construct of interest. For example, literature in sociology has suggested that a construct called *alienation* has three independent dimensions: normlessness, powerlessness, and social estrangement. A test designed to measure alienation should have a number of items designed to measure each of these three dimensions respectively. Through a factor analysis of item scores on this test, we can identify the number of factors underlying the items and which item is associated with which factor. For our alienation test, if a factor analysis yields more or less than three factors, the construct validity of inferring from the test score to the degree of alienation is suspect. If items designed to measure, for instance, powerlessness do not cluster around a single factor but are scattered across all three factors, the construct validity of the score is also suspect.

Statistically, if item scores are manifestations of an underlying factor structure, the observed intercorrelations among the items can be reproduced mathematically from the correlations between the factors and the items. For example, if Items 1 and 2 in a test are two different manifestations of a single common factor F and the measurement errors of Items 1 and 2 are not related (recall classical theory), then the correlation between Items 1 and 2 should equal the correlation between F and Item 1 multiplied by the correlation between F and Item 2. If all underlying common factors are mutually independent, the correlation between a factor and an item is called *factor loading*. In other words, the correlation matrix among all items can be reproduced by various cross-products of factor loadings. Because of measurement errors, it is rare that a simple factor structure can totally reproduce the item correlation matrix. Generally, only when the number of factors equals the number of items can the correlation matrix be totally reproduced. A measure of the extent to which each factor contributes to the reproduction of the correlation matrix is the proportion of item variance accounted for by the factor.

The Process of Factor Analysis

In factor analysis, a single factor structure is initially postulated. This factor is identified by statistically generating an imaginary variable that has maximum factor loadings with the items. Hence, this factor would account for the maximum possible amount of item variance. The unaccounted for item variance may be due to the existence of a more complex factor structure or measurement error. In any event, a second imaginary variable (2nd factor) that is independent of the first factor is then generated. This factor would account for the maximum possible portion of the remaining item variance. Next, another independent factor is generated (or extracted) to account for the maximum amount of the remaining variance. This process is repeated until all item variances are accounted for.

In this manner, the early factors account for substantial portions of item variance and have high loadings. The later factors account for trivial amounts of variance, the existence of which are probably attributable to random measurement error. Given that we have hypothesized that the items are manifestations of a small number of common factors, we need to sift the genuine factors from the trivial factors that may be attributable to random measurement error. A decision has to be made as to which of these numerous factors to retain and which to discard. Two common criteria used are the Kaiser criterion, which discards a factor if the factor does not account for at least one item's worth of variance, and the Scree Test, which discards factors at the point when the change of proportion of accounted for variance from one factor to the next becomes stable. Through these or other criteria, a small number of factors is retained.

This can be used as an initial check on construct validity. Specifically, the number of factors retained should be equal to the number of dimensions within the internal structure of the construct. Caution, however, that Zwick and Velicer (1986) found that using the Kaiser criterion will generally overestimate the number of factors. The Scree Test criterion was found to be less biased. Additionally, Hulin, Drasgow, and Parsons (1983) demonstrated that if the items are scored dichotomously, ordinary factor analysis will overestimate the number of factors. For dichotomous data, a factor analysis based on tetrachoric correlations (e.g., Wilson, Wood, & Gibbons, 1987) should be used.

After the number of factors are judged to be appropriate, it is necessary to examine which items are associated with which factor. This can be done by examining the factor loadings for each item. Those items that are designed to measure the same dimension should all have high loadings on the same factor. The judgment of loadings cannot be performed until the factors are "rotated." Recall that the first factor accounts for most item variance. Thus, this factor would have high loadings with all items and the successive factors would have successively lower loadings with the items. This does not imply a one-factor structure. Rather, the loadings are an artifact of the statistical strategy employed. To arrive at more meaningful factors, the initial set of factors are "rotated" so that the accounted for variance is distributed more evenly among the factors. Dependent on the theoretical relationships among the dimensions of the construct represented by these factors, the factors are rotated in an orthogonal or an oblique manner. An orthogonal rotation is used when the dimensions are theoretically independent of one another. An oblique rotation is used when they are mutually related. The most common method used is an orthogonal rotation technique known as *varimax rotation*.

After the rotation process, a final set of factors is extracted. One can then examine the matrix of all factor loadings to identify those items that "belong together." Specifically, all the items with high loadings within the same factor can be considered manifestations of the same factor. The items within the same factor can be examined to determine what these items have in common conceptually and assign a label to reflect this commonality. The labels assigned to these factors should also reflect the nature of these dimensions. When the items that are supposed to be manifestations of the same dimension do "belong together" within the same factor, evidence of the internal structure aspect of construct validity is obtained.

THE RELIABILITY/VALIDITY CONTINUUM

Although there is an apparent conceptual difference between reliability and validity, when the common statistical evidences used to support reliability and validity are considered, the distinction between the two becomes blurred. Consider, for example, a situation in which a new shortened version of an old test is constructed. Scores on both the new and the old tests are gathered and the correlation between the two sets of scores is estimated. For the purpose of investigating whether the new version can adequately replace the old one, we would consider this correlation as evidence of criterion-related validity with the old test as the criterion. However, an alternative way of looking at this situation is that the new test is composed of items drawn from the same universe and that the two tests are parallel tests. Hence, the correlation is indicative of reliability rather than validity.

The distinction between reliability and validity is not always clear-cut. This is because reliability and validity are matters of degree on a continuum. Based on the classical concept of reliability, Lord and Novick (1968) pointed out that the reliability of a test score is just its validity with respect to a parallel test. Similarly, Campbell and Fiske (1959) suggested that reliability is the correlation between two maximally similar measures whereas validity is the correlation between two maximally dissimilar measures. Hence, reliability and validity are simply different points along a continuum of correlations between measures.

MULTITRAIT-MULTIMETHOD MATRIX

The reliability–validity continuum suggests that reliability, which is a correlation between two maximally similar measures, is at one end of the continuum. Validity, the correlation between two maximally dissimilar measures *of the same construct,* is at the other end of the continuum. If we extend this continuum beyond validity, we would reach the point of a correlation between two maximally dissimilar measures *of different constructs.* As we move from reliability toward the correlation of dissimilar measures of different constructs, we would expect the correlation to decrease. Campbell and Fisk (1959) suggested that these three points along the correlation continuum be distinguished as follows: (a) The correlation between two maximally similar measures of the same construct is reliability; (b) the correlation between two maximally dissimilar measures of the same construct provides evidence of *convergent validity;* and (c) the difference between the convergent validity coefficient and the correlation between two maximally dissimilar measures of two different constructs provides evidence of *discriminant validity.* Conceptually, one would expect the correlation for reliability to be higher than that for convergent validity, which is in turn higher than the correlation between two maximally dissimilar measures of two different traits.

They further suggested a sensible way of organizing these multiple sources of correlation coefficients in the form of a *multitrait-multimethod* matrix, which would permit a visual assessment of reliability and validity. Table 11.1 describes the general scheme of a multitrait-multimethod matrix. This is a matrix of intercorrelations among scores from various methods of measuring various traits or constructs. In this matrix, three different traits (X, Y, and Z) are each measured by three different methods (1, 2, and 3). Each cell entry in the matrix represents the correlation between the corresponding marginal trait/method combinations. For example, the entry in the cell corresponding to Method $1-$Trait Y and Method $1-$Trait X would be the correlation between the scores from these two measurement procedures. To facilitate visual inspection, redundant correlations are removed from the matrix in Table 11.1. The resulting matrix contains clusters of correlation coefficients.

To facilitate discussion, symbols rather than numerical values of

TABLE 11.1
Multitrait-Multimethod Matrix

	Trait	Method 1			Method 2			Method 3		
		X	Y	Z	X	Y	Z	X	Y	Z
Method 1	X	r								
	Y	dv1	r							
	Z	dv1	dv1	r						
Method 2	X	cv			r					
	Y	dv2	cv		dv1	r				
	Z	dv2	dv2	cv	dv1	dv1	r			
Method 3	X	cv			cv			r		
	Y	dv2	cv		dv2	cv		dv1	r	
	Z	dv2	dv2	cv	dv2	dv2	cv	dv1	dv1	r

correlation coefficients have been placed into the cells of Table 11.1. A correlation between the same method measuring the same trait (i.e., reliability) is represented by *r*. A correlation between two different methods of measuring the same trait (i.e., convergent validity) is represent by *cv*. A correlation between the same method measuring two different traits (i.e., a form of discriminant validity) is represented by *dv1*. Finally, a correlation between two different methods measuring two different traits (i.e., another form of discriminant validity) is represented by *dv2*.

The actual correlation values in this matrix can be examined visually to assess the reliability and validity of various methods of measuring various traits. For these methods to be reliable and valid, the multitrait-multimethod matrix should contain a number of characteristics. First, all *r* values should be high because these are reliability estimates. Second, all *cv* values should be significantly different from zero and have reasonably high values for evidence of convergent validity. Third, the *cv* values should be higher than the *dv2* values for evidence of discriminant validity. Similarly, the *cv* values should also be higher than the *dv1* values for additional evidence of discriminant validity. The pattern of *dv1* and *dv2* values within each triangle should be similar.

A GENERALIZABILITY PERSPECTIVE OF VALIDITY

A useful conceptual extension of the multitrait-multimethod paradigm and the reliability–validity continuum is a sampling model of validity (Kane, 1982). If test scores are invariant across different methods of measurement, then test scores from one set of measurement conditions can sustain inference under other sets of measurement conditions (Messick, 1989). Thus, the test score is not only a reliable indicator of the true score within a single set of measurement conditions, but an indicator of the universe score across different measurement conditions. This is analogous to the stability of scores across maximally dissimilar measures. Hence, the generalizability across different methods of measurement is an indicator of the validity of the test scores. The generalizability within each method would indicate the extent to which the true score as defined under the particular measurement conditions of the method can be represented by the observed score. This is analogous to the stability across maximally similar measures. Hence, it indicates the reliability of each individual method.

In a study by Breland, Camp, Jones, Morris, and Rock (1987), for example, each student wrote six essays. Two of the essays were written in a narrative mode, two in an expository mode, and two in a persuasive mode. Score invariance within each mode would indicate the reliability of test scores in reflecting the true scores of narrative, expository, and persuasive skills respectively. However, score invariance across all three modes would indicate the validity of using these modes to assess a general compositional skill.

Statistically, within a multi-facet generalizability D-study with method of measurement as one of the facets, using σ_s^2 to represent the true variance, σ_m^2 to represent the main effect variance component due to the facet of methods of measurement, and σ_e^2 to represent the sum of all other relevant variance components, the coefficient (Kane, 1982):

$$E\rho^2 \ = \ \sigma_s^2/(\sigma_s^2 \ + \ \sigma_m^2 \ + \ \sigma_e^2) \tag{11.1}$$

is a validity coefficient indicating the extent to which scores are invariant across methods of measurement. If the facet of methods is treated as fixed, the D-study would indicate the extent to which scores are invariant within a given set of measurement conditions. Therefore:

$$E\rho^2 \ = \ (\sigma_s^2 \ + \ \sigma_m^2)/(\sigma_s^2 \ + \ \sigma_m^2 \ + \ \sigma_e^2) \tag{11.2}$$

is a reliability coefficient indicating the extent to which measurement errors are absent from the score within a particular measurement method. What constitutes the levels of the method facet depends on the universe to which inferences are made. If the levels of the method facet are different test item formats such as multiple-choice, true-false, open-ended, and so on (e.g., Crocker & Algina, 1986), Equation 11.1 would lead to an indicator of the validity of using scores from any of these formats to reflect the true score *as measured through paper-and-pencil tests*. Results from applying Equation 11.2, however, would indicate the reliability of using a given format.

PART 5

APPLIED ISSUES

CHAPTER 12

Criterion-Referenced Testing

The term *criterion-referenced* testing was suggested by Glaser and Klaus (1962). A criterion-referenced test is one in which the scores are interpreted relative to a well-defined domain of behaviors and characteristics, rather than how well a person performs relative to how others perform. Typically, the score for an examinee is expressed as the proportion of the items the examinee has answered correctly. This is used as an estimate of the proportion of the domain of knowledge, skills, behaviors, and/or characteristics the examinee has mastered. Over the past three decades, there has been a substantial increase in testing activities related to criterion-referenced testing.

Physically, there is little apparent difference between a criterion-referenced test and a norm-referenced test. The difference is in how scores are to be interpreted. A criterion-referenced test is one that is developed carefully to enhance the capability of the score to reflect some absolute domain. Depending on how scores are to be interpreted, the same test can be both norm-referenced and criterion-referenced (Nitko, 1984).

Psychometrically, however, there is a considerable amount of difference between a score interpreted in a criterion-referenced fashion and one that is interpreted in a norm-referenced fashion. The reason is that for a criterion-referenced score interpretation there is an absolute domain. Scores on the test need to correspond accurately to this absolute standard.

Conventional evidence of reliability does not assure that the observed score accurately reflects the absolute score in the domain and is thus necessary but insufficient. In this chapter, some of the issues beyond conventional reliability and validity are addressed.

RELIABILITY OF TEST SCORES

When scores are to be interpreted in relation to an absolute criterion domain, it is not enough that the observed score is a linear transformation of the true score. The observed score needs to be a faithful reflection of the true score. In other words, it is not enough that the observed score has a small amount of random error, it should not systematically deviate from the true score. Consider the extreme hypothetical situation depicted in Table 12.1. Test A and Test B can be considered to be any two parallel tests (e.g., test-retest) and the numbers in the table are proportion-correct scores obtained by the subjects in these two parallel tests. The scores are to be interpreted in a criterion-referenced fashion in that they reflect the proportion of the criterion domain the subjects have mastered.

Classical Theory

If the reliability of these scores were to be estimated through a classical approach, a Pearson's *r* would be calculated as an estimate of the reliability coefficient. Consequently, we would obtain a perfect reliability coefficient. This happens because scores on Test B are a perfect linear transformation of those on Test A in that subjects *systematically* scored an additional 50% of the items correct in Test B. For norm-referenced testing, these tests are

TABLE 12.1
Hypothetical Proportion-Correct Scores Obtained in Two Parallel Tests

Subject	Score on	
	Test A	*Test B*
A	0.40	0.90
B	0.35	0.85
C	0.30	0.80
D	0.25	0.75
E	0.20	0.70
F	0.15	0.65
G	0.10	0.60
H	0.05	0.55
I	0.00	0.50

indeed perfectly reliable in that the rank-orders of the subjects are identical on both tests. In other words, classical reliability cannot detect systematic score variations and is appropriate for norm-referenced testing only.

If the scores in Table 12.1 were to be interpreted in a criterion-referenced manner, these tests cannot be considered perfectly reliable. The individual scores are to reflect the proportion of the absolute domain that the subjects have mastered. The two tests show different proportions. The systematic increase in scores needs to be taken into consideration as well, because both random and systematic variations affect how well the observed proportion-correct score can represent the true proportion-of-domain-mastered score.

Generalizability Theory

In generalizability theory, the systematic variation of scores across a facet is represented by the main effect variance component of the facet. Let us say that the two parallel tests in Table 12.1 are a test and a retest. In this case, we have a single-facet crossed design with time as the facet. The systematic variation in scores is reflected by the main effect variance component due to time, or σ_T^2. The amount of measurement error for criterion-referenced interpretation is the sum of both random and systematic variations, or the sum of the main effect time variance, σ_T^2, and the interaction between time and subject, σ_{sT}^2. This sum is referred to as the *absolute error variance* and is denoted by $\sigma^2(\Delta)$, which for our example is ($\sigma_T^2 + \sigma_{sT}^2$). The reliability of the observed score is (Brennan & Kane, 1977):

$$\Phi = \sigma_s^2/(\sigma_s^2 + \sigma_T^2 + \sigma_{sT}^2), \tag{12.1}$$

where σ_s^2 is the subject main effect variance component. To distinguish the absolute nature of this reliability coefficient, Φ is frequently referred to as the *dependability* index, as opposed to the generalizability coefficient for norm-referenced testing.

To generalize to other measurement designs, the absolute error variance $\sigma^2(\Delta)$ is the sum of all main effect and interaction variance components except the main effect due to the object of measurement. In the case of a fixed facet, the main effect of the fixed facet and the interaction between the fixed facet and the object of measurement are also excluded from $\sigma^2(\Delta)$. The generalized Φ is $\sigma_s^2/[\sigma_s^2 + \sigma^2(\Delta)]$ where σ_s^2 is the main effect variance of the object of measurement. In the case of a fixed facet, the interaction between that facet and the object of measurement should be included in both the denominator and the numerator.

Item Response Theory

The item response theory analog to a reliability coefficient is the test information function. The use of the test information function in the presence of systematic error is a more complicated matter. Because the θ scale is arbitrary and a z-score metric is generally used, the subjects in Table 12.1 would probably obtain identical θ scores on both tests in spite of the systematic variation. Thus, the information values are identical on both tests. However, this is assuming that all items in the tests have identical item characteristics. When they do not, which is most likely to be the case, subjects would obtain different θ values on the two tests that are not linear transformations of one another. This would indicate that either the assumptions of unidimensionality and local independence are violated, or that the items in the two tests represent two different domains. In practice, when two tests are assumed to be parallel, observed differences of θ scores on the two tests are frequently attributed to the arbitrariness of the θ scale. A linear transformation is performed to *equate* the two tests. (*Equating* is addressed in chapter 15.) Hence, the systematic error is not detected.

STANDARD SETTING

Tests are frequently used to classify individuals into categories. Individuals are categorized based on their scores being above or below certain cut scores. When scores are interpreted in a norm-referenced fashion, cut scores are determined by the proportion of people to be classified into certain groups. For example, using a deviation IQ score of 130 as the cut score for a gifted education program is essentially defining a gifted child as one whose IQ score is in the top 2% to 3% of all children of the same age. When a college uses an SAT score of, say, 1,200 as the cut score for admission, the college is essentially saying that they will only admit the top 16% of all potential applicants.

It would defeat the purpose of criterion-referenced testing if cut scores are determined in the above norm-referenced fashion. Rather, cut scores should be determined by what skills, knowledge, and so forth are required. A general approach is to find a cut score that would distinguish those who have adequately mastered the domain from those who have not. This is primarily a judgmental process. There are two alternatives to this judgmental process: Judgment of groups and judgment of test contents.

Judgment of Groups

If we can somehow identify existing groups of people who are masters and nonmasters of the content domain, test data from these individuals can be used to identify the appropriate cut score. This approach is referred to as the *contrasting groups method* (Nedelsky, 1954). Figure 12.1 provides a graphic illustration of determining the cut score through this method. This figure shows the two different score distributions among masters and nonmasters. No matter which score along the scale is chosen as the cut score between masters and nonmasters, there will be some amount of misclassification. Using the score corresponding to the intersection of the two distributions, however, leads to the minimum amount of misclassification. Therefore, given the distributions, that is the best cut score.

Essentially, this method requires judgments from content experts as to who the masters and nonmasters are without the use of the test. An inherent limitation is that these judgments are not always consistent. The same subject may be considered a master or a nonmaster by different judges. A situation in which the contrasting groups method is quite appropriate is one that is commonly referred to as *credit-by-examination.* In this situation, a student who wishes to earn the credits for a course of instruction without actually attending the course may do so by demonstrating his/her competence through a test. If the student passes this test, the student is assumed to have mastery of the subject area and is awarded the credits. For this situation, the master–nonmastery classification is relatively clear-cut. Students in the past who have attended that course and passed would be logical masters whereas those who have attended but failed the course would be nonmasters.

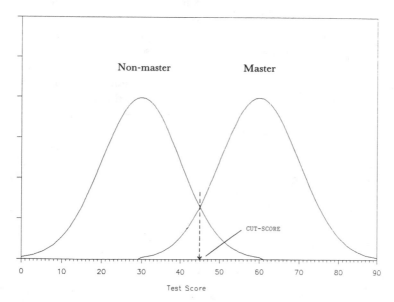

Figure 12.1.   Contrasting Groups

An alternative to the contrasting groups method is the *borderline group method* (Nedelsky, 1954; Zieky & Livingston, 1977). With this method, content experts meet and discuss the characteristics of a minimally competent barely passing individual. Based on these characteristics, a sample of borderline subjects are identified. The test is administered to this sample and the median score from this sample is used as the cut score.

Judgment of Test Contents

An alternative approach is to employ expert judges to *systematically* judge the contents of the test rather than the groups. There are numerous variations in this approach. The most common variants are the *Angoff method* (Angoff, 1984), the *Ebel method* (Ebel, 1972), and the *Nedelsky method* (Nedelsky, 1954). These methods are generally quite similar.

With the Angoff method, each judge is asked to state the probability that a minimally competent person can answer each item correctly. With K judges used for an N-item test, the best cut score is:

$$\lambda = (\sum_{i=1}^{N} \sum_{j=1}^{K} p_{ij})/K, \tag{12.2}$$

where λ is the final cut score and P_{ij} is the probability that a minimally competent person can answer the ith item correctly as assessed by the jth judge.

The Nedelsky method is appropriate for a test with multiple-choice items only. In this method, judges are asked to assess item-by-item how many distractors in each item can a minimally competent person eliminate. It is then assumed that the person would guess randomly from the remaining choices. Thus, for an ith item with m choices and the jth judge thinks that the minimally competent person can eliminate x_{ij} distractors, the probability that the person can answer the ith item correctly as viewed by the jth judge is:

$$p_{ij} = 1/(m_i - x_{ij}). \tag{12.3}$$

The p_{ij} values thus obtained for all items from all judges can be applied to Equation 12.2 to derive the cut score.

The Ebel method is more elaborated and takes into account such factors as item difficulty and the importance of an item relative to the domain being measured. Judges are to assign items into categories according to the difficulty and importance of each item. Within each category, a judge is to assess the proportion of items a minimally competent person can answer correctly. These are then the P_{ij} values for the items in that category. With these P_{ij} values, Equation 12.2 can be applied to find λ.

Combining Judgments of Contents and Empirical Evidence

A fundamental problem shared by methods involving judgments of test contents is the lack of consensus among the expert judges. Methods have been developed to improve the consistency of judgment across judges or to adjust the cut score based on empirical evidence. Jaeger (1982), suggested a combination of the Angoff method and a modified Delphi consensus-seeking procedure to arrive at a cut score with smaller across-judge variance. In this process, actual test information is provided to judges and the judges are asked to revise their judgments in light of the new information.

Kane (1987) suggested that information from an item response theoretic analysis can be used to assess the quality of judgment and revise the cut score. Conceptually, if θ^* on the θ scale corresponds to the cut score λ on the true score ξ scale, then the discrepancy between expert judgment and empirical data can be assessed by the difference between $P(\theta^*)$ estimated from an IRT analysis and P_{ij} as assessed by the jth judge. The optimal cut score can then be derived by identifying the θ that minimizes this discrepancy.

CLASSIFICATION RELIABILITY

From our earlier discussion of generalizability theory, for a given measurement procedure there can be many reliability coefficients, depending on such variables as the object of measurement and the measurement condition. A mastery-nonmastery decision is not so much a change of object of measurement or measurement condition, rather it is a change of the scales of both the true and observed scores from a continuous scale to a dichotomy.

For the purpose of a mastery-nonmastery decision, it is important that the dichotomous decision is reliable, that is, consistent. Let us look at a preschool screening test the sole purpose of which is to identify children who are likely to be "problematic." With neither diagnosis nor inference made from the test score regarding some ability construct, it is more important to establish the reliability and validity of the decision than to establish those of the observed score (Suen, Mardell-Czudnowski, & Goldenberg, 1989). However, the reliability of the observed score influences the reliability of the decision (Brennan & Kane, 1977; Livingston, 1972). This influence decreases as the cut score approaches the extremes of 0% or 100% correct. There are two basic approaches to the assessment of classification reliability: Threshold loss functions and squared-error loss functions.

Threshold Loss Functions

A threshold loss function estimates the extent to which an examinee is consistently classified as a master or a nonmaster over repeated administration of the test. This can be estimated from scores on two parallel tests (e.g., test-retest, equivalent forms) or from a single administration of the test.

Methods Requiring Two Administrations.   Table 12.2 is a 2×2 table depicting the proportions of examinees classified as masters and nonmasters by two parallel tests. In this table, a is the proportion of examinees classified as masters by Test A and as nonmasters by Test B, b is the proportion classified as masters by both tests, and so on. The total (or marginal) proportion of examinees classified as masters by Test A is P_A, q_A is the proportion classified as nonmasters by Test A, P_B is proportion of masters by Test B and q_B is the proportion of nonmasters by Test B. For a test to have a high classification reliability, cells b and c should be large and a and d should be small.

Hambleton and Novick (1973) suggested that the classification reliability

TABLE 12.2
Two-by-two Contingency Table of Mastery-Nonmastery Classifications

		Parallel Test B		
		Nonmaster	Master	
Parallel Test A	Master	a	b	P_A
	Nonmaster	c	d	q_A
		q_B	P_B	1

of the test can be estimated from a *proportion agreement* index. This is the sum of the proportions of subjects who are classified as masters by both parallel tests and those who are classified as nonmasters by both parallel tests. Using the notations in Table 12.2, the proportion agreement index is:

$$\hat{p}_o = b + c. \tag{12.4}$$

The use of $\hat{p}_o$ as an indicator of classification reliability, however, can be misleading because the observed $\hat{p}_o$ is inflated by *chance agreement*. Recall from the discussion of likelihood function in chapter 8 that when two events are unrelated, the probability of their joint occurrence is the product of the probabilities of occurrence of each of the two events. Therefore, even if the two tests in Table 12.2 are completely unrelated (e.g., Test A is a test of geology and Test B is one of English literature), the proportions of subjects in cells b and c are not expected to be zero but are the products $p_A p_B$ and $q_A q_B$. In other words, $\hat{p}_o$ is unlikely to be zero. This non-zero p_o is not indicative of the decision reliability of Test A or Test B. Rather, it is the probability of chance joint occurrence of the two classifications, or *chance agreement*.

When the classification reliability of a test is assessed through $\hat{p}_o$, the observed $\hat{p}_o$ value is spuriously inflated by this chance agreement. The degree of inflation due to chance in a given observed $\hat{p}_o$ becomes more severe as the passing rate on the test becomes extreme. Cohen (1960) developed a kappa coefficient that assesses the degree of agreements after the removal of chance agreement. Statistically, using the notations in Table 12.2, kappa is:

$$\begin{aligned} \varkappa &= (p_o - p_e)/(1 - p_e), \\ &= \frac{b + c - p_A p_B - q_A q_B}{1 - p_A p_B - q_A q_B}, \end{aligned} \tag{12.5}$$

where p_e is chance agreement. Swaminathan, Hambleton, and Algina (1974) suggested that the kappa estimated from two parallel tests can be used to estimate the classification reliability of the test.

Methods For Single Administration.   A limitation of the above method is that two administrations of the test are needed to obtain data to estimate $\hat{p}_o$ and kappa. Based on the assumption that the joint distribution of scores for two parallel tests has the form of a beta-binomial distribution, Huynh (1976a) and Subkoviak (1976) developed methods to estimate p_o and kappa based on data from a single administration.

With the Huynh method (1976a), the *KR*-21 reliability estimate from the single administration of the test is used to estimated the parameters of the beta-binomial distribution, that is, α and β. Specifically,

$$\hat{\alpha} = [-1 + (1/KR_{21})]\hat{\mu}, \tag{12.6}$$

and

$$\hat{\beta} = -\hat{\alpha} + (n/KR_{21}) - n, \tag{12.7}$$

where μ is the mean raw score across examinees and n is the number of items in the test. With α and β estimated, the joint probability of obtaining a raw score of X in the first test and a raw score of Y in a second administration can be estimated through the binomial probability distribution (a rather complicated process). If the joint probability of obtaining a raw score of X in the first test and a raw score of Y in the second test is $f(X, Y)$, then the probability of a consistent nonmastery decision based on a cut score of λ is:

$$\hat{p}_{00} = \sum_{X, Y=0}^{\lambda-1} f(X, Y) \tag{12.8}$$

or the sum of $f(X, Y)$ across all values of X and Y below. The probability of being classified as nonmaster by a single test is:

$$\hat{p}_0 = \sum_{X=0}^{\lambda-1} \sum_{Y=0}^{n} f(X, Y) \tag{12.9}$$

The proportion agreement index and kappa coefficient can be estimated through:

$$\hat{p}_o = 1 + 2(\hat{p}_{00} - p_0) \tag{12.10}$$

and

$$\varkappa = (\hat{p}_{00} - \hat{p}_0^2)/(\hat{p}_0 - \hat{p}_0^2). \tag{12.11}$$

With the Subkoviak (1976, 1984) method, if the mean raw score (number of items correct) of the examinees in the single administration of an n-item test is μ, then the probability of a correct item response for an examinee with a score of x is:

$$\hat{p}_x = KR_{20}(x/n) + (1 - KR_{20})(\mu/n).$$ (12.12)

Given this probability $\hat{p}_x$, the probability of obtaining a raw score of x or higher ($\hat{P}_x$) can be estimated from a binomial distribution. The values of $\hat{p}_o$ and $\hat{p}_e$ can be estimated through:

$$\hat{p}_o = \frac{\Sigma N_x[1 - 2(\hat{P}_x - \hat{P}_x^2)]}{N},$$ (12.13)

and

$$\hat{p}_e = 1 - 2\left[\frac{\Sigma N_x\hat{P}_x}{N} - (\frac{\Sigma N_x\hat{P}_x}{N})^2\right],$$ (12.14)

where N_x is the number of examinees with a raw score of x and N is the total number of examinees in the sample. These estimated values of $\hat{p}_o$ and $\hat{p}_e$ can be applied to Equation 12.5 to estimate $\hat{x}$. The appropriateness of the use of either the Huynh method of the Subkoviak method depends on the appropriateness of the joint binomial distribution assumption. In general, both methods yield very similar results. Subkoviak (1984) provided a comparison of these threshold loss functions.

Squared-error Loss Functions

An alternative view of decision reliability is that it is not a simple mastery–nonmastery decision. Rather, such a decision is based on the score on a test. Decisions are made based on the difference between the true score and the cut score. If the difference between the true score and the cut score is large, we would have a reliable decision. On the other hand, if this difference is trivial, the reliability of the decision is suspect. Therefore, instead of a simple master–nonmaster dichotomy, we need to take into consideration how far a person's true score is from the cut score. This line of reasoning is also supported by Lord's (1959a) derivation that the standard error of measurement decreases as the score approaches the extremes. Therefore, the more extreme the cut score, the more reliable the classification.

Classical Theory. Conceptually, the farther the distance between a person's true score and the cut score, the more reliable the decision. Decisions made in a situation in which the true scores of most people are very close to the cut score are less reliable than those made in a situation in which the true scores are farther away from the cut score. In the former case, the scores of most people are close to the cut score and are therefore susceptible to misclassification. An indicator of this distance from the cut score is $(\mu - \lambda)^2$, where μ is the mean true score of the subjects and λ is the cut score. The higher this squared value, the more reliable the decisions.

In reality, true scores are unknown. However, the error of representing the true score based on the observed score is indicated by the error variance. Therefore, the reliability of the decision is a combination of the distance of the mean true score from the cut score *and* the reliability of using the observed score to represent the true score. Based on this reasoning, Livingston (1972) combined $(\mu - \lambda)^2$ with the classical reliability coefficient and developed the K^2 index. This index is defined as:

$$K^2 = \frac{\sigma_t^2 + (\mu - \lambda)^2}{\sigma_x^2 + (\mu - \lambda)^2},$$

(12.15)

where σ_t^2 is the true variance and σ_i^2 is the observed variance. Within classical theory, σ_t^2 can be estimated from σ_x^2 multiplied by the classical reliability coefficient. Further, the observed mean score $\overline{X}$ from a sample is an unbiased estimate of μ. Therefore, from a set of sample data, K^2 can be estimated by:

$$\hat{K}^2 = \frac{\sigma_x^2(KR_{20}) + (\overline{X} - \lambda)^2}{\sigma_x^2 + (X - \lambda)^2}.$$

(12.16)

When the cut score equals the mean score, the variance between the cut score and the mean becomes zero. Hence, in this situation, K^2 equals the classical KR-20 coefficient.

Generalizability Theory.   A limitation of the K^2 index is that, like its Pearson's r counterpart in classical theory, it does not take into account systematic score variation. Brennan and Kane (1977) proposed an index which is the generalizability analog of K^2 with the exception that the error variance is the absolute error variance instead of the classical relative error variance. Specifically, the reliability of decisions relative to the cut score is conceptually:

$$\Phi(\lambda) = \frac{\sigma_s^2 + (\mu - \lambda)^2}{\sigma_s^2 + \sigma^2(\Delta) + (\mu - \lambda)^2}.$$

(12.17)

The μ in Equation 12.17 is the grand mean score in the universe of items and subjects, which is unknown. Instead, we only have sample mean $\overline{X}$. Brennan and Kane (1977) further demonstrated that $(\overline{X} - \lambda)^2$ is a biased estimate of $(\mu - \lambda)^2$. To obtain an unbiased estimate of $(\mu - \lambda)^2$, the sampling error of $\overline{X}$ needs to be taken into consideration. Recall from chapter 5, the sampling error of using $\overline{X}$ to represent μ is $\sigma^2(\overline{X})$ and is estimated through Equation 5.23. An unbiased estimate of $(\mu - \lambda)^2$ is thus $(\overline{X} - \lambda)^2 - \sigma^2(\overline{X})$. Therefore, an unbiased estimate of $\Phi(\lambda)$ based on sample data is:

$$\Phi(\lambda) = \frac{\sigma_s^2 + (\overline{X} - \lambda)^2 - \sigma^2(\overline{X})}{\sigma_s^2 + \sigma^2(\Delta) + (X - \lambda)^2 - \sigma^2(\overline{X})}. \tag{12.18}$$

As with K^2, $\Phi(\lambda)$ is equal to its score reliability counterpart Φ when the cut score λ equals μ. However, when the cut score equals the sample mean $\overline{X}$, $\Phi(\lambda)$ equals the classical KR-21 reliability coefficient (Brennan, 1983). Because of the inclusion of the absolute error variance, for the same data and same cut score, $\Phi(\lambda)$ can be expected to be lower in value than K^2. Additionally, as the cut score approaches 0% or 100%, $\Phi(\lambda)$ increases. In other words, Φ can be considered to be the upper bound of $\Phi(\lambda)$.

IRT Method

Huynh (1985) suggested that the single-administration threshold loss function for a test can be estimated through item response theory. Specifically, the conditional probability that an examinee with a particular θ score will have a raw score of X on parallel Test A and a raw score of Y on parallel Test B is:

$$f(X, Y|\theta) = L(X|\theta)L(Y|\theta), \tag{12.19}$$

where $L(X|\theta)$ and $L(Y|\theta)$ are the conditional likelihood functions of obtaining X and Y raw scores, given θ. If there are m possible discrete θ values, then the unconditional joint probability of X and Y is:

$$f(X, Y) = \sum_{i=1}^{m} f(X, Y|\theta_i)p(\theta_i), \tag{12.20}$$

where $p(\theta_i)$ is the marginal probability of obtaining a θ of θ_i value. The joint probability $f(X, Y)$ can be applied to Equations 12.8 through 12.11 to estimate p_o and κ.

An alternative perspective of classification reliability within the IRT framework is that the reliability of a mastery decision can be assessed through the test information function at the θ score that corresponds to the true score ξ, which in turn corresponds to the cut score λ. A high information value would indicate a low error variance. An advantage of IRT in this regard is the flexibility to select items from the appropriate domain with a high item information function value at the cut score. This would ensure maximum classification reliability. Caution needs to be taken in this selection process to ensure that content relevance and representativeness are maintained.

Methods to Minimize Threshold Loss

The cut score λ is conceptually on the true score scale. However, mastery–nonmastery decisions are made based on observed scores. A subject whose observed score is below the cut score may have a true score above or below λ. Threshold losses, or misclassifications, are caused by errors due to using the observed score as an indicator of true score. Table 12.3 shows the relationship between observed and true scores. Note that this table is different from Table 12.2 in that Table 12.3 depicts the classifications based on observed and true scores whereas Table 12.2 depicts the classifications based on parallel tests. Cell a in Table 12.3 is the proportion of *false positives* and Cell d is the proportion of *false negatives*. The amount of threshold loss is minimized when Cells a and d are minimized. Huynh (1976b) and Huynh and Saunders (1980) suggested that these can

TABLE 12.3
Mastery-Nonmastery Classifications Based on Observed and True Scores

		Decision Based on True Score		
		Nonmaster	Master	
Decision Based on Observed Score	Master	a	b	p_O
	Nonmaster	c	d	q_O
		q_T	p_T	1

be minimized if an appropriate observed cut score C_o can be derived from the true cut score λ. Specifically, for an N-item test, the most appropriate C_o is:

$$\hat{C}_o = \frac{N - KR_{21}}{KR_{21}}\lambda + \frac{KR_{21} - 1}{KR_{21}}\mu_x + .5, \qquad (12.21)$$

where KR_{21} is the classical KR-21 reliability coefficient and $\hat{\mu}_x$ is the mean score on the test.

VALIDITY OF MASTERY DECISION

The issues of validity for a criterion-referenced test are not different from those for a norm-referenced test. All the concerns about content, criterion-related, and construct validation apply equally to criterion-referenced tests. Additionally, the various methods of inquiry, including the multitrait-multimethod matrix, factor analysis, and the generalizability model of validity also apply to criterion-referenced testing. If the generalizability approach described by Kane (1982) is applied to the validation of a criterion-referenced test, however, the absolute error variance $\sigma^2(\Delta)$ should be used instead of the relative error variance $\sigma^2(\delta)$.

When a cut score is used to classify individuals into masters and nonmasters, however, it is also necessary to determine the validity of the classification decision: Do people classified as masters prove to be competent in reality? This is in fact a question of criterion-related validity (Nitko, 1983; Suen, 1988). If an alternative method of determining mastery and nonmastery can be identified, this can be used as a criterion-measure. The correspondence between the mastery decision based on the test and that based on the criterion measure can be used as evidence of criterion-related validity. If the test scores are intended to be used to predict on-the-job competence, actual on-the-job competence as judged by the person's supervisor can be used as the criterion measure. If the scores on a test are intended to identify preschool children who potentially would require special education, actual placement information for a sample of children after they have entered school can be used as the criterion measure, as long as the scores were not actually used for placement for this group of children (e.g., Mardell-Czudnowski, Goldenberg, Suen, & Fries, 1988).

Table 12.4 depicts the 2×2 table between decisions made based on observed test scores and those based on the criterion measure. As with Tables 12.2 and 12.3, the higher the values of Cells b and c, the stronger

TABLE 12.4
Criterion-related Validity of Mastery-Nonmastery Classifications

		Classification Based on Criterion Measure		
		Nonmaster	Master	
Decision Based on Test Score	Master	a	b	p_t
	Nonmaster	c	d	q_t
		q_C	p_C	1

the evidence of criterion-related validity of the decision. The sum of Cells *b* and *c* is sometimes referred to as the *hit rate*.

Based on the information in Table 12.4, a number of other indicators of the quality of the test scores can also be derived (e.g., Diamond, 1987). Specifically, the proportion b/p_c is known as *sensitivity* or *copositivity*, c/q_c is known as *specificity* or *conegativity*, a/p_t is known as *overidentification* or *overreferral*, and d/q_t is known as *underidentification* or *underreferral*.

CHAPTER 13

Direct Observation
of Behavior

$\mathbf{A}$ major limitation of conventional testing, whether the scores are to be interpreted in a norm-referenced or a criterion-referenced fashion, is the amount of inference one has to make from the test score to some underlying construct. Because of the inherent uncertainty involved in the large inferential leap from test score to the construct, many, particularly among operant behaviorists, have suggested that measurement of individuals should be confined to directly observable overt behaviors.

Many in the field have referred to a systematic direct observation of human or animal behavior as the *sine qua non* of science (cf. Ary, Jacobs, & Razavieh, 1985; Gelfand & Hartmann, 1975). It has been hailed as the hallmark of applied behavior analysis (Ciminero, Calhoun, & Adams, 1977) and as the greatest contribution of behavior modification to the treatment of human problems (Johnston & Bolstad, 1973). It has often been considered virtually bias free and axiomatically valid (Cone & Foster, 1982). Behavioral observational data is often used as the yardstick against which the validity of data from other measurement procedures are judged. Other advantages of the use of direct observation are described by Fiske (1978) and by Wiggins (1973).

In spite of the past confidence in the direct observation of behavior as a method of measurement, it has become increasingly clear that the superiority of scores from behavioral observation over other means of measurement cannot be axiomatically assumed (Suen & Ary, 1989). In any event, direct observational data are not automatically reliable and valid. The quality of these data in terms of reliability and validity must be assessed (Cone, 1977).

IDEOGRAPHIC-SAMPLE AND NOMOTHETIC-SIGN MEASURE

Data from the direct observation of overt behavior may be used for different purposes with different interpretations. Some uses of these data require only a low level of inference. In these cases, the issues of reliability and validity are more relaxed. In other cases, a considerable amount of inference is made and adequate evidence of reliability and validity is required.

Scores from the direct observation of behavior have been used with different views of what the scores are supposed to reflect. These views can be largely grouped under the classical distinction between operant behaviorism and cognitive psychology (Suen, 1988) or social behaviorists and trait theorists (Messick, 1989). While many have maintained the Skinnerian view that data should reflect objectively verifiable behaviors only (Skinner, 1945), there have been numerous behavioral observation situations in which data are used to reflect trait-like variables, or otherwise psychological constructs. A common use of behavioral observation methods is in the area of *performance assessment*. With performance assessment, an examinee's behavior is observed. Based on the observed behavior, inferences are made regarding the examinee's competence. This use typifies a construct orientation of observational data and interpretations go beyond the overt observable behavior.

In other words, data from the direct observation of overt behavior in a particular observation session may be used strictly as a *sample* of the subject's target behavior of interest. This use of observational data is referred to as *ideographic* observation. With this orientation, no inference is made beyond the behavior itself. The overt and observable behavior of a subject is the object of measurement. Alternatively, observational data may be used as a *sign* of some unobservable construct. In this case, the behavior observed is considered one of the many possible manifestations of the construct. This use of observational data is referred to as *nomothetic* observation (cf. Cone, 1986; Messick, 1989; Suen, 1988). With nomothetic observation, inferences are made from the observable behavior to the construct.

From a psychometric perspective, a major difference between an ideographic-sample and a nomothetic-sign orientation is that, with ideographic observations, a critërion-referenced score interpretation is most appropriate (Suen, 1988). This is because the "domain" of interest is the occurrences and nonoccurrences of some particular behavior. This is an absolute domain in that there is an absolute zero (i.e., behavior never occurs). The score (e.g., frequency of occurrence) has an absolute external point of reference and is interpretable by itself without regard to the scores of other subjects. With nomothetic observations, however, data may be interpreted in a norm-referenced or a criterion-referenced manner.

DIMENSIONS OF BEHAVIOR

Overt behaviors, whether observed directly or through an electronic medium such as a videotape, may be quantified through a rating scale or a quantitative record of occurrences and nonoccurrences. For ideographic observation, a quantitative record is most frequently used; whereas for nomothetic observation, a rating scale or a quantitative record may be used. A quantitative record may be derived from a global checklist (e.g., recording whether a particular behavior has occurred or not) or a detailed record (e.g., when, how often, and how long did the behavior occur). When a rating scale is used, the behavior is quantified through the assignment of scores by an observer based on the observer's perception. Scores may reflect the perceived quality, quantity, or simply the overall impression of the rater. A typical example of this type of rating is the observation of the performance of a diver in an Olympics competition by a number of raters and scores are assigned based on a set of criteria.

When a quantitative record is desired, however, scores are to reflect the occurrences and nonoccurrences of particular target behaviors. A detailed quantitative record of behavioral occurrences has been summarized in numerous scoring terms such as mean bout duration, duration, incidence, frequency, and so forth. These are basically numerical transformations of three basic quantitative dimensions of behavior: *prevalence, frequency,* and *pattern.* Prevalence is the proportion of time the behavior of interest occupies. Frequency is the number of times within a given period the behavior is *initiated.* Pattern is the change of prevalence or frequency over time. From these three dimensions, other quantitative descriptors are derived. For instance, *rate* is frequency of occurrence per time unit. *Duration* is prevalence multiplied by the length of the observation session and *Mean bout duration* is duration divided by frequency.

TIME SAMPLING AND SCORING ERROR

Whether a rating scale, a global checklist, or a detailed record is used in behavioral observation, random measurement error is of concern. When

behavior occurrences are recorded in detail, however, additional systematic recording error not detectable through reliability assessment may be
introduced into the score as a result of using particular methods of
recording.

Observation Sessions

A fundamental difference between behavioral observation and conventional paper-and-pencil testing is that behaviors occur over the time
continuum. Unlike items or subjects, time has no natural discrete units.
When to observe is as important a question as how to observe and whom
to observe. Typically, the time continuum is divided into a number of
blocks and only those that are appropriate are used as the time blocks of
observations (e.g., class period as a time block to observe in-class
behavior). These chosen time blocks are called *observation sessions.* Behavioral observations take place within these observation sessions. These
observation sessions may be scored at the time of the observation session.
Alternatively, they may be videotaped and scored at a later time.

Continuous and Discrete Recording

Within each observation session, behavior occurrences and nonoccurrences
may be recorded in a *continuous* or *discrete* manner along the time continuum. Continuous within-session observation may be scored through
real-time recording or *frequency tally,* depending on the dimension of interest.
With real-time recording, the subject(s) is observed continuously
throughout the observation session, and the exact clock time for the
initiation and termination of each behavior occurrence is recorded. This is
the ideal method of recording but is not always realistic (cf. Suen & Ary,
1989). When frequency tally is used, the subject is also observed continuously and the number of times a particular behavior is initiated is
recorded. When continuous real-time recording or frequency tally is not
possible, too obtrusive, or too expensive, *time sampling* techniques are used.

Time Sampling

In time sampling (Altmann, 1974; Bindra & Blond, 1958; Goodenough,
1928; Olson, 1929; Powell, Martindale, & Kulp, 1975; Suen & Ary, 1986),
the observation session is divided into a number of discrete units of time
called *intervals.* Behavior occurrences and nonoccurrences are recorded for
each interval. There are three alternative methods of time sample record-

ing: partial-interval, momentary, and whole-interval recording. With *partial-interval* recording, an interval is assigned a score of 1 if the behavior occurs at all and a score of 0 is assigned only if the behavior *never* occurs within an interval. With *momentary recording,* the subject is observed only at the last moment of the interval and a score of 1 is assigned to the interval if the behavior is occurring at that moment; otherwise, the interval is scored 0. With *whole-interval recording,* an interval is scored 1 only if the behavior occupies the entire interval; otherwise, the interval is scored 0. Through either of the time sampling methods, a chain of 1s and 0s is produced for the observation session representing the occurrences and nonoccurrences of behavior. Various quantitative summary scores of the behavior can be derived from this chain of dichotomous scores. For instance, the sum of the interval scores divided by the number of intervals is an estimate of prevalence. The number of 0–1 sequences in the chain is an estimate of frequency.

Unfortunately, the use of time sampling techniques to estimate prevalence and frequency can be biased and the amount of systematic error is not discernible from reliability assessments. Therefore, the systematic error needs to be removed through design or *post hoc* statistical techniques. Specifically, all three time sampling methods tend to underestimate frequency. Partial-interval recording tends to produce a systematic overestimate of prevalence. Whole-interval recording tends to produce a systematic underestimate of prevalence. Using momentary recording to estimate prevalence, however, is unbiased.

Conditions Necessary for Unbiased Time Sampling

The biased effects of time sampling on the estimates of behavioral dimensions can be eliminated if the observation session is divided into intervals of proper length. Specifically, if the shortest behavioral bout within the session is b and the shortest *interresponse time* (period of time between behavior occurrences) is t, for time sampling to produce unbiased estimates of frequency, the length of observation intervals must meet the following conditions (Suen & Ary, 1986):

$$\left. \begin{array}{l} i < b \quad \text{and} < 0.5t \quad \text{for partial-interval recording} \\ i < b \quad \text{and} < t \quad \text{for momentary recording} \\ \text{and} \quad i < 0.5b \quad \text{and} < t \quad \text{for whole-interval recording} \end{array} \right\} \quad (13.1)$$

When these conditions are met, a count of the number of 0–1 paired sequences in the chain of score will produce an unbiased estimate of frequency, $\hat{f}$. If the first interval is scored 1, $\hat{f}$ is adjusted by $+1$. When the conditions in Equation 13.1 are met, unbiased estimates of prevalence can also be estimated through:

$$
\left.
\begin{aligned}
p &= (x - \hat{f})/n && \text{for partial-interval recording} \\
p &= x/n && \text{for momentary recording} \\
\text{and} \quad p &= (x + \hat{f})/n && \text{for whole-interval recording}
\end{aligned}
\right\} \tag{13.2}
$$

where p is the estimated prevalence, x is the sum of interval scores across all intervals, $\hat{f}$ is the unbiased frequency estimate, and n is the number of intervals in the observation session.

In reality, the shortest bout b and the shortest interresponse time t are unknown. If prior information from either expert judges or prior continuous observation is available, the probability that the conditions in Equation 13.1 are violated can be assessed. Specifically, if the mean of the prior distribution of b is $\bar{b}$ and the mean of the prior distribution of t is $\bar{t}$, the probability that the conditions are violated by using a particular interval length of i can be assessed through:

$$
P_e = \sum_{j=0}^{i} \left[\frac{e^{-\bar{b}}\bar{b}^j}{j!} + \frac{e^{-.5\bar{t}}(.5\bar{t})^j}{j!} \right] \tag{13.3}
$$

for partial-interval recording,

$$
P_e = \sum_{j=0}^{i} \left[\frac{e^{-\bar{b}}\bar{b}^j}{j!} + \frac{e^{-\bar{t}}\bar{t}^j}{j!} \right] \tag{13.4}
$$

for momentary recording, and

$$
P_e = \sum_{j=0}^{i} \left[\frac{e^{-.5\bar{b}}(.5\bar{b})^j}{j!} + \frac{e^{-\bar{t}}\bar{t}^j}{j!} \right] \tag{13.5}
$$

for whole-interval recording. These probabilities can be assessed for different interval lengths until a tolerably low probability is attained. In general, the shorter the interval length i, the less the probability of violating the conditions outlined in Equation 13.1. Once the appropriate interval length is identified, time-sampling observation can be used to produce unbiased estimates of prevalence and frequency. Most recently, further refinements of these conditions and correction procedures have been proposed. Interested readers should consult Quera (1989).

RELIABILITY

In earlier years, because data from the direct observation of behavior had been assumed to be reliable and valid by definition, issues of reliability had been generally ignored (cf. Johnson & Bolstad, 1973). It has been determined since that scores from direct observation of behavior are not exempted from reliability and validity considerations (Cone, 1977; Hartmann, 1977, 1982; Kazdin, 1977; Johnson & Bolstad, 1973). Because different observers observing the same behavior can produce different scores, minimally, score reliability needs to be assessed.

Threshold Loss Function Analog

The most common approach to the assessment of observational data reliability is through *interobserver agreement* indices (e.g., Hartmann, 1977, 1982; Kazdin, 1977). These approaches are similar to the threshold loss function approach in criterion-referenced testing but are applied to data from observers. Specifically, two independent observers record the occurrences and nonoccurrences of the same target behavior of interest within an observation session using one of the time sampling methods to generate discrete dichotomous scores of occurrences and nonoccurrences. The correspondence of the interval-by-interval scores from the two observers can be cast onto a 2×2 table in a manner similar to Table 12.2 in the previous chapter. In this case, two observers are analogous to two parallel tests. The proportions in this table would be proportions of intervals for a single subject rather than proportions of all subjects. From this table, p_o and $\varkappa$ can be estimated as defined in Equations 12.4 and 12.5. In general, because of the probability of chance agreement, the use of $\varkappa$ instead of p_o is recommended (Hartmann, 1977; Suen & Ary, 1989; Suen & Lee, 1985).

Classical Reliability Analog

Although p_o and $\varkappa$ can be used to assess interobserver agreement, conceptually these indices are not directly comparable to the classical concept of proportion of true variance (Berk, 1979; Suen, 1988). An alternative is to treat the two observers as an analog of two classically parallel tests. With this view, the Pearson's r between the two sets of interval-by-interval scores would be conceptually equivalent to a classical reliability index. Because the interval-by-interval scores are dichotomous, this Pearson's r is equivalent to a ϕ coefficient and is indicative of the reliability of scores from any single similar observer drawn from the same universe of observers. This ϕ coefficient can best be described as an index of *intraobserver reliability* (Martin & Bateson, 1986; Suen, 1988).

The Generalizability Approach

Many (e.g., Bakeman & Gottman, 1986; Cone, 1977; Kazdin, 1977) have suggested that neither interobserver agreement nor intraobserver reliability is adequate for the assessment of observational score reliability. Unlike conventional paper-and-pencil tests in which many facets can be fixed (or standardized), observations of behavior take place in real-time as behaviors occur. Numerous environmental factors at the time of measurement cannot be controlled or fixed. The observer facet is but one of the many potential sources of measurement error. Minimally, the facets of scoring method, quality and quantity of observer training, and situational variables within the observation session should be considered (Kazdin, 1977). Consequently, many (e.g., Berk, 1979; Cone, 1977; Hartmann, 1982; Mitchell, 1979; Suen, Ary, & Greenspan, in press) have contended that a multi-facet generalizability assessment is particularly suited for the assessment of the reliability of data obtained through direct behavioral observation.

In the generalizability assessment of observational data, what constitutes true variance is not always clear-cut. When data are gathered through the direct observation of behavior, a major limitation is that each observer can only observe a very small number of subjects. To observe a large sample of subjects would imply a prohibitively expensive endeavor for an average researcher. Therefore, observational methods are typically used with a small sample of subjects. In many cases, these methods are used in *single-subject research* designs (e.g., Kratochwill, 1978). With an extremely small sample of subjects, the variance across subjects are inherently unstable. With a single-subject research design, there is simply no variance across subjects. In these situations, true variance is not necessarily subject variance. In other words, for many behavioral observation situations, the object of measurement is not individual subjects. In most cases, the object of measurement is "the subject's behavior *in time.*" As such, variance across time intervals or observation sessions is the true variance of interest.

Another important consideration in the generalizability assessment of behavioral observation data is whether the data are to be interpreted as ideographic-samples of the overt behavior or nomothetic-signs of a construct. As discussed previously, an ideographic-sample interpretation implies a criterion-referenced interpretation. As such, the absolute error variance and Brennan and Kane's (1977) dependability index are of interest. For a nomothetic-sign interpretation, however, scores may be interpreted in a criterion-referenced or a norm-referenced manner. Hence, the absolute error variance as well as the relative error variance may be of interest and either the G-coefficient or the dependability index may be appropriate.

Sample Sizes

As discussed earlier, due to the demand on resources, behavioral observation methods are typically conducted on a small sample of subjects. For the purpose of reference, we call these procedures of inquiry single-subject research. With single-subject research, the dimension of subjects is severely limited in the universe of admissible observations. More specifically, the dimension of subject is fixed to one subject with no variance. The evidence of reliability only applies to that single subject's behavior over time. Using the same observation procedure for other subjects may or may not lead to reliability scores. The reliability for other subjects for a particular observation procedure derived through single-subject observations may be determined through replications with other subjects having similar or different characteristics and under similar or different measurement conditions (Hersen & Barlow, 1976; Homer, Peterson, & Wonderlich, 1983).

VALIDITY

In the accumulation of evidence of validity for observational scores, two independent characteristics of the score of interest need to be taken into consideration. First, it is necessary to discern whether the score is used as an ideographic-sample or a nomothetic-sign. Second, the level of complexity of the behavior needs to be identified.

The behavior of interest for observation may fall into one of two general categories: molecular behavior and molar behavior. *Molecular behaviors* are individually recognizable specific behaviors for which further breakdown into components becomes meaningless (e.g., in-seat vs. out-of-seat). These behaviors, frequently derived through a process of systematic reduction of a phenomenon to a single directly observable overt behavior dimension are widely used among operant behaviorists. *Molar behaviors* are categories of behaviors with meaningful component behaviors. For example, "inappropriate disruptive behavior" in a classroom is a molar behavior for which finer molecular behaviors such as "talking out of order," and "throwing objects" may be meaningful component behaviors.

When the sample-sign and the molecular-molar dichotomies are combined, we have four different types of behavioral measures: molecular sample, molecular sign, molar sample, and molar sign. For example, the prevalence of a child's reading behavior in a study hall during an observation session as an indication of the prevalence of the child's reading behavior in the study hall would be a molecular sample measure. On the other hand, the prevalence of a child's reading behavior *when asked to do so* during an observation session as an indication of the child's "compliance" would be a molecular sign measure. The prevalence of inappropriate disruptive behavior in class during an observation session as an indication of the level of inappropriate disruptive behavior would be a molar sample measure. The frequencies of verbal behaviors such as criticism, disagreement, interruption, sarcasm, and so on between two spouses as elements of a molar behavior called *aversive communication,* which in turn indicates a construct of *marital discord* would be an example of a molar sign measure. These four types of behavioral measures imply different levels of inference and thus require different amounts of evidence of validity.

Content Validity

With a molecular sample measure, the question of content validity evidence reduces to one of a match between the behavior observed and the universe of admissible observations. In other words, depending on which facet is fixed, the observed behavior measure may be judged as relevant and representative or not. Scores on the reading behavior of a child obtained from an observation session in class may be judged as relevant and representative indicators of the universe of "reading behavior in class" but may not be indicative of "reading behavior" in general. When the universe of admissible observations is properly restricted, content validity of a molecular sample measure can be self-evident.

For a molecular sign measure, the observed molecular behavior is assumed to be a manifestation of the construct. For this type of behavioral measure, the questions of relevance and representativeness translate to: (a) Is the chosen molecular behavior among the various possible manifestations of the construct? (b) Is the chosen molecular behavior an adequate observable sign of the construct? For instance, *reading when asked to* is probably one of the manifestations of *compliance.* However, it may not be an adequate representation of *compliance.* In addition to these two questions, the proper identification of the universe of admissible observations is of concern as well.

A molar sample measure is a summary label for a category of molecular sample measures. The content validity for each component molecular sample measure as well as the overall molar sample measure need to be assessed. The relevance and representativeness of each molecular sample measure can be judged relative to its own universe of admissible observations. Additionally, the relevance and representativeness of the molar sample measure can be judged as to whether all molecular sample behaviors are relevant and if the molecular sample behaviors together form a representative sample of all molecular behaviors in this category. For example, a molar sample measure of *self-care activity* obtained from summing molecular measures of *eating* and *drinking* but not *grooming* and *dressing* probably would have poor representativeness.

For a molar sign measure, the content validity considerations include those of the molecular sign and molar sample measures. Additionally, the question of whether the particular molar behavior is an adequate manifestation of the construct needs to be considered. Whether aversive communication is an adequate manifestation of marital discord, for instance, needs to be considered.

Criterion-related Validity

As with any other measurement procedures, criterion-related validity is related to the intended use of the behavioral observation scores. The key is the identification of the proper criterion measure for the intended use. For a molecular sample measure not intended to predict any criterion other than the molecular behavior itself, criterion-related validity considerations reduces to a question of *observer accuracy*. Observer accuracy, also known as *criterion-referenced agreement* and *transductional accuracy,* is assessed by examining the degree of correspondence between data recorded by an observer and those defined as criterion measures. Common criterion measures for observer accuracy include scores from a "master" observer or from a continuous observation. Other means of attaining criterion measures include preparing a script for a sequence of pre-orchestrated behaviors with known quantities. Actors are used to act out the script and observers are used to record the behaviors of the actor. The correspondence between the data recorded and the known quantities would serve as evidence of observer accuracy or criterion-related validity.

Construct Validity

Construct validity is important for nomothetic-sign measures only. This is because, with an ideographic-sample measure, no inference is made to a construct. With a molecular sign measure, only external structure can be assessed since a molecular behavior cannot be meaningfully decomposed to investigate whether its internal structure is consistent with the structure of the construct. For a molar sign measure, however, the correspondence between the internal and external structures of the behavioral measure and those of the construct need to be assessed. For instance, a factor analysis may be conducted on the constituent molecular behaviors of the molar sign behavior to investigate the interrelationships among the molecular behaviors.

CHAPTER 14

Detection
of Item Bias

In addition to the core theoretical considerations of reliability and validity and their variations for criterion-referenced testing and behavioral observation, there are a number of other important theoretic-conceptual considerations in the construction and use of educational and psychological tests. These include issues of test bias, equating, interpretation of group and individual scores, and answer changing. The issues of detecting biased items in a test are discussed in this chapter. Other issues are discussed in chapter 15.

TEST BIAS

Test bias is a critical issue. As uses of educational and psychological tests continue to proliferate, an increasing number of decisions that have profound effects on individuals' lives are being made based on test scores. The problem of possible gender and/or ethnic biases in the use of many tests have drawn an increasing amount of concern among test users as well as the public in general. Court decisions have been made in some instances to prohibit the use of certain tests for admission decisions because of evidence that these tests are biased against female and/or minority examinees.

Test bias is essentially a problem of validity of inferences made from and/or uses of test scores (Berk, 1982). Given that a test is never perfect and there can be many sources of score variation, scores on many tests do in fact reflect to some degree variables other than the intended construct. This lack of unidimensionality implies a threat to the validity of inferences and uses of test scores. In a very general sense, the inferences and uses of scores on such tests can be considered biased against individuals with certain characteristics on the unintended variable. For example, when the scores on a math test also reflects reading ability, using the score to infer math aptitude can be biased against poor readers.

The term *test bias* as used today, however, is in a more restricted sense. Specifically, when the unintended variables being reflected by the test score are certain types of demographic variables such as gender, ethnicity, and socio-economic background, the use of these test scores for certain inferences or decisions may give unfair advantages to certain groups of individuals. When this occurs, the test is said to be biased. Therefore, a more appropriately restricted definition of a biased test is one the score on which reflects not only the quantity of the intended construct, but some other socio-demographic variables as well. For example, with our previous math test the score on which reflects both math and reading abilities, scores for students whose primary language at home is not English (e.g., Hispanic and Asian students) and have lower English reading abilities may be adversely affected. In this case, using scores from this test as indicators of math aptitude can be biased against those for whom English is a second language.

The issue of test bias is very complex both conceptually and statistically (Shepard, 1982). As an issue, it is emotionally and politically sensitive. Further complications include issues of culture-free tests, culture-fair tests, bias in inferences made from test scores, bias in predictions based on test scores, bias in selection decisions based on test scores, and bias within the content of each item. These complex and interrelated issues cannot be adequately treated in this portion of a chapter. Readers are suggested to consult in-depth discussions such as Berk (1982), Bond (1981), Cole and Moss (1989), and Jensen (1980).

ITEM BIAS

In the following discussion, we focus on methods to detect bias within an item only. A biased item is also referred to as an item with *differential item functioning* (dif). A test is composed of items. In general, a first step in eliminating bias effects on the use of the test scores is to ascertain that scores on individual items are not biased. It should be noted, however, that the absence of biased items is a necessary but insufficient safeguard against biased uses of or inferences from total test scores (Berk, 1982).

To minimize possible biased items, considerations need to be given during the item construction stage to remain sensitive to possible psychological effects of the context of the items on individuals from different groups, to avoid the use of biased language, and to ensure the experiential context of items do take into account the variety of social and environmental experiences for different groups of examinees. Systematic procedures have been developed to enhance the judgments of possible bias items. Typically, expert judges with different ethnicities and genders are used to write items and/or judge contents of items for possible biased effects. Additionally, many test publishers have developed guidelines for the development of unbiased items. Tittle (1982) provided a concise summary of these systematic judgmental procedures.

Although it is necessary to construct items carefully to avoid possible item bias, there is no guarantee that a carefully constructed item is not biased. A number of statistical methods have been developed to assess the possibility of item bias based on test data. Four common approaches are the *delta-plot,* the *chi-square,* the *Mantel-Haenszel* and the *item response theoretic* approach.

THE DELTA-PLOT APPROACH

An intuitive view of item bias is that if the true item difficulty indices (i.e., p values) estimated separately for two groups, call them a majority and a minority group, are different, the item is biased against the group with the lower p value. That is, the item is more difficult for one group than it is for the other. This view is reasonable but inadequate. Recall that p values are sample-dependent. Two different p values for two different groups may be due to different ability levels in the two samples.

However, even if the two groups have different levels of ability, the rank order of item difficulties across the different items in the test should remain the same for both groups. That is, if item 7 is more difficult than item 8 for the majority group, it should also be true for the minority group. A biased item is then one the p value of which ranks differently among the p values of all other items for the two groups. A method to detect such an item would be to estimate the regression equation between the two sets of item p values for the two groups. The observed p values can then be plotted against this regression line. Items with points departing substantially from this regression line are then biased items.

Unfortunately, the relationship between two sets of p values from two groups is inherently nonlinear and is inconvenient to estimate (Lord,

1980). The nonlinearity is due to the fact that the regression line has to pass through the points (1,1) and (0,0) for those items that both groups can answer correctly and those that both groups cannot answer correctly. Any differences in p values in between these two points would then render the relationship nonlinear.

Angoff (1984) and Angoff and Ford (1973) suggested the use of the delta-plot, instead of p values, to partly overcome the problem of nonlinearity. A delta value is an inverse normal transformation of the p value. Specifically, the delta value for the ith group for the jth item with an item difficulty of p_{ij} is:

$$\Delta_{ij} = 4\pi_{ij} + 13, \tag{14.1}$$

where π_{ij} is the z score that cuts off p_{ij} proportion of the cases in a unit normal distribution. The two sets of delta values for two groups, A and B, can be plotted against one another and the principal axis for this plot would have the linear form of $\Delta_{Bj} = b\Delta_{Aj} + a$, where b is the slope and a the intercept. The values of a and b can be estimated through (Angoff & Ford, 1973):

$$\hat{a} = \frac{(\hat{\sigma}_A^2 - \hat{\sigma}_B^2) \pm \sqrt{(\hat{\sigma}_B^2 - \hat{\sigma}_A^2) + 4r_{AB}^2 \hat{\sigma}_A^2 \hat{\sigma}_B^2}}{2r_{AB}\hat{\sigma}_A\hat{\sigma}_B}, \tag{14.2}$$

and

$$\hat{b} = \hat{\mu}_B - \hat{a}\hat{\mu}_A, \tag{14.3}$$

where μ_A, μ_B, σ_A, and σ_B are the means and standard deviations of the delta values across items for groups A and B, and r_{AB} is the Pearson's correlation between the two sets of delta values. If all delta values are closely clustered around this axis, the items can be assumed not to be biased. Items with pairs of delta values departing substantially from this axis can be considered biased. To measure the extent of departure from the axis, a d_i index can be estimated for the ith item through:

$$d_i = \frac{\hat{a}\Delta_{Ai} - \Delta_{Bi} + \hat{b}}{\sqrt{\hat{a}^2 + 1}}, \tag{14.4}$$

where Δ_{Ai} and Δ_{Bi} are the delta values for the ith item for groups A and B. This d_i value indicates the perpendicular distance from the actual delta values to the principal axis. Items with particularly large values of d_i are likely to be biased. The contents of these items need to be examined for possible revision. Lord (1980) and Angoff (1982) pointed out, however, that the failure of a point to lie on the principal axis may be attributable to guessing, differences in discrimination and/or ability.

THE CHI-SQUARE APPROACH

A limitation of the delta-plot approach is that the p value does not take into consideration within-group difference in ability levels. Recall that the classical ICC assumes the same p value for all ability levels. A more precise comparison of p values between two groups is a comparison by ability level. That is, if the item is not biased, given the same ability level, members of two different groups should have the same probability of a correct response. When examinees with the same ability but different group memberships have different probabilities of a correct response, the item can be considered biased.

An approach based on this reasoning is the chi-square approach. With this approach, members of the majority and the minority groups in the sample are each divided into a number of ability levels. Because a reliable observed total score is to be used to indicate level of ability, it is a good basis for classifying individuals into ability levels. A separate p value can be estimated for each individual ability level within each of the two groups. The total amount of discrepancies in p values between the two groups across different ability levels would be a good indication of item bias. Figure 14.1 provides a pictorial representation of such an analysis. In this figure, members of two groups are each divided into five ability levels based on observed total score. The first level consists of examinees with scores between 0 and 20, the second level between 21 and 40, and so on. Separate p values are computed for the two groups within each ability level. The differences between the two p values would be the measure of possible item bias.

Scheuneman's Chi-square

Because of random score fluctuation, some degree of discrepancy is expected between the two p values for the two groups. Scheuneman (1979) suggested that item bias can be measured by the extent to which the differences in p values between the two groups are beyond chance expectation. Specifically, Scheuneman suggested the use of a $\chi^2_{correct}$ statistic. To compute Scheuneman's $\chi^2_{correct}$ for majority/minority groups A and B, each of the two groups are divided into K ability intervals. Let O_{Aj} and O_{Bj} represent the observed number of individuals who have answered

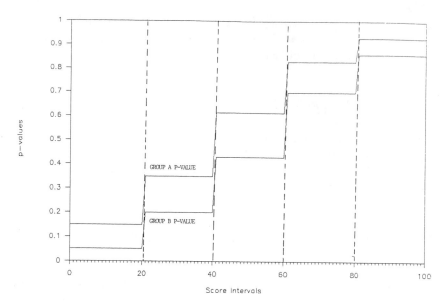

Figure 14.1.   Chi-square Test of Item Bias

a particular item correctly in Group A jth interval and Group B jth interval respectively. Also let N_{Aj} and N_{Bj} represent the number of individuals in Group A jth interval and Group B jth interval respectively. The marginal proportion for the jth interval, $P_{\cdot j}$, is then defined as:

$$P_{\cdot j} = (O_{Aj} + O_{Bj})/(N_{Aj} + N_{Bj}). \tag{14.5}$$

The expected frequencies of correct responses for Group A and Group B in the jth interval are:

$$E_{Aj} = P_{\cdot j}N_{Aj}, \tag{14.6}$$

and

$$E_{Bj} = P_{\cdot j}N_{Bj}, \tag{14.7}$$

respectively. The χ^2_{correct} statistic can then be computed across the K ability intervals by:

$$\chi^2_{\text{correct}} = \sum_{j=1}^{K} \frac{(E_{Aj} - O_{Aj})^2}{E_{Aj}} + \sum_{j=1}^{K} \frac{(E_{Bj} - O_{Bj})^2}{E_{Bj}}. \tag{14.8}$$

This χ^2 can be evaluated against $K - 1$ degrees of freedom in a χ^2 distribution. If the χ^2 is larger than the critical value at a desired alphalevel, the two groups can be considered significantly different and the item considered biased. When more than two groups are compared, Equation 14.8 can be extended to include Groups C, D, and so forth. The resulting χ^2 is then evaluated against $(I - 1)(K - 1)$ degrees of freedom, where I is the number of majority/minority groups.

Camilli's Chi-square

A drawback of Scheuneman's χ^2_{correct} statistic is that it only takes into consideration correct responses. Because incorrect response patterns are excluded, the resulting statistic may not approximate a χ^2 distribution (Scheuneman, 1979). To remedy this problem, Camilli (See Ironson, 1982) proposed the use of a χ^2_{full} statistic. Essentially, the process described above to compute χ^2_{correct} can be repeated, using the observed number of individuals who have answered the item incorrectly in each group in each ability interval to replace O_{Aj} and O_{Bj} accordingly. This repeated process would yield a $\chi^2_{\text{incorrect}}$ statistic. The value of χ^2_{full} is the sum of χ^2_{correct} and $\chi^2_{\text{incorrect}}$ and is evaluated against $(I - 1)J$ degrees of freedom.

THE MANTEL-HAENSZEL APPROACH

Most recently, Holland and Thayer (1988) suggested that a statistical technique developed by Mantel and Haenszel (1959) for cancer research can be applied in educational testing to detect different item functioning (DIF), or item bias. In applying the Mantel-Haenszel procedure to detect DIF, subjects in the analysis are divided into two groups: a *focal* group and a *reference* group. The focal group is consisted of subjects for whom we are interested to determine if an item functions differently. The reference group is consisted of subjects against whom the focal group is compared. For example, if we are interested in whether an item functions differently for minority subjects, a group of minority examinees would form the focal group whereas a group of majority examinees would form the reference group. The two groups must be matched on some variable directly related to the construct being measured. A common criterion used to match the two group on ability is the total score on the test.

Once the matched groups are identified, the performances of the two groups are then analyzed item-by-item. Specifically, an odds ratio, α, is computed for the ith item through:

$$\alpha_i = \frac{P_{ri}q_{fi}}{P_{fi}q_{ri}}, \tag{14.9}$$

where p_{ri} is the proportion of subjects in the reference group who have responded correctly to the ith item, q_{ri} is the proportion of the reference group who have responded incorrectly, p_{fi} is the proportion in the focal group who have responded correctly and q_{fi} is the proportion in the focal group who have responded incorrectly. The values of α_i ranges from 0 to ∞ with an α_i of 1 indicating that the ith item has no differential item functioning, or bias. An α_i value of greater than 1 indicates the item functions differentially across the two groups in favor of the reference group.

To facilitate interpretation, the odds ratio can be transformed to the delta scale as described in Equation 14.4 with a mean of 13 and a standard deviation of 4. The result is referred to as the MH D-DIF index. Based on the MH D-DIF index, items can be classified into three types (cf. Wild, McPeek, & Zieky, 1989; Zwick & Ercikan, 1989). Type A items are those with MH D-DIF values of less than 1 and is statistically not significantly different from zero. This type of items are nonproblematic. Type B items are those with MH D-DIF values significantly different from 1 and either has an absolute value of at least 1 but less than 1.5 or has an absolute value of at least 1 but not significantly different from 1 at the .05 level. Type C items are those with MH D-DIF values of greater than 1.5 and statistically significantly greater than 1. Type B items may be used if necessary. Type C items should be avoided. Types B and C exhibit differential item functioning and, when used, would disadvantage one group of examinees. It is important to point out, however, that the differential item functioning of Types B and C may or may not be an indication of bias. Further analyses of these items are needed to determine if group membership is the reason for the DIF.

THE ITEM RESPONSE THEORETIC APPROACH

There are two primary approaches to the detection of item bias through item response theory: Comparison of ICC's and comparison of item parameters between the majority and the minority group. A third alternative has been suggested by Wright, Mead, and Draba (1976) and by Linn and Harnisch (1981). In this third approach, comparisons are made on how well the actual data fit the IRT model between the two groups. This method contains a number of conceptual and statistical problems and is generally not recommended (Shepard, Camilli, & Averill, 1981; Hambleton & Swaminathan, 1985). However, Shepard et al. (1981) also suggested that this method can be appropriate when the number of subjects in one of the two groups is too small for meaningful estimation of item parameters in IRT. The division of subjects in each group into ability intervals in the chi-square approach can be considered an imprecise approximation to the item response theoretic approach of comparing ICCs.

Comparison of ICCs

From the perspective of item response theory, if the ICCs for the same item on the same θ scale are different between the majority and the minority group, the item is biased. Figure 14.2 depicts the ICCs of the same item for a majority group and a minority group. Note that for examinees with the same ability, the probability of a correct response is higher for the majority group than that for the minority group. This indicates that the item is biased against the minority group. A different and more subtle form of item bias, generally not detectable judgmentally, is the type of item bias depicted in Fig. 14.3. Note in this figure that the item is biased against minority members who have low ability levels. However, it is also biased against *majority* members with high ability.

These types of bias can be detected through an analysis of the two ICCs. The use of ICCs for two groups on an item follows the same principle as that of the chi-square method, but has a substantially greater degree of precision in that subjects are not grouped into large ability intervals. Specifically, the difference between the two ICCs can be measured by the

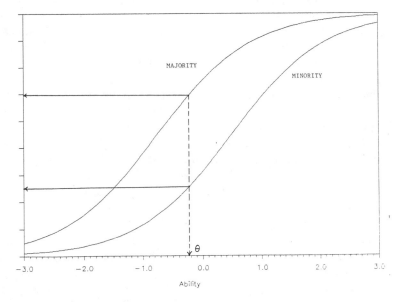

Figure 14.2.   A Biased Item

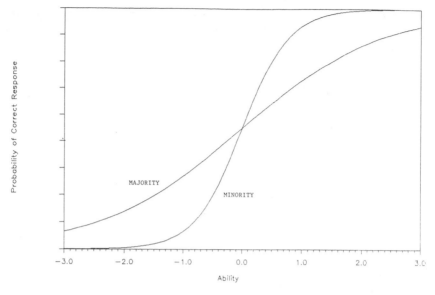

Figure 14.3.   Another Biased Item

total area enclosed between the two ICCs. This area represents the discrepancies in probabilities of correct responses between the two groups.

For the convenience of calculation, the θ scale can be divided into very small discrete intervals at increments of δ_θ (e.g., $\delta_\theta = .005$). For practical purposes, the θ scale can be further limited into a finite scale between -3 and $+3$. In other words, the θ scale between -3 and $+3$ is divided into numerous discrete intervals δ_σ in width. The values of $P_i(\theta)$ for the ith item for both groups at the mid point of the jth interval, $P_{Ai}(\theta_j)$ and $P_{Bi}(\theta_j)$, can be estimated for the two groups. This can be accomplished by estimating the item parameters for the ith item separately for the two groups through one of the item calibration procedures and the equating of the scales between the two groups. (*Equating* is discussed in the next chapter.) The difference between these two $P(\theta)$ values would be the discrepancy in probability between the two groups at precisely a θ value equal to the mid point of that interval. This difference multiplied by the width δ_θ would very closely approximate the area between the two ICCs within this small interval. Summing across all intervals would conceptually provide a close approximation of the area between the two ICCs.

This would prove to be correct for situations represented by Figure 14.2. For situations represented by Fig. 14.3, however, summing across all intervals would lead to a sum of zero. Hence, a more generalized approach is to remove the effects of negative differences through the use of absolute values or the use of squared values. Specifically, Rudner (1977) suggested that the absolute area, A_{1i}, between the ICC for Group X and that for Group Y on the ith item can be assessed through:

$$A_{1i} = \sum_{\theta=-3}^{+3} |P_{Xi}(\theta_j) - P_{Yi}(\theta_j)| \delta_\theta. \tag{14.10}$$

Alternatively, Linn, Levine, Hastings, and Wardrop (1981) proposed the use of:

$$A_{2i} = \sum_{\theta=-3}^{+3} \{[P_{Xi}(\theta_j) - P_{Yi}(\theta_j)^2] \delta_\theta\}^{1/2}. \tag{14.11}$$

as an index of the size of the area. The larger the value of A_{1i} or A_{2i}, the more likely that the ith item is biased.

Comparison of Item Parameters

An alternative to comparing ICCs to assess the discrepancies in $P_i(\theta)$ values between two groups in the form of A_{1i} or A_{2i} is to compare the item parameters directly. The principle behind comparing item parameters is the same as that for comparing ICCs. If two groups have the same ICCs on a particular item, they also have the same item parameter values. When they have different ICCs, the item parameters would also be different.

Based on Rao's (1965) multivariate chi-square, the differences in item parameters on the same item between two groups can be assessed through a chi-square procedure (Hambleton & Swaminathan, 1985). If the item parameter vector for the ith item for Group A is $\mathbf{x}_{Ai}$ [i.e., $\mathbf{x}_{Ai} = (a_{Ai}, b_{Ai}, c_{Ai})$] and that for Group B is $\mathbf{x}_{Bi}$, then, the difference in item parameters can be assessed through:

$$Q_i = (\mathbf{x}_{Ai} - \mathbf{x}_{Bi})'(\mathbf{I}_{Ai}^{-1} + \mathbf{I}_{Bi}^{-1})^{-1}(\mathbf{x}_{Ai} - \mathbf{x}_{Bi}), \tag{14.12}$$

where $\mathbf{I}_{Ai}^{-1}$ and $\mathbf{I}_{Bi}^{-1}$ are the inverses of the item information matrices for Group A and Group B. Conceptually, these inversed information matrices are the matrices of the variances and covariances around each estimate of item parameters. The exact mathematical elements in these information matrices can be found in Hambleton and Swaminathan (1985, p. 134). Q_i has a chi-square distribution with degrees of freedom equal to the number of item parameters in the logistic model used. Thus, Q_i can be evaluated against the critical value in a chi-square distribution with degrees of freedom equal to the number of item parameters at the desired alpha level. If Q_i is larger than this critical value, the ith item is biased.

Equation 14.11 becomes substantially simplified if the chosen IRT model is a 1-parameter Rasch model. In this situation, only the parameters

b_{Ai} and b_{Bi} are of interest. The vector $\mathbf{x}$ in Equation 14.11 reduces to a scalar of a single b parameter estimate for each group and the inversed information function reduces to the variance around the estimated b for each group. Hence, for a Rasch model,

$$Q_i = (b_{Ai} - b_{Bi})'(V_{Ai} + V_{Bi})^{-1}(b_{Ai} - b_{Bi})$$
$$= (b_{Ai} - b_{Bi})^2/(V_{Ai} + V_{Bi}), \tag{14.13}$$

where V_{Ai} and V_{Bi} are the variances around b_{Ai} and b_{Bi}. This Q_i is evaluated against a chi-square distribution with one degree of freedom. Because the chi-square distribution for one degree of freedom is equivalent to the square of a unit normal z distribution, Wright et al. (1976) suggested an alternative z score approach for the Rasch model:

$$z_i = (b_{Ai} - b_{Bi})/(V_{Ai} + V_{Bi})^{1/2} \tag{14.14}$$

which is equivalent to the square root of the value of Equation 14.12 and can be evaluated against a z distribution. For example, if the chosen alpha value is 0.05 and z_i is greater than 1.96, one may conclude that the ith item is biased.

CHOICE OF METHOD

With the large variety of methods to detect item bias, an obvious dilemma is which method produces the best results. Conceptually, the item response theoretic approach is most appealing. However, its conceptual advantage is somewhat moderated by the practical issues of sample size. Recall from chapter 9 that the joint estimation of item and ability parameters generally require large number of items and sample of examinees. In the assessment of item bias, the examinees are further divided into two or more subgroups, thereupon substantially reducing the sample size of examinees. To arrive at reliable item parameter estimates, the sample size for each of the subgroups must meet the rather high minimum requirements as described in chapter 9. Except for large-scale testing programs, this requirement is generally unrealistic for an average researcher.

It has been found that indices derived from the delta-plot approach, the chi-square approach, and the item response theoretic approach are moderately highly correlated (Burrill, 1982). Unfortunately, this fact does not provide evidence that these approaches are interchangeable; nor does it provide guidance in the choice of approach. This is because, whereas a high correlation suggests linear transformation over the range of items, identification of biased items is made on an item-by-item basis.

If the number of subjects in each subgroup is sufficiently large for item parameter estimation, either of the two item response theoretic approaches would offer a conceptually superior indicator of item bias. When these large sample sizes are not attainable, either the delta-plot or the chi-square approach will produce reasonable indicators of item bias with moderate sample sizes. Crocker and Algina (1986) suggested that sample sizes of between 100 and 200 examinees in each group are sufficient for these methods.

The Mantel-Haenszel procedure is relatively new and its use is not widespread yet. It is primarily used today at the Educational Testing Service to detect bias in large-scale testing programs. Its advantages and disadvantages are not clear at this time.

CHAPTER 15

Other Conceptual and Technical Issues

In the previous three chapters, we reviewed three particular applied issues: criterion-referenced testing, behavioral observation, and item bias. All three issues are directly related to the core theoretical problems of reliability and validity, which have been the central concern of this book. Specifically, for criterion-referenced testing and behavioral observation, additional considerations of reliability and validity, beyond those of conventional norm-referenced, paper-and-pencil tests are needed. Test bias is a specific, direct, and important threat to the validity of score interpretation and use.

There are many other applied measurement issues that are not immediately related to the theoretical concerns of reliability and validity. However, they may have direct influence on the proper interpretation and use of test scores, and hence may affect validity indirectly. Several of these issues are considered briefly in this chapter. Additionally, some emerging conceptual and technical trends in psychometrics are discussed briefly.

EQUATING

Equating becomes an important issue for proper score interpretation when there is more than one form of a test. It is a process through which correspondence of scores on different forms of the test is established. An obvious prerequisite to equating scores on two or more forms of a test is that all forms of the test must measure the same identical construct.

A number of applied situations necessitate equating. For instance, over a period of time after a test has been administered repeatedly to various individuals, items in the test gradually become known to future examinees. Continued use of the test would provide unfair advantage to examinees who have information of test items. In this type of situation, it is necessary to construct and use an equivalent form of the test with different items. Equating scores across different forms of the same test is referred to as *horizontal equating*.

In a different situation, different forms of a test are designed for different levels of difficulty. For instance, a test may have a form appropriate for 4th-grade level students and one appropriate for 5th-grade students. Students whose ability levels are at the extremes of their grade levels and who take the version of the test appropriate for their own grade level may obtain scores that are inherently unreliable (recall that reliability is a function of ability level). For example, a 5th-grade student with extremely low ability taking the 4th-grade level version of the test may obtain unreliable scores. In this case, the 5th-grade student may be administered the 4th-grade test instead to attain a better estimate of ability. Because the items for different grade levels are different, it becomes necessary to equate scores across different levels in order to properly interpret scores in out-of-level testing. The equating of scores across test versions for different levels is referred to as *vertical equating*.

Data Collection Designs

In order to equate test scores, empirical data are needed. Equating is not possible for certain data collection designs. The data collection procedure used must provide some type of commonality between the two sets of test data obtained from two different forms of the test. This commonality may be in terms of subjects or in terms of items. There are a number of acceptable data collection designs (cf. Petersen, Kolen, & Hoover, 1989); some are more elaborated than others. These designs are basically extensions or variations of three basic designs: *counterbalanced, equivalent groups,* and *anchor test*.

The counterbalanced design is most comprehensive but difficult to attain. In this design, a sample of subjects is randomly assigned into two subgroups. Both subgroups are administered both forms of the tests. However, to control for possible effects due to the order in which the two forms are given, one subgroup is given one form first to be followed by the second form while the other subgroup is given the second form first. The drawback of this design is that each subject would have to take two forms of the test, which can be time-consuming and, in many situations, impractical.

With the equivalent groups design, subjects are again randomly assigned to two subgroups and the two subgroups are given a different form of the test each. With the anchor test design, a small number of common items designed to measure the same construct are embedded in both forms of the test. The two forms with the embedded items are then administered to the two randomly assigned subgroups. The set of common items embedded is called the *anchor test*. Responses to the anchor test can be used as the basis for equating.

Linear and Equipercentile Method

A common approach to equating is *linear equating*. This approach is based on the equivalence of z scores. Specifically, a particular raw score X_1 on Form A is equivalent to a raw score Y_1 on Form B if both X_1 and Y_1 have identical z scores. Because z scores are linear transformations of raw scores, the X raw scores on Form A can be transformed to the Y raw scores on Form B through a linear transformation:

$$Y = bx + a. \tag{15.1}$$

If data are collected through the equivalent group design, the values of the slope b and the intercept a can be estimated through (Angoff, 1984):

$$\hat{b} = \hat{\sigma}_Y/\hat{\sigma}_X \tag{15.2}$$

and

$$\hat{a} = \hat{\mu}_Y - \hat{b}\hat{\mu}_X, \tag{15.3}$$

where σ_X, σ_Y, μ_X, and μ_Y are the standard deviations and means of the scores on Form A and Form B respectively. If the data are gathered through a counterbalanced design, the values of b and a can be estimated through:

$$\hat{b} = [(\hat{\sigma}_{Y1}^2 + \hat{\sigma}_{Y2}^2)/(\hat{\sigma}_{X1}^2 + \hat{\sigma}_{X2}^2)]^{1/2}, \tag{15.4}$$

and

$$\hat{a} = 0.5[\hat{\mu}_{Y1} + \hat{\mu}_{Y2} - b(\hat{\mu}_{X1} + \hat{\mu}_{X2})], \tag{15.5}$$

where σ_{X1}^2 and σ_{X2}^2 are the X score variances on Form A for Groups 1 and 2, σ_{Y1}^2 and σ_{Y2}^2 are the Y score variances on Form B for Groups 1 and 2, μ_{X1} and μ_{X2} are the mean X scores on Form A for Groups 1 and 2, and μ_{Y2} and μ_{Y2} are the mean Y scores on Form A for Groups 1 and 2 respectively. Equating through data obtained in an anchor test design is essentially similar to that for equivalent groups design as outlined in Equations 15.1 through 15.3. However, the estimates of μ_X, μ_Y, σ_X, and σ_Y have to be modified through knowledge of the anchor test. Specifically, a linear regression of the X scores on Form A on the scores, U, on the anchor test can be performed to derive a regression slope b_{XU}. A similar analysis is performed on Group 2 to obtain the slope b_{YU}. The mean and standard deviations of X and Y can then be modified through:

$$\hat{\mu}_X = \overline{X} + b_{XU}(\overline{U} - \overline{U}_1), \tag{15.6}$$

$$\hat{\mu}_Y = \overline{Y} + b_{YU}(\overline{U} - \overline{U}_2), \tag{15.7}$$

$$\hat{\sigma}_X^2 = s_X^2 + b_{XU}^2(s_U^2 - s_{U1}^2), \tag{15.8}$$

$$\hat{\sigma}_Y^2 = s_Y^2 + b_{YU}^2(s_U^2 - s_{U2}^2), \tag{15.9}$$

where $\overline{X}$ and $\overline{Y}$ are the observed mean scores of X and Y, s_X^2 and s_Y^2 are the observed sample variances of X and Y, $\overline{U}$ and s_U^2 are the mean and variance of the anchor test across both groups of examinees, $\overline{U}_1$ and s_{U1}^2 are the mean and variance of the anchor test for Group 1 and $\overline{U}$ and s_{U2}^2 are the mean and variance of the anchor test for Group 2. The adjusted mean and standard deviation estimates in Equations 15.6 through 15.9 can be applied directly to Equations 15.1 through 15.3 to equate the scores on the two forms of the test. Angoff (1984) provided methods to estimate the standard error around the derived equivalent score on the Y scale through either of the three data collection designs.

An assumption that justifies the equating of test scores through linear equating is that the distributions of scores on the two forms are similar. Only when this is true can we claim that two raw scores with equivalent z scores are equivalent. When the two distributions are different, the relationship between their scores is curvilinear; thus, a linear equating procedure becomes inappropriate. In these situations, the *equipercentile* approach is preferred (Angoff, 1984).

With the equipercentile approach, raw scores are converted to percentile rank scores. The raw scores on the two forms with the same percentile rank are then equivalent. Figure 15.1 shows the raw score distributions of two

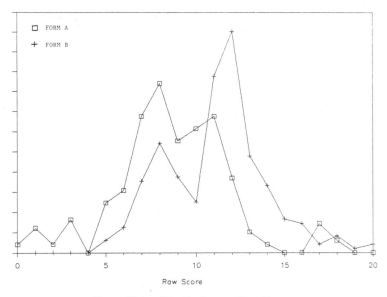

Figure 15.1.   Distributions on Two Forms

forms of a test. The distributions are quite different between the two forms. Thus, linear equating is not appropriate.

The raw scores on the two forms in Fig. 15.1 were converted to percentile ranks based on their respective score distributions. The resulting correspondence between raw scores and percentile ranks is presented in Fig. 15.2. Raw scores with the same percentile ranks are considered equivalent. For example, in Fig. 15.2, a raw score of 6.2 on Form A is equivalent to a raw score of 8 on Form B. Similarly, a raw score of 11 on Form A is equivalent to a raw score of 13.7 on Form B.

IRT Methods

Conceptually, equating through item response theory is straightforward. Computationally, however, it can be quite formidable. Because item parameters are invariant across different samples of subjects and the θ score is not test-dependent, a subject taking different tests made up of items that measure the same construct should theoretically obtain the same θ score. Unfortunately, the indeterminacy of the θ scales implies that θ scores obtained from two forms of a test are on different metrics when the two forms are calibrated separately. This suggests that the θ metric for Form B is an unknown linear transformation of that for Form A. That is:

$$\theta_B = \beta\theta_A + \alpha \tag{15.10}$$

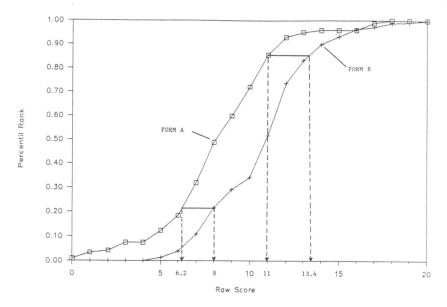

Figure 15.2. Percentiles on Two Forms

If the values of α and β can be estimated, θ scores from Form A can be transformed to the same θ metric as that of Form B through Equation 15.10; and thus θ scores are equated. Stocking and Lord (1983) suggested that the θ scores are equated when a subject's true score on Form A, ξ_A, is identical to the subject's true score on Form B, ξ_B. The error in using any pair of α and β values can be represented by the function:

$$F = \frac{1}{N} \sum_{i=1}^{N} (\xi_{Ai} - \xi_{Bi})^2 \tag{15.11}$$

where N is the number of examinees. Stocking and Lord demonstrated that F is a function of α and β. The optimal values of α and β are then those that correspond to the minimum value of F. In other words, the best α and β values are those corresponding to the point at which the first derivative of F becomes zero. As with the estimation of item and ability parameters, α and β cannot be estimated directly. Rather, an optimization algorithm is used to search for these values. Hambleton and Swaminathan (1985) suggested that the Newton-Raphson process may be appropriate. Stocking and Lord (1983) suggested the use of a multivariate minimization algorithm described by Davidon (1959) and Fletcher and Powell (1963).

Because θ scores are not very useful for communicating with test users, the true score metric is often desirable. When the true score, ξ, is used, it is necessary to equate scores on the true score metric instead of the θ score metric. Once α and β are estimated through the process described, the true scores on Forms A and B can be equated through:

$$\xi_B = \sum_{i=1}^{m} P_i(\beta\theta_A + \alpha), \tag{15.12}$$

where ξ_B is the true score on Form B, m is the number of items in Form B, and θ_A is a subject's θ score on Form A.

GROUP VERSUS INDIVIDUAL SCORE INTERPRETATION

An important but frequently overlooked issue in test score interpretation is the difference between group scores and individual scores. Conceptually, it is obvious that a group mean score is not the same as an individual score. What is frequently overlooked is that the variances of group mean score distributions are quite different from those of individual score distributions. A common inappropriate practice is to evaluate a group mean score based on the distribution of individual scores. For example, a test has been administered to a large national sample of individual students and obtained a mean score of 50 and a standard deviation of 10. A school district has adopted this test for local testing and found that the mean score for the district is 60. The school administrator compares this score against the "national norm" and interprets the mean of 60 as indicating that "the typical student in the district scores one standard deviation above the national mean" or "the typical student in the district is at the 84th percentile of the nation." Neither of these interpretations is appropriate (Note: Some, e.g., Baglin, 1986, suggested that these interpretations can be appropriate if the exact procedure used in calculating group scores is reported clearly so as to allow for comparison).

The error stems from comparing a *group mean* against a distribution of *individual* scores. For instance, it is not surprising to find individual students with perfect test scores. These are simply outstanding students. However, it would be practically impossible to find the mean for a school district to be the perfect test score. For this to happen implies that every single student in the district must obtain a perfect score. Therefore, group mean scores generally cluster around the grand mean more tightly than do individual scores. That is, the distribution of group means has a smaller variance than that of individual scores. Researchers (e.g., Angoff, 1984; Lindquist, 1930; Lord, 1959b) have found that the variance of individual scores is generally 2 to 2.5 times that of the variance of school means. Feldt and Brennan (1989) reported a situation in which the variance of group means was 3.9 times that of individual scores. Based on the 2 to 2.5 figure, the school district with a mean of 60 in this discussion is not one standard deviation above the mean, but is 2 to 2.5 standard deviations above the grand mean of all school district means. In general, using individual score distribution as a basis to judge school performance, a school with a mean below the grand mean of individuals will overestimate its performance. On the other hand, a school with a mean above the grand mean will underestimate its performance.

SIMPSON'S PARADOX

Related to the problem of mixing individual score interpretation with group score interpretation is a problem of inferring group scores from subgroup scores or vice versa. In general, group scores can be expected to be the weighted average of subgroup scores, as weighted by subgroup sample sizes. However, this is not always true when there is an interaction between subgroup membership and test performance.

When there is an interaction, a potential problem that can occur is a phenomenon known as *Simpson's paradox* (Paik, 1985; Simpson, 1951). In a Simpson's paradox, the implication from a group score is inconsistent with those from the constituent subgroup scores. Wainer (1986a) reported an occurrence of Simpson's paradox related to the increase in Scholastic Aptitude Test (SAT) between 1980 and 1984. Ordinarily, we would logically expect that the mean gain score for the entire group would be a weighted average of the gain scores from different subgroups (e.g., majority and minority groups). In this situation, however, the mean gain score for the overall group was found to be 7 whereas that for the white subgroup was 8 points and that for the nonwhite subgroup was 15 points. That is, the total group mean gain score was lower than the mean gain score for each of the subgroups. Bickel, Hammel, and O'Connell (1975), Novick (1982) and Paik (1985) provided examples of Simpson's paradox applied to college admission situations in which the process of admission decision-making can be viewed as adversative to a certain group when judged from the overall statistic, but is adversative to another group when judged from subgroup statistics.

Tables 15.1a through 15.1c provide an illustration of Simpson's paradox. Table 15.1a contains the admission information for a hypothetical college at a certain year. There are 4,000 male and 4,000 female applicants. From this table, proportionately, more male applicants (50%) were admitted than female applicants (40%). Concerns of equity regarding the admission policy may be raised. That is, it appears that the admission policy is adversative to female applicants.

TABLE 15.1a
Overall Admission Pattern of Hypothetical College

		Gender of Applicants		
		Male	Female	
Admission Status	Admitted	2,000 (50%)	1,600 (40%)	3,600
	Not Admitted	2,000	2,400	4,400
	All Applicants	4,000	4,000	8,000

TABLE 15.1b
Undergraduate Admission Pattern

		Gender of Applicants		
		Male	Female	
Admission Status	Admitted	1,800 (60%)	700 (70%)	2,500
	Not Admitted	1,200	300	1,500
	All Undergrad. Applicants	3,000	1,000	4,000

Let us further assume that of the 8,000 applicants, 4,000 applied for admissions to the graduate school and 4,000 applied for admissions to the undergraduate school. The graduate and undergraduate admission patterns are as depicted in Tables 15.1b and 15.1c. Note that the sums of various frequencies in Tables 15.1b and 15.1c do correspond to those in

TABLE 15.1c
Graduate Admission Pattern

		Gender of Applicants		
		Male	Female	
Admission Status	Admitted	200 (20%)	900 (30%)	1,100
	Not Admitted	800	2,100	2,900
	All Graduate Applicants	1,000	3,000	4,000

Table 15.1a. In other words, Tables 15.1b and 15.1c are possible breakdowns of Table 15.1a. When we examine Tables 15.1b and 15.1c, however, we find that in both cases, more females were admitted proportionately than males. We have a paradoxical situation in which both the statements: "Overall, the admission policy of the college is adversative to female applicants," and "For both graduate and undergraduate programs, the admission policy is adversative to male applicants" appear correct. These apparent self-contradictory statements are result of the interaction between undergraduate versus graduate and gender. Note that the marginal frequencies are different between graduate and undergraduate applicants.

The possible existence of Simpson's paradox suggests that different conclusions can be drawn from the same set of test data, dependent on whether one is looking at the overall group score or subgroup scores. Because of Simpson's paradox, Brennan (1988) pointed out that the exact unit of analysis to which a policy or statement applies needs to be clearly specified prior to score interpretation. Other potential pitfalls in aggregating and segregating subgroup and population scores are discussed in Novick (1982), Brennan (1988), and Wainer (1986b).

ANSWER-CHANGING

As pointed out in our discussion of guessing, examinee's test-taking behavior is not well-understood today. One of the issues related to test-taking behavior is answer-changing. That is, an examinee decides that the response given to a question earlier during the test is not correct and changes the response to a different one. For example, in a multiple-choice test, an examinee is not certain of the correct choice for a particular item. The examinee provided a tentative choice. Later, the examinee decides to change that choice to a different one.

Conventional wisdom and common advice given to test takers is, when uncertain, stick to the first impression because one's initial impressions are most likely to be correct (cf. Benjamin, Cavell, & Shallenberger, 1984; Stoffer, Davis, & Brown, 1977). There does not seem to be any sound foundation for this advice. Empirical research (e.g., Beck, 1978; Brunworth, 1987; Crocker & Benson, 1980; Edwards & Marshall, 1977; Lehman, 1928; Smith & Moore, 1976) has consistently shown that, when an examinee changes an answer, the probability of changing from a wrong to a right response is higher than either changing from a wrong to a wrong or from a right to a wrong response. It is clear that, when an examinee thinks that a previous response might not be correct, it is to the examinee's advantage to change to a response that the examinee thinks might be better. What is not clear, however, is how answer changing may affect the reliability and validity of test scores. Lynch and Smith (1975, p. 224) speculated that when examinees stick to the first impression and do not go over the exam reliability and validity of the test score are reduced. Additional research is needed to investigate the effects of answer-changing on the psychometric properties of test scores.

ADAPTIVE TESTING

Conventional paper-and-pencil tests require that all examinees respond to all items in the test. This is rather inefficient and often undesirable. For those examinees with very low ability, they are required to attempt all items although these items are too difficult and frustrating for them. On the other hand, for examinees with very high ability, most of the items are too easy and boring. Some (e.g., Ingebo, 1987) have suggested that requiring examinees to respond to items with inappropriate levels of difficulty may be viewed as a form of mental abuse. It would save a considerable amount of testing time if only items with the appropriate level of difficulty are administered to an examinee. Such an approach would also maximize the motivation of examinees in that they are less likely to be bored or frustrated by items of inappropriate difficulty levels.

A testing approach in which attempts are made to administer only items of appropriate difficulty level to each individual examinee is known as *adaptive testing* or *tailored testing*. Adaptive testing is not new. With many existing intelligence and achievement tests, for instance, items are administered one at a time from the easiest item to the most difficult one. When a test-taker fails to provide the correct response to a certain number of consecutive items, the testing process is terminated for that individual and no further items on the same construct are administered.

What is new with adaptive testing today is the flexibility afforded by computer technology combined with item response theory. Lord's (1971, 1977, 1980) and Weiss's (1976, 1978, 1983) work laid the theoretical foundation for modern adaptive testing. There are a variety of adaptive testing strategies. These include *fixed branching, variable branching* (Weiss & Betz, 1973; Weiss, 1974), *two-stage testing* (Lord, 1980) and *testlets* (Wainer & Kiely, 1987). These are different strategies of deciding what items to present to an examinee next after the examinee has responded to an item. The basic idea common across these strategies is that an examinee first be presented with an item or short test of moderate difficulty from a large pool of items previously calibrated through item response theory. Which item or test will be presented next is determined by the examinee's response to the initial item or short test. At each step, new items or short tests are selected based on which items in the pool would be most appropriate for the examinee. Specifically, the θ score for the examinee is estimated based on responses to items already presented. Items with maximum information function around that θ value are selected next. The θ score is re-estimated at each step to determine the next item. This process is repeated until either a specific number of items have been administered, a sufficiently small standard error of measurement is reached, or there is no more appropriate item available in the pool (Warm, 1978).

With computerized adaptive testing, there is an apparent advantage of efficiency. Ward (1984), for instance, suggested that the length of a test can be reduced by 50% to 60% through computerized adaptive testing without a loss of accuracy. McBride and Martin (1983) reported that for personnel testing applications satisfactory reliability levels were attained for ability estimated from adaptive tests with as few as 5 and 9 items. Additionally, adaptive testing can minimize the concerns for test security (Linn, 1986) and yield scores that promote accurate selection and classification decisions (McBride and Martin, 1983). McBride and Martin also reported that stronger evidence of criterion-related validity was obtained for adaptive testing than its conventional fixed-form paper-and-pencil counterpart in that scores from the adaptive test correlated more highly with scores on criterion tests. Other than the inherent conceptual and practical difficulties in estimating item and ability parameters in item response theory, it appears that the limitations for large-scale applications of computerized adaptive testing today are the need for large numbers of computers, computer networks, or workstations (Linn, 1986) and the identification of the best strategy of item selection and presentation (e.g.,

Wainer & Kiely, 1987). The inherent difficulties of item and ability parameter estimation can be minimized through the use of the Rasch model. The widespread availability of computer networks and workstations for testing purposes is rapidly becoming a reality (Deringer, 1986). It appears that the use of adaptive testing is becoming practical.

THE ROLE OF TECHNOLOGY

Prior to the current rapid advancement in video and computer technology, the role of technology in testing has been primarily limited to test scoring through optical scanners and analysis of test scores through computer statistical software. However, video and computer technology is playing an increasing role in the construction and administration of tests. Computerized interactive adaptive testing is but one of the many potential applications of new technology to improve the testing process itself. Minimally, computer technology such as various input devices (e.g., blow tubes, light pen, mouse) can be employed to improve the access to testing for individuals with physical handicaps. For the measurement of certain constructs (e.g., social competence), the use of interactive video discs, hypermedia, and computers in combination may provide stronger evidence of ecological validity. Large-scale observation-based performance assessment without the potentially serious consequences of on-the-job error (e.g., testing skills of airplane pilots, skills of nuclear submarine personnel) can be accomplished through computer simulation. Today, numerous tests can be administered interactively through computers.

One of the existing uses of technology in testing is to generate items or whole tests through computer. For example, Millman (1980) and Olympia (1975) have developed computer software to generate test items in science courses. Braby, Parrish, Guitard, and Aagard (1978) developed computerized test generators for the testing of military personnel. A program by Fremer and Anastasio (1969) is designed to generate tests to measure specific skills such as spelling, and Vicker (1973) designed a program to generate tests of computer programming knowledge. Roid (1986) provided a review of how computer technology has influenced test development, test administration, test scoring, as well as test interpretation. With the fast improvement in video and computer technology, the role of technology in the testing process, beyond routine scoring, can be expected to increase dramatically.

THE ROLE OF COGNITIVE THEORY

A major criticism of existing mainstream psychometric theories is that they are essentially statistical or mathematical theories with little psychological or behavioral theoretic foundations (e.g., Anastasi, 1967; Glaser, 1981; Glass, 1986; Hunt, 1986; Kempf, 1983; Messick, 1984a, 1984b; Sternberg, 1984). That is to say, psychometric theories contain substantially more *-metric* with little *psycho-*. There is a certain degree of separation between cognitive theory and psychometric theory today.

Increasingly, however, we see the body of knowledge in cognitive psychology being carefully integrated into the test design as well as evaluation of these tests. For example, Kempf (1983) suggested a qualitative evaluation design based on a cognitive model (Siegler, 1976) that children accumulate knowledge in a stepwise manner, to replace a quantitative measurement of knowledge. Smith (1987) combined O'Conner's (1940) cognitive theory of vocabulary acquisition with Andrich's (1978) polychotomous Rasch model to develop and analyze a general English vocabulary test. Results of his study supported both the advantage of Andrich's model as well as the validity of O'Conner's theory of vocabulary acquisition. Tatsuoka (1983; 1987) developed a Rule Space model to diagnose erroneous cognitive rules of operation in arithmetic and found that cognitive subtasks appeared to systematically influence the parameters of an ICC. Other examples of combining cognitive psychological theory with the mathematically-oriented psychometric theory can be found in Embretson (1983), Gustaffson (1984), Haertel and Calfee (1983), Harnisch (1983), Johnston (1983), Messick (1984b), and Sternberg (1984). It can be expected that knowledge in cognitive psychology will play a major role in the construction and validation of educational and psychological tests in the future.

THE ROLE OF MATHEMATICAL PROGRAMMING

As cognitive theoretic elements are being integrated into the psychometric process, the quantitative aspects of psychometric theory have also become increasingly sophisticated, complex, and rigorous. Increasingly, conventional statistical techniques are found to be inadequate for the extremely complex problems of psychometrics. Complex mathematical/computer optimization algorithms are being employed more frequently. These techniques, used to be found almost exclusively in business operations research, have become common in psychometric analyses. A brief conceptual introduction to optimization algorithms was presented in chapter 2.

The application of optimization and other mathematical search algorithms and strategies in psychometrics is most commonly found today in the resolution of the complex mathematics of item response theory. The use of the Newton-Raphson process represents one of the numerous applications of these algorithms. Examples of applications of other mathematical algorithms or strategies in item response theory include Stocking and Lord's (1983) use of a multivariate minimization algorithm in equating, Bock and Aitkin's (1981) use of an EM algorithm for marginal maximum likelihood estimation, Adema's (1989) use of linear programming in two-stage adaptive testing, and Xiao's (1989) use of the Golden Section Search strategy in adaptive testing.

The employment of these types of mathematical algorithms in psychometrics is not limited to the area of item response theory. For instance, Suen and Lee (1985) employed a linear programming strategy to facilitate the comparison between two threshold loss functions. Sanders, Theunissen, and Baas (1989) developed what amounts to a multivariate Spearman-Brown process to search for the optimal combination of number of levels for each facet in a multi-facet generalizability D-study. In their approach, a branch-and-bound integer programming strategy is employed.

It has been said that statistics is a prerequisite to psychometrics. It appears that knowledge of statistics commonly taught in graduate level education and psychology curricular today may no longer be sufficient to keep pace with the mathematical complexity of new developments in some areas of psychometrics. If the employment of mathematical programming techniques continues to expand in psychometrics, it is quite possible that future training programs in psychometric may require training in mathematical optimization programming as well.

The general trend of psychometrics appears to be one of integrating cognitive psychological theory on the one hand and increasing mathematical sophistication and complexity on the other. This simultaneous growth in both the *psycho-* and the *-metric* aspects of test theory is a healthy one and, when combined with the flexibility of adaptive testing and of video and computer technology, appears to be in agreement with Messick's (1984b) statement that "to better serve both theory and practice, new approaches to achievement measurement should be more complex, dynamic, and cognitive."

References

Adema, J. J. (1989, March). *Two-stage test construction by linear programming.* Paper presented at the Fifth International Objective Measurement Workshop, Berkeley, CA.

Akemann, C. A., Bruckner, A. M., Robertson, J. B., Simons, S., & Weiss, M. L. (1983). Conditional correlation phenomena with application to university admission strategies. *Journal of Educational Statistics, 8,* 5–44.

Altmann, J. (1974). Observational study of behavior: Sampling methods. *Behaviour, 49,* 227–267.

Anastasi, A. (1967). Psychology, psychologists and psychological testing. *American Psychologist, 22,* 297–306.

Andersen, E. B. (1973a). A goodness of fit test for the Rasch model. *Psychometrika, 38,* 123–140.

Andersen, E. B. (1973b). Conditional inference in multiple choice questionnaires. *British Journal of Mathematical and Statistical Psychology, 26,* 31–44.

Andrich, D. (1978). A rating formulation for ordered response categories. *Psychometrika, 43,* 561–573.

Angoff, W. H. (1984). Scales, norms, and equivalent scores. Princeton, NJ: Educational Testing Service. (Reprinted from R. L. Thorndike Ed., *Educational Measurement* 2nd Ed., Washington, DC: American Council on Education, 1971).

Angoff, W. H. (1982). Use of difficulty and discrimination indices for detecting item bias. In R. A. Berk (Ed.), *Handbook of methods for detecting test bias* (pp. 96–116). Baltimore, MD: Johns Hopkins University Press.

Angoff, W. H., & Ford, S. F. (1973). Item-race interaction on a test of scholastic aptitude. *Journal of Educational Measurement, 10,* 95–105.

Ary, D., Jacobs, L. C., & Razavieh, A. (1985). *Introduction to research in education* (3rd ed.). New York: Holt, Rinehart, and Winston.

Baglin, R. F. (1986). A problem in calculating group scores on norm-referenced tests. *Journal of Educational Measurement, 23,* 57–68.

Bakeman, R., & Gottman, J. M. (1986). *Observing interaction: An introduction to sequential analysis.* London: Cambridge University Press.

Bartke, J. J. (1966). The intraclass correlation coefficient as a measure of reliability. *Psychological Report, 19,* 3–11.

Beck, M. D. (1978). The effect of item response changes on scores on an elementary reading achievement test. *Journal of Educational Research, 71,* 153–156.

Bejar, I. I. (1983). Achievement testing: Recent advances. In J. L. Sullivan and R. G. Niemi (Eds.), *Quantitative applications in the social sciences.* (No. 07-036). Beverly Hills, CA: Sage.

Bell, J. F. (1985). Generalizability theory: The software problem. *Journal of Educational Statistics, 10*(1), 19–29.

Benjamin, L. T., Cavell, T. A., & Shallenberger, W. R. (1984). Staying with initial answers on objective tests: Is it a myth? *Teaching of Psychology, 11,* 133–141.

Berk, R. A. (1979). Generalizability of behavioral observation: A clarification of interobserver agreement and interobserver reliability. *American Journal of Mental Deficiency, 83,* 460–472.

Berk, R. A. (Ed.) (1982). *Handbook of methods for detecting test bias.* Baltimore, MD: The Johns Hopkins University Press.

Berk, R. A. (1984). Selecting the index of reliability. In R. A. Berk (Ed.), *A guide to criterion-referenced test construction* (pp. 231–266). Baltimore, MD: The Johns Hopkins University Press.

Beuchert, A. K., & Mendoza, J. L. (1979). A Monte Carlo comparison of ten item discrimination indices. *Journal of Educational Measurement, 16,* 109–118.

Bickel, P. J., Hammel, E. A., & O'Connell, J. W. (1975). Sex bias in graduate admissions: Data from Berkeley. *Science, 187,* 398–404.

Bindra, D., & Blond, J. (1958). A time-sample method for measuring general activity and its components. *Canadian Journal of Psychology, 12,* 74–76.

Binet, A., & Simon, T. H. (1916). *The development of intelligence in young children.* Vineland, NJ: The Training School.

Birnbaum, A. (1957). *Efficient design and use of tests of a mental ability for various decision-making problems.* (Series Report No. 58-16. Project No. 7755-23). USAF School of Aviation Medicine, Randolph Air Force Base, Texas.

Birnbaum, A. (1968). Some latent trait models and their use in inferring an examinee's ability. In F. M. Lord & M. R. Novick, *Statistical theories of mental test scores* (pp. 397–479). Reading, MA: Addison-Wesley.

Bliss, L. B. (1980). A test of Lord's assumption regarding examinee guessing behavior on multiple choice tests using elementary school children. *Journal of Educational Measurement, 17,* 147–153.

Bock, R. D., & Aitkin, M. (1981). Marginal maximum likelihood estimation of item parameters: An application of an EM algorithm. *Psychometrika, 46,* 443–459.

Bock, R. D., & Lieberman, M. (1970). Fitting a response model for n dichotomously scored items. *Psychometrika, 35,* 179–197.

Bohrnstedt, G. W. (1970). Reliability and validity assessment in attitude measurement. In G. F. Summers (Ed.), *Attitude measurement* (pp. 80–99). Chicago: Rand McNally.

Bond, L. (1981). Bias in mental tests. In B. F. Green (Ed.), *New directions for testing and measurement: Issues in testing — coaching, disclosure and ethnic bias,* No. 11 (pp. 55–77). San Francisco: Jossey-Bass.

Braby, M., Parrish, W. F., Guitard, C. R., & Aagard, J. A. (1978). *Computer-aided authoring of programmed instruction for teaching symbol recognition.* (TAEG Report No. 58). Orlando, FL: U.S. Navy Training Analysis and Evaluation Group.

Breland, H. M., Camp, R., Jones, R. J., Morris, M. M., & Rock, D. A. (1987). *Assessing writing skill* (Research Monograph No. 11). New York: College Entrance Examination Board.

Brennan, R. L. (1983). *Elements of Generalizability Theory.* Iowa City, IA: ACT.

Brennan, R. L. (1984a, April). *Some statistical issues in Generalizability Theory.* Paper presented at the annual meeting of the American Educational Research Association, New Orleans.

Brennan, R. L. (1988). Methodological problems and paradoxes: Aggregation/disaggregation issues. *MWERA Researcher,* Spring, 2–7.

Brennan, R. L., & Kane, M. T. (1977). An index of dependability for mastery tests. *Journal of Educational Measurement, 14,* 277–289.

Brunworth, D. W. (1987). *Answer-changing gains and losses related to reasons, confidence, beliefs, and item characteristics.* Unpublished doctoral dissertation, Northern Illinois University, De-Kalb, IL.

Burrill, L. E. (1982). Comparative studies of item bias methods. In R. A. Berk (Ed.), *Handbook of methods for detecting test bias* (pp. 161–179). Baltimore, MD: The Johns Hopkins University Press.

Burt, C. (1936). The analysis of examination marks. In P. Hartog and E. C. Rhodes (Eds.), *The marks of examiners* (pp. 245–314). London: Macmillan.

Campbell, D. T., & Fiske, D. W. (1959). Convergent and discriminant validation by the multitrait-multimethod matrix. *Psychological Bulletin, 56,* 81–105.

Carver, R. (1978). The case against statistical significance testing. *Harvard Educational Review, 48,* 378–399.

Ciminero, A. R., Calhoun, K. S., & Adams, H. E. (Eds.) (1977). *Handbook of behavioral assessment.* New York: Wiley.

Cohen, J. A. (1960). A coefficient of agreement for nominal scales. *Educational and Psychological Measurement, 20,* 37–46.

Cole, N. S., & Moss, P. A. (1989). Bias in test use. In R. L. Linn (Ed.), *Educational Measurement* (3rd ed., pp. 201–220). New York: Macmillan.

Cone, J. D. (1977). The relevance of reliability and validity for behavioral assessment. *Behavior Therapy, 8,* 411–426.

Cone, J. D. (1986). Ideographic, nomothetic, and related perspectives in behavioral assessment. In R. O. Nelson & S. C. Hayes (Eds.), *Conceptual foundations of behavioral assessment* (pp. 111–128). New York: Guilford.

Cone, J. D., & Foster, S. L. (1982). Direct observation in clinical psychology. In P. C. Kendall & J. N. Butcher (Eds.), *Handbook of research methods in clinical psychology.* New York: Wiley.

Cook, L. L., Eignor, D. R., & Taft, H. L. (1984, April). *A comparative study of curriculum effects on the stability of IRT and conventional item parameter estimates.* Paper presented at the annual meeting of the American Educational Research Association, Montreal.

Crick, J. E., & Brennan, R. L. (1983). *GENOVA: A generalized analysis of variance system.* Iowa City, IA: ACT.

Crocker, L., & Algina, J. (1986). *Introduction to classical and modern test theory.* New York: Holt, Rinehart and Winston.

Crocker, L., & Benson, J. (1980). Does answer-changing affect test quality? *Measurement and Evaluation in Guidance, 12,* 233–239.

Cronbach, L. J. (1971). Test validation. In R. L. Thorndike (Ed.), *Educational measurement* (2nd ed. Washington, DC: American Council on Education.

Cronbach, L. J. (1984). *Essentials of psychological testing* (4th ed.). New York: Harper and Row.

Cronbach, L. J., Gleser, G. C., Nanda, H., & Rajaratnam, N. (1972). *The dependability of behavioral measurements: Theory of generalizability for scores and profiles.* New York: John Wiley and Sons.

Darlington, R. B. (1970). Some techniques for maximizing a test's validity when the criterion variable is unobserved. *Journal of Educational Measurement, 7,* 1–14.

Davidon, W. C. (1959). *Variable metric method for minimization* (Research and Development Report ANLK-5990; rev. ed.). Argonne, IL: Argonne National Laboratory, U.S. Atomic Energy Commission.

Dempster, A. P., Laird, N. M., & Rubin, D. B. (1977). Maximum likelihood from incomplete data via the EM algorithm (with discussion). *Journal of the Royal Statistical Society,* Series B, *39,* 1–38.

Deringer, D. K. (1986). Technology advances that may change test design for the future. In E. E. Freeman (Ed.), *The redesign of testing for the 21st century. Proceedings of the 1985 ETS Invitational Conference* (pp. 35–44). Princeton, NJ: Educational Testing Service.

Diamond, J., & Evans, W. (1973). The correction for guessing. *Review of Educational Research, 43,* 181–191.

Diamond, K. E. (1987). Predicting school problems from school developmental screening. *Journal of the Division for Early Childhood, 11,* 247–253.

Dixon, W. J., & Brown, M. B. (Eds.) (1979). *BMDP-79 biomedical computer programs, P series.* Los Angeles: University of California Press.

Dorans, N. J., & Kingston, N. M. (1985). The effects of violations of unidimensionality on the estimation of item and ability parameters and on item response theory equating of the GRE Verbal scale. *Journal of Educational Measurement, 22,* 249–262.

Ebel, R. L. (1951). Estimation of the reliability of ratings. *Psychometrika, 16,* 407–425.

Ebel, R. L. (1972). *Essentials of educational measurement* (2nd Ed.). Englewood Cliffs, NJ: Prentice-Hall.

Edwards, K. A., & Marshall, C. (1977). First impressions on tests: Some new findings. *Teaching of Psychology, 4,* 193–195.

Embretson, S. (1983). Construct validity: Construct representation versus nomothetic span. *Psychological Bulletin, 93,* 179–197.

Feldt, L. S., & Brennan, R. L. (1989). Reliability. In R. L. Linn (Ed.), *Educational measurement* (3rd ed.), (pp. 105–146). New York: Macmillan.

Fisher, R. A. (1921). On the "probable error" of a coefficient of correlation deduced from a small sample. *Metron, 1* (4), 1–32.

Fiske, D. W. (1978). *Strategies for personality research: The observation versus interpretation of behavior.* San Francisco: Jossey-Bass.

Fletcher, R., & Powell, M. J. D. (1963). A rapidly convergent descent method for minimization. *The Computer Journal, 6,* 163–168.

Forsyth, R., Saisangjan, U., & Gillmer, J. (1981). Some empirical results related to the robustness of the Rasch model. *Applied Psychological Measurement, 5,* 175–186.

Fremer, J., & Anastasio, E. J. (1969). Computer-assisted test writing—I (Spelling items). *Journal of Educational Measurement, 6,* 69–74.

Gelfand, D. M., & Hartmann, D. P. (1975). *Child behavior analysis and therapy.* New York: Pergamon.

Gillmore, G. M., Kane, M. T., & Naccarato, R. W. (1978). The generalizability of student ratings of instruction: Estimation of the teacher and course components. *Journal of Educational Measurement, 15,* 1–13.

Glaser, R. (1981). The future of testing: A research agenda for cognitive psychology and psychometrics. *American Psychologist, 36,* 923–936.

Glaser, R., & Klaus, D. J. (1962). Proficiency measurement: Assessing human performances. In R. M. Gagne (Ed.), *Psychological principles in systems development* (pp.419–474). New York: Holt, Rinehart, and Winston.

Glass, G. V. (1986). Testing old, testing new: Schoolboy psychology and the allocation of intellectual resources. In B. S. Plake & J. C. Witt (Eds.), *The future of testing* (pp. 9–28). Hillsdale, NJ: Lawrence Erlbaum Associates.

Goodenough, F. L. (1928). Measuring behavior traits by means of repeated short samples. *Journal of Juvenile Research, 12,* 230–235.

Gronlund, N. E. (1981). *Measurement and evaluation in teaching* (4th ed.). New York: Macmillan.

Guion, R. M. (1977). Content validity—The source of my discontent. *Applied Psychological Measurement, 1,* 1–10.

Guion, R. M. (1980). On trinitarian doctrines of validity. *Professional Psychology, 11,* 385–398.

Gulliksen, H. (1950). *Theory of mental tests.* New York: Wiley.

Gustaffson, J. (1984). A unifying model for the structure of intellectual abilities. *Intelligence, 8,* 179–203.

Guttman, L. A. (1944). A basis for scaling qualitative data. *American Sociological Review, 9,* 139–150.

Haberman, S. (1975). Maximum likelihood estimates in exponential response models. *Technical Report.* Chicago: University of Chicago.

Haertel, E., & Calfee, R. (1983). School achievement: Thinking about what to test. *Journal of Educational Measurement, 20,* 119–132.

Haggard, E. A. (1958). *Intraclass correlation and the analysis of variance.* New York: Dryden Press.

Hambleton, R. K. (1980). Test score validity and standard-setting methods. In R. A. Berk (Ed.), *Criterion-referenced measurement: The state of the art* (pp. 80–123). Baltimore: Johns Hopkins University Press.

Hambleton, R. K. (1989). Principles and selected applications of item response theory. In R. L. Linn (Ed.), *Educational measurement* (3rd ed.). (pp. 147–200). New York: Macmillan.

Hambleton, R. K., & Murray, L. (1983). Some goodness of fit investigations for item response models. In R. K. Hambleton (Ed.), *Applications of item response theory.* Vancouver: Educational Research Institute of British Columbia.

Hambleton, R. K., & Novick, M. R. (1973). Toward an integration of theory and method for criterion-referenced tests. *Journal of Educational Measurement, 10,* 159–170.

Hambleton, R. K., & Swaminathan, H. (1985). *Item response theory: Principles and applications.* pp.147–200. Hingham, MA: Kluwer.

Harnisch, D. L. (1983). Item response patterns: Applications for educational practice. *Journal of Educational Measurement, 20,* 119–206.

Hartmann, D. P. (1977). Considerations in the choice of interobserver reliability estimates. *Journal of Applied Behavior Analysis, 10,* 103–116.

Hartmann, D. P. (1982). Assessing the dependability of observational data. In D. P. Hartmann (Ed.), *Using observers to study behavior* (pp.51–66). San Francisco: Jossey-Bass.

Hersen, M., & Barlow, D. H. (1976). *Single case experimental designs.* New York: Pergamon.

Heuer, E., & Wiersma, W. (1977). A design for the content validation of standardized achievement tests. *AIGE Forum, 2*(3), 18–20.

Holland, P. W., & Thayer, D. T. (1988). Differential item functioning and the Mantel-Haenszel procedure. In H. Wainer & H. Brain (Eds.), *Test Validity.* Hillsdale, NJ: Lawrence Erlbaum Associates.

Homer, A. L., Peterson, L., & Wonderlich, S. A. (1983). Subject selection in applied behavior analysis. *The Behavior Analyst, 6,* 39–45.

Hoyt, C. J. (1941). Test reliability estimated by analysis of variance. *Psychometrika, 6,* 153–160.

Hulin, C. L., Drasgow, F., & Parsons, C. K. (1983). *Item response theory: Applications to psychological measurement.* Homewood, IL: Dow Jones-Irwin.

Hulin, C. L., Lissak, R. I., & Drasgow, F. (1982). Recovery of two- and three-parameter logistic item characteristic curves: A Monte Carlo study. *Applied Psychological Measurement, 6,* 249–260.

Hunt, E. (1986). Cognitive research and future test design. In E. E. Freeman (Ed.), *The redesign of testing for the 21st century, Proceedings of the 1985 ETS Invitational Conference* (pp. 9–24). Princeton, NJ: Educational Testing Service.

Huynh, H. (1976a). On the reliability of decisions in domain-referenced testing. *Journal of Educational Measurement, 13,* 253-264.

Huynh, H. (1976b). Statistical considerations of mastery scores. *Psychometrika, 41,* 65-78.

Huynh, H. (1985, April). *Projection of decision consistency indices based on latent trait models.* Paper presented at the Annual Meeting of the American Educational Research Association, Chicago.

Huynh, H., & Saunders, J. C. (1980). Accuracy of two procedures for estimating reliability of mastery tests. *Journal of Educational Measurement, 17,* 351-358.

Ingebo, G. (1987, April). *Riding the Rasch tiger.* Paper presented at the annual meeting of the National Council on Measurement in Education, Washington, D.C.

Ironson, G. H. (1982). Use of chi-square and latent trait approaches for detecting item bias. In R. A. Berk (Ed.), *Handbook of methods for detecting test bias* (pp. 117-160). Baltimore, MD: Johns Hopkins University Press.

Jackson, D. N. (1977). Distinguishing trait and method variance in multitrait-multimethod matrices: A reply to Golding. *Multivariate Behavioral Research, 12,* 99-110.

Jackson, R. W. B., & Ferguson, G. (1941). *Studies on the reliability of tests.* Toronto: University of Toronto.

Jaeger, R. M. (1982). An iterative structured judgment process for establishing standards on competency tests: Theory and application. *Educational Evaluation and Policy Analysis, 4,* 461-475.

Jensen, A. R. (1980). *Bias in mental testing.* New York: Free Press.

Johnson, S. M., & Bolstad, O. D. (1973). Methodological issues in naturalistic observation: Some problems and solutions for field research. In L. A. Hamerlynck, L. C. Hardy, & E. J. Mash (Eds.), *Behavior change: Methodology, concepts, and practice* (pp. 7-67). Champaign, IL: Research Press.

Johnston, P. H. (1983). *Reading comprehension assessment: A cognitive basis.* Newark, DE: International Reading Association.

Jöreskog, K. G., & Sörbom, D. (1979). *Advances in factor analysis and structural equation models.* Cambridge, MA: Abt Books.

Jöreskog, K. G., & Sörbom, D. (1983). *LISREL VI users guide.* Uppsala: Department of Statistics.

Kale, B. K. (1962). On the solution of likelihood equation by iteration processes: The multiparametric case. *Biometrika, 49,* 479-486.

Kane, M. T. (1982). A sampling model for validity. *Applied Psychological Measurement, 6,* 125-160.

Kane, M. T. (1987). On the use of IRT models with judgmental standard setting procedures. *Journal of Educational Measurement, 24* (4), 333-345.

Kazdin, A. E. (1977). Artifacts, bias, and complexity of assessment: The ABC's of reliability. *Journal of Applied Behavior Analysis, 10,* 141-150.

Kelley, T. L. (1939). Selection of upper and lower groups for the validation of test items. *Journal of Educational Psychology, 30,* 17-24.

Kempf, W. (1983). Some theoretical concerns about applying latent trait models in educational testing. In S. B. Anderson & J. S. Helmick (Eds.), *On educational testing* (pp. 252-270). San Francisco: Jossey-Bass.

Kendall, M. G., & Stuart, A. (1973). *The advanced theory of statistics* (Vol. 2). New York: Hafner.

Klein, S. P., & Kosecoff, J. P. (1975). *Determining how well a test measures your objectives.* (CSE Report No. 94). Los Angeles: Center for the Study of Evaluation, University of California.

Kratochwill, T. R. (Ed.) (1978). *Single subject research: Strategies for evaluating change.* New York: Academic Press.

Lawley, D. N. (1944). On problems connected with item selection and test construction. *Proceedings of the royal society of Edingburgh, 6,* 273–287.

Lehman, H. C. (1928). Does it pay to change initial decisions in a true-false test? *School and Society, 28,* 456–458.

Lennon, R. T. (1956). Assumptions underlying the use of content validity. *Educational and Psychological Measurement, 16,* 294–304.

Liebman, J., Lasdon, L., Shrage, L., & Waren, A. (1986). *Modeling and optimization with GINO.* Palo Alto, CA: Scientific Press.

Lindquist, E. F. (1930). Factors determining reliability of test norms. *Journal of Educational Psychology, 21,* 512–520.

Lindquist, E. F. (1953). *Design and analysis of experiments in psychology and education.* Boston: Houghton-Mifflin.

Linn, R. L. (1980). Issues of validity for criterion-referenced measures. *Applied Psychological Measurement, 4,* 547–561.

Linn, R. L. (1986). Barriers to new test designs. In E. E. Freeman (Ed.), *The redesign of testing for the 21st century, Proceedings of the 1985 ETS Invitational Conference* (pp. 69–80). Princeton, NJ: Educational Testing Service.

Linn, R. L., & Harnisch, D. L. (1981). Interactions between item content and group membership on achievement test items. *Journal of Educational Measurement, 18,* 109–118.

Linn, R. L., Levine, M. V., Hastings, C. N., & Wardrop, J. L. (1981). An investigation of item bias in a test of reading comprehension. *Applied Psychological Measurement, 5,* 159–173.

Livingston, S. A. (1972). Criterion-referenced applications of classical test theory. *Journal of Educational Measurement, 9,* 13–26.

Loevinger, J. (1957). Objective tests as instruments of psychological theory. *Psychological Reports, 3,* (9), 635–694.

Lord, F. M. (1952a). A theory of test scores. *Psychometric Monograph,* No. 7.

Lord, F. M. (1952b). The relationship of the reliability of multiple choice items to the distribution of item difficulties. *Psychometrika, 18,* 181–194.

Lord, F. M. (1953). The relation of test score to the trait underlying the test. *Educational and Psychological Measurement, 13,* 517–548.

Lord, F. M. (1957). Do tests of the same length have the same standard error of measurement? *Educational and Psychological Measurement, 17,* 510–521.

Lord, F. M. (1959a). Tests of the same length do have the same standard error of measurement. *Educational and Psychological Measurement, 19* (2), 233–239.

Lord, F. M. (1959b). Test norms and sampling theory. *Journal of Experimental Education, 27,* 247–263.

Lord, F. M. (1971). The self-scoring flexilevel test. *Journal of Educational Measurement, 8,* 147–151.

Lord, F. M. (1974). Estimation of latent ability and item parameters when there are omitted responses. *Psychometrika, 39,* 247–264.

Lord, F. M. (1975). Formula scoring and number-right scoring. *Journal of Educational Measurement, 12,* 7–12.

Lord, F. M. (1977). A broad-range tailored test of verbal ability. *Applied Psychological Measurement, 1,* 95–100.

Lord, F. M. (1980). *Applications of item response theory to practical testing problems.* Hillsdale, NJ: Lawrence Erlbaum Associates.

Lord, F. M. (1986). Maximum likelihood and Bayesian parameter estimation in item response theory. *Journal of Educational Measurement, 23,* 157–162.

Lord, F. M., & Novick, M. R. (1968). *Statistical theories of mental test scores.* Reading, MA: Addison-Wesley.

Loyd, B. H, (1988). Implications of item response theory for the measurement practitioner. *Applied Measurement in Education, 1,* 135–143.

Loyd, B. H., & Hoover, H. D. (1980). Vertical equating using the Rasch model. *Journal of Educational Measurement, 17,* 179–193.

Lumsden, J. (1976). Test theory. In M. R. Rosenzweig & L. W. Porter (Eds.), *Annual review of psychology.* Palo Alto, CA: Annual Review Inc.

Lyman, H. B. (1978). *Test scores and what they mean* (3rd ed.). Englewood Cliffs, NJ: Prentice-Hall.

Lynch, D. O., & Smith, B. C. (1975). Item response changes: Effects on test scores. *Measurement and Evaluation in Guidance, 7,* 220–224.

Mantel, N., & Haenszel, W. (1959). Statistical aspects of the analysis of data from retrospective studies of disease. *Journal of the National Cancer Institute, 22,* 719–748.

Maranell, G. M. (Ed.) (1974). *Scaling: A sourcebook for behavioral scientists.* Chicago: Aldine.

Marcoulides, G. A. (1987). *An alternative method for variance component estimation: Applications to generalizability theory.* Unpublished doctoral dissertation, University of California, Los Angeles.

Mardell-Czudnowski, C., Goldenberg, D., Suen, H. K., & Fries, R. K. (1988). Predictive validity of the DIAL-R. *Diagnostique, 14,* 55–62.

Martin, P., & Bateson, P. (1986). *Measuring behavior: An introductory guide.* London: Cambridge University Press.

McBride, J. R., & Martin, J. T. (1983). Reliability and validity of adaptive ability tests in a military setting. In D. J. Weiss (Ed.), *New horizons in testing: Latent trait theory and computerized adaptive testing* (pp. 223–236). New York: Academic Press.

Messick, S. (1975). The standard problem: Meaning and values in measurement and evaluation. *American Psychologist, 30,* 955–966.

Messick, S. (1984a). The psychology of educational measurement. *Journal of Educational Measurement, 21,* 215–237.

Messick, S. (1984b). Abilities and knowledge in educational achievement testing: The assessment of dynamic cognitive structures. In B. S. Plake (Ed.), *Social and technical issues in testing: Implications for test construction and usage* (pp. 156–172). Hillsdale, NJ: Lawrence Erlbaum Associates.

Messick, S. (1989). Validity. In R. L. Linn (Ed.), *Educational Measurement* (3rd ed.), (pp. 13–104). New York: Macmillan.

Millman, J. (1980). Computer-based item generation. In R. A. Berk (Ed.), *Criterion-referenced measurement: The state of the art.* Baltimore, MD: Johns Hopkins University Press.

Mislevy, R. J., & Bock, R. D. (1984). *BILOG-2 user's guide.* Mooresville, IN: Scientific Software.

Mislevy, R. J., & Stocking, M. L. (1987). *A consumer's guide to LOGIST and BILOG.* Research Report RR-87-43. Princeton, NJ: Educational Testing Service.

Mitchell, S. K. (1979). Interobserver agreement, reliability, and generalizability of data collected in observational studies. *Psychological Bulletin, 86,* 376–390.

Murtagh, B. A., & Saunders, M. A. (1987). *MINOS 5.1 user's guide.* (Report SOL 83-30R). Palo Alto, CA: Stanford University.

Nedelsky, L. (1954). Absolute grading standards for objective tests. *Educational and Psychological Measurement, 14,* 3–19.

Nitko, A. J. (1983). *Educational tests and measurement: An introduction.* New York: Harcourt Brace Jovanovich.

Nitko, A. J. (1984). Defining "criterion-referenced test". In R. A. Berk (Ed.), *A guide to criterion-referenced test construction* (pp. 8–28). Baltimore: Johns Hopkins University Press.

Novick, M. R. (1982). Educational testing: Inferences in relevant subpopulations. *Educational Researcher, 11,* 4–10.

Nunnally, J. C. (1978). *Psychometric theory.* New York: McGraw-Hill.

O'Conner, J. (1940). *Unsolved business problems*. Boston: Johnson O'Conner Research Foundation.

Olson, W. C. (1929). *The measurement of nervous habits in normal children*. Minneapolis: University of Minnesota Press.

Olympia, P. L., Jr. (1975). Computer generation of truly repeatable examinations. *Educational Technology, 14,* 53–55.

Paik, M. (1985). A graphic representation of a three-way contingency table: Simpson's paradox and correlation. *The American Statistician, 39,* 53–54.

Petersen, N. S., Kolen, M. J., & Hoover, H. D. (1989). Scaling, norming, and equating. In R. L. Linn (Ed.), *Educational Measurement* (3rd ed., pp. 221–262). New York: Macmillan.

Powell, J., Martindale, A., & Kulp, S. (1975). An evaluation of time-sample measures of behavior. *Journal of Applied Behavior Analysis, 8,* 463–469.

Quera, V. (1989). Estimación de frecuencia y duración en el muestreo temporal de la conducta. *Anuario de Psicologia, 43* (4).

Rasch, G. (1980). *Probabilistic models for some intelligence and attainment tests*. Chicago: The University of Chicago Press.

Rentz, R. R., & Bashaw, W. L. (1977). The National Reference Scale for reading: An application of the Rasch model. *Journal of Educational Measurement, 14,* 161–180.

Richardson, M. W. (1936). The relationship between difficulty and the differential validity of a test. *Psychometrika, 1,* 33–49.

Rao, C. R. (1965). *Linear statistical inference and its application*. New York: Wiley.

Roid, G. H. (1986). Computer technology in testing. In B. S. Plake & J. C. Witt (Eds.), *The future of testing* (pp. 29–69). Hillsdale, NJ: Lawrence Erlbaum Associates.

Ross, J. (1966). An empirical study of a logistic mental test model. *Psychometrika, 31,* 325–340.

Rovinelli, R. J., & Hambleton, R. K. (1977). On the use of content specialists in the assessment of criterion-referenced test item validity. *Dutch Journal of Educational Research, 2,* 49–60.

Rudner, L. M. (1977, April). *An approach to biased item identification using latent trait measurement theory*. Paper presented at the annual meeting of the American Educational Research Association, New York.

Samejima, F. (1973). A comment on Birnbaum's three parameter logistic model in the latent trait theory. *Psychometrika, 38,* 221–223.

Samuelson, P. A. (1968). How deviant can you be? *Journal of the American Statistical Association, 63,* 1522–1525.

Sanders, P. F., Theunissen, T. J. J. M., & Baas, S. M. (1989, March). *The optimization of decision studies*. Paper presented at the Fifth International Objective Measurement Workshop, Berkeley, CA.

SAS Institute Inc. (1985). *SAS user's guide: Statistics, Version 5 edition*. Cary, NC: SAS Institute Inc.

Scheuneman, J. D. (1979). A new method of assessing bias in test items. *Journal of Educational Measurement, 16,* 143–152.

Schmidt, F. L. (1977). The Urry method of approximating the item parameters of latent trait theory. *Educational and Psychological Measurement, 37,* 613–620.

Shavelson, R. J., & Webb, N. M. (1981). Generalizability theory: 1973–1980. *British Journal of Mathematical and Statistical Psychology, 34,* 133–166.

Shavelson, R. J., Webb, N. M., & Rowley, G. L. (1989). Generalizability theory. *American Psychologist, 44,* 922–932.

Shepard, L. A. (1982). Definitions of bias. In R. A. Berk (Ed.), *Handbook of methods for detecting test bias,* (pp. 1–8). Baltimore, MD: The Johns Hopkins University Press.

Shepard, L. A. (1984). Setting performance standards. In R. A. Berk (Ed.), *A guide to criterion-referenced test construction,* (pp. 169–198). Baltimore, MD: The Johns Hopkins University Press.

Shepard, L. A., Camilli, G., & Averill, M. (1981). Comparison of procedures for detecting test-item bias with both internal and external ability criteria. *Journal of Educational Statistics, 6*, 317–375.

Siegler, R. S. (1976). Three aspects of cognitive development. *Cognitive Psychology, 8*, 481–520.

Simpson, E. H. (1951). The interpretation of interaction in contingency tables. *Journal of the Royal Statistical Society,* Series B, *13*, 238–241.

Skinner, B. F. (1945). The operational analysis of psychological terms. *Psychological Review, 52*, 270–277.

Slinde, J. A., & Linn, R. L. (1978). An exploration of the adequacy of the Rasch model for the problem of vertical equating. *Journal of Educational Measurement, 15*, 23–35.

Smith, A., & Moore, J. C. (1976). The effects of changing answers on scores of non-test-sophisticated examinees. *Measurement and Evaluation in Guidance, 8*, 252–254.

Smith, P. (1978). Sampling errors of variance components in small sample multifacet generalizability studies. *Journal of Educational Measurement, 3*, 319–346.

Smith, R. M. (1987). Assessing partial knowledge in vocabulary. *Journal of Educational Measurement, 24*, 217–231.

Stamp, J. C. (1929). *Some economic factors in modern life.* London: P. S. King and Son.

Sternberg, R. J. (1981). Testing and cognitive psychology. *American Psychologist. 36*, 1181–1189.

Sternberg, R. J. (1984). What cognitive psychology can (and cannot) do for test development. In B. S. Plake (Ed.), *Social and technical issues in testing: Implications for test construction and usage* (pp. 39–60). Hillsdale, NJ: Lawrence Erlbaum Associates.

Stocking, M. L., & Lord, F. M. (1983). Developing a common metric in item response theory. *Applied Psychological Measurement, 7*, 201–210.

Stoffer, G. R., Davis, K. E., & Brown, J. B. (1977). The consequences of changing initial answers on objective tests: A stable effect and a stable misconception. *Journal of Educational Research, 70*, 272–277.

Subkoviak, M. J. (1976). Estimating reliability from a single administration of a mastery test. *Journal of Educational Measurement, 13*, 265–276.

Subkoviak, M. J. (1984). Estimating the reliability of mastery-nonmastery classifications. In R. A. Berk (Ed.), *A guide to criterion-referenced test construction* (pp. 267–291). Baltimore: Johns Hopkins University Press.

Suen, H. K. (1988). Agreement, reliability, accuracy, and validity: Toward a clarification. *Behavioral Assessment, 10*, 343–366.

Suen, H. K., & Ary, D. (1986). Poisson cumulative probabilities of systematic errors in single-subject and multiple-subject time sampling. *Behavioral Assessment, 8*, 31–38.

Suen, H. K., & Ary, D. (1989). *Analyzing quantitative behavioral observation data.* Hillsdale, NJ: Lawrence Erlbaum Associates.

Suen, H. K., Ary, D., & Ary, R. (1986). A note on the relationship among eight indices of interobserver agreement. *Behavioral Assessment, 8*, 301–303.

Suen, H. K., Ary, D., & Greenspan, S. (In press). Generalizability assessment of behavioral observation data. In R. Gaylord-Ross (Ed.), *Research methods in special education.* New York: Teachers College Press.

Suen, H. K., & Lee, P. S. C. (1985). Effects of the use of percentage agreement on behavioral observation reliabilities: A reassessment. *Journal of Psychopathology and Behavioral Assessment, 7*, 221–234.

Suen, H. K., & Lee, P. S. C. (1989, March) *Nonlinear optimization: A perspective of IRT parameter estimation.* Paper presented at the Fifth International Objective Measurement Workshop, Berkeley, CA.

Suen, H. K., Mardell-Czudnowski, C., & Goldenberg, D. (1989). Classification reliability of the DIAL-R preschool screening test. *Educational and Psychological Measurement,* Autumn.

Swaminathan, H., and Gifford, J. A. (1983). Estimation of parameters in the three parameter latent trait model. In D. Weiss (Ed.), *New Horizons in Testing* (pp. 9–33). New York: Academic Press.

Swaminathan, H., & Gifford, J. A. (1985). Bayesian estimation in the two-parameter logistic model. *Psychometrika, 50,* 349–364.

Swaminathan, H., & Gifford, J. A. (1986). Bayesian estimation in the three-parameter logistic model. *Psychometrika, 51,* 589–601.

Swaminathan, H., Hambleton, R. K., & Algina, J. (1974). Reliability of criterion-referenced tests: A decision-theoretic formulation. *Journal of Educational Measurement, 11,* 263–267.

Tatsuoka, K. K. (1983). Rule space: An approach for dealing with misconceptions based on item response theory. *Journal of Educational Measurement, 20,* 345–354.

Tatsuoka, K. K. (1987). Validation of cognitive sensitivity for item response curve. *Journal of Educational Measurement, 24,* 233–245.

Tenopyr, M. L. (1977). Content-construct confusion. *Personnel Psychology, 30,* 47–54.

Thissen, D. M. (1982). Marginal maximum likelihood estimation for the one-parameter logistic model. *Psychometrika, 47,* 175–186.

Tittle, C. K. (1982). Use of judgmental methods in item bias studies. In R. A. Berk (Ed.), *Handbook of methods for detecting bias* (pp. 31–63). Baltimore: Johns Hopkins University Press.

Traub, R. E. (1983). A priori considerations in choosing an item response model. In R. K. Hambleton (Ed.), *Applications of item response theory.* Vancouver, BC: Educational Research Institute of British Columbia.

Traub, R. E., & Wolf, R. G. (1981). Latent trait theories and assessment of educational achievement. In D. C. Berliner (Ed.), *Review of research in education 9.* Washington, DC: American Educational Research Association.

Tucker, L. R. (1946). Maximum validity of a test with equivalent items. *Psychometrika, 11,* 1–13.

Tucker, L. R. (1962). Factor analysis of relevance judgments: An approach to content validity. *Proceedings: 1961 Invitational Conference on Testing Problems* (pp. 29–38). Princeton, NJ: Educational Testing Service.

Tuinman, J. J., Farr, R., & Bianton, B. E. (1972). Increases in test scores as a function of material rewards. *Journal of Educational Measurement, 9,* 218–220.

Urry, V. W. (1974). Approximations to item parameters of mental test models and their uses. *Educational and Psychological Measurement, 34,* 253–269.

Urry, V. W. (1976). *Ancillary estimators for the item parameters of mental tests.* Washington, DC: Personnel Research and Development Center, U.S. Civil Service Commission.

Urry, V. W. (1977). Tailored testing: A successful application of latent trait theory. *Journal of Educational Measurement, 14,* 181–196.

Vernon, P. E. (1962). The determinants of reading comprehension. *Educational and Psychological Measurement, 22,* 269–286.

Vicker, F. D. (1973). Creative test generators. *Educational Technology, 13,* 43–44.

Wainer, H. (1986a) Minority contributions to the SAT score turnaround: An example of Simpson's paradox. *Journal of Educational Statistics, 11,* 239–244.

Wainer, H. (1986b). Five pitfalls encountered while trying to compare states on their SAT scores. *Journal of Educational Measurement, 23,* 69–81.

Wainer, H., & Kiely, G. (1987). Item clusters and computerized adaptive testing: A case for testlets. *Journal of Educational Measurement, 24,* 185–201.

Waller, M. I. (1981). A procedure for comparing logistic latent trait models. *Journal of Educational Measurement, 18,* 119–125.

Ward, W. C. (1984). Using microcomputers to administer tests. *Educational Measurement: Issues and practice, 3,* 16–20.

Ward, W. C. (1986). Measurement research that will change test design for the future. In E.

E. Freeman (Ed.), *The redesign of testing for the 21st century, Proceedings of the 1985 ETS Invitational Conference* (pp. 25–34). Princeton, NJ: Educational Testing Service.

Warm, T. A. (1978). *A primer of item response theory.* Springfield, VA: National Technical Information Services.

Webb, N. M., & Shavelson, R. J. (1981). Multivariate generalizability of general educational development ratings. *Journal of Educational Measurement, 18,* 13–22.

Webb, N. M., Shavelson, R. J., & Maddahian, E. (1983). Multivariate generalizability theory. In L. J. Fyans, Jr. (Ed.), *Generalizability theory: Inferences and practical applications* (pp. 67–81). San Francisco: Jossey-Bass.

Weiss, D. J. (1974). *Strategies of adaptive measurement.* (Research Report 74-5). Minneapolis: University of Minnesota, Psychometric Methods Program, Department of Psychology.

Weiss, D. J. (1976). Adaptive testing research at Minnesota: Overview, recent results, and future directions. In C. L. Clark (Ed.), *Proceedings of the First Conference on Computerized Adaptive Testing* (pp. 24–35). Washington, DC: United States Civil Service Commission.

Weiss, D. J. (Ed.). (1978). *Proceedings of the 1977 computerized adaptive testing conference.* Minneapolis: University of Minnesota.

Weiss, D. J. (Ed.). (1983). *New horizons in testing: Latent trait test theory and computerized adaptive testing.* New York: Academic Press.

Weiss, D. J., & Betz, N. E. (1973). *Ability measurement: Conventional or adaptive?* (Research Report 73-1). Minneapolis: University of Minnesota, Psychometric Methods Program, Department of Psychology.

Werts, C. E., Jöreskog, K. G., & Linn, R. L. (1972). A multitrait-multimethod model for studying growth. *Educational and Psychological Measurement, 32,* 655–678.

Wiggins, J. S. (1973). *Personality and prediction: Principles of personality assessment.* Reading, MA: Addison-Wesley.

Wild, C. L., McPeck, W. M., & Zieky, M. (1989, March). *Decision making with DIF data.* Paper presented at the National Council on Measurement in Education, San Francisco.

Wilson, D. T., Wood, R., & Gibbons, R. T. (1987). *TESTFACET-2 user's guide.* Mooresville, IN: Scientific Software.

Wingersky, M. S. (1983). LOGIST: A program for computing maximum likelihood procedures for logistic test models. In R. K. Hambleton (Ed.), *Applications of item response theory* (pp. 45–56). Vancouver, BC: Educational Research Institute of British Columbia.

Wright, B. D. (1968). Sample-free test calibration and person measurement. *Proceedings of the 1967 invitational conference on testing problems.* Princeton, NJ: Educational Testing Service.

Wright, B. D. (1977). Solving measurement problems with the Rasch model. *Journal of Educational Measurement, 14,* 97–166.

Wright, B. D., Mead, R., & Draba, R. (1976). *Detecting and correcting item bias with a logistic response model.* Research Memorandum No. 22. Chicago: University of Chicago, Statistical Laboratory, Department of Education.

Wright, B. D., & Stone, M. H. (1979). *Best test design.* Chicago: MESA.

Xiao, B. (1989, March). *Golden section search strategies for computerized adaptive testing.* Paper presented at the Fifth International Objective Measurement Workshop, Berkeley, CA.

Yen, W. M. (1981). Using simulation results to choose a latent trait model. *Applied Psychological Measurement, 5,* 245–262.

Zieky, M. J., & Livingston, S. A. (1977). *Manual for setting standards on the Basic Skills Assessment Tests.* Princeton, NJ: Educational Testing Service.

Zwick, R., & Ercikan, K. (1989). Analysis of differential item functioning in the NAEP assessment. *Journal of Educational Measurement, 26,* 55–60.

Zwick, W. R., & Velicer, W. F. (1986). Comparison of five rules for determining the number of components to retain. *Psychological Bulletin, 99*(3), 432–442.

Author Index

Subject Index